After the
Party

For Simone, Misha and Maya ... my life

To Mutti, for life and love

To all the Wallaces and Gromits,
people of courage

After the Party

Party

A Personal and Political Journey Inside the ANC

Andrew Feinstein

JONATHAN BALL PUBLISHERS
Johannesburg & Cape Town

© Andrew Feinstein, 2007

The author has asserted his moral rights.
Published in 2007 in trade paperback by
JONATHAN BALL PUBLISHERS (PTY) LTD
P O Box 33977
Jeppestown
2043

Reprinted three times in 2007

ISBN 978 1 86842 262 3

Editing and index by Frances Perryer
Typesetting and reproduction of text by Etienne van Duyker,
Cape Town
Printed and bound by CTP Book Printers,
Duminy Road, Parow, Cape

ACKNOWLEDGEMENTS

Thanks to the following for permission to reprint their work:

Ad. Donker/Publisher and Mongane Wally Serote for 'For Don M. – Banned' and an extract from 'City Johannesburg'

Harcourt Education for an extract from Ngugi Wa Thiong'o's *Devil on the Cross*

Sara Roy, for extracts from 'Living with the Holocaust: The Journey of a Child of Holocaust Survivors', in Adam Shatz (ed), *Prophets Outcast*. New York: Nation Books, 2004, and from 'A Jewish Plea' in Nubar Hovsepian (ed), *The War on Lebanon: A Reader*. Northampton MA: Interlink Publishing, 2007

Zapiro for cartoons 'Arms Deal Horrorscope' and 'Scopa's Arms Probe Study Group'

Stephen Watson for an extract from 'The Mountain'

Faber & Faber Ltd and Adam Zagajewski for an extract from 'An Unfinished House'

Every effort has been made to contact the copyright holders. Those copyright holders whom we have been unable to contact are requested to contact the publisher, so that the omission can be remedied in the event of a reprint.

CONTENTS

'After all, there is such a thing as truth.'

Victor Serge
The Case of Comrade Tulayev

ABBREVIATIONS

ADS	African Defence Systems
AG	Auditor-General
ANC	African National Congress
ARVs	anti-retrovirals
AWB	Afrikaanse Weerstandsbeweging
Azapo	Azanian People's Organisation
Azasm	Azanian Students Movement
BC	Black Consciousness
CBM	Consultative Business Movement
Codesa	Conference for a Democratic South Africa
Cosatu	Congress of South African Trade Unions
DA	Democratic Alliance
FoTAC	Friends of the Treatment Action Campaign
GEAR	Growth, Equality and Redistribution strategy
GFC	German Frigate Consortium
IBA	Independent Broadcasting Authority
Idasa	Institute for Democracy in South Africa
IMF	International Monetary Fund
JIT	Joint Investigating Team
LIFT	Lead In Fighter Trainer
MCC	Medicines Control Council
MDC	Movement for Democratic Change
Merg	Macroeconomic Research Group
MK	Umkhonto we Sizwe
MTCTP	Mother to Child Treatment Plan
NEC	National Executive Committee
Nedlac	National Education, Development and Labour Council
NEPAD	New Partnership for Africa's Development

NP	National Party
NTF	National Tourism Forum
NWC	ANC National Working Committee
PAC	Pan-Africanist Congress
PFMA	Public Finance Management Act
PMA	Pharmaceutical Manufacturer's Association
PWV	Pretoria-Witwatersrand-Vereeniging
RDP	Reconstruction and Development Programme
SAAF	South African Air Force
SACP	South African Communist Party
SAMA	South African Musicians' Association
Sanco	South African National Civic Organisation
Scopa	Standing Committee on Public Accounts
SFO	Serious Fraud Office, UK
Shawco	Student Health and Welfare Centres Organisation
TRC	Truth and Reconciliation Commission
UDF	United Democratic Front
WTO	World Trade Organisation

'This is in no wise apathy against politics in general, but against a species of politics.'

Karl Marx
New York *Tribune*
4 September 1852

PREFACE

This has been a difficult book to write. Not just because of the inherent difficulty of conveying my experience in words. Nor because I had to leave two jobs that I enjoyed to be able to publish it. But because within the culture of the African National Congress (ANC) it is implicitly accepted that one does not talk publicly about what happens inside the organisation. Especially if what is happening is controversial or at odds with the party line.

Despite my deep respect for a large number of people within the ANC I have decided to be completely open about my time in the organisation because I believe it is in the best interests of South Africa to know about both the many triumphs and some of the more shameful episodes in our short democratic history. I do so in the hope that this knowledge will contribute to the re-creation of a more open, honest, principled and accountable politics in the country. And because I do believe that 'after all, there is such a thing as truth'.

During my time in government I took verbatim notes on a Psion mini computer. These have proved an invaluable record of meetings, conversations and random thoughts. In addition, I have wherever possible verified the events described with other people involved in the specific incidents, meetings and discussions. Similarly where I have been given information by a source I have made every effort to substantiate that insight with at least one additional source and often more.

I would like to thank the countless people who have given of their time to check drafts and facts, who have excavated memories and, in some instances, relived painful experiences. For obvious reasons I am unable to thank many of these people by name. You all know who you are. And I am very grateful to you.

Barbara Hogan has devoted her life to the ANC and the cause

of freedom, democracy and accountability in South Africa. She has been a friend, a support and the wisest possible counsel since I first entered government in 1994. She is brave, honest and great fun. I owe her a personal and political debt that I will never be able to repay satisfactorily.

Gavin Woods is a man of courage and conviction. Despite our political differences we were united in the pursuit of truth. It was a difficult journey made easier by his incorruptibility and his stoicism. Along the way we became friends. I am proud to still call him a friend.

Some people inspire others without knowing it. Zackie Achmat is such a person. I am honoured to know him and to have observed his bravery, his stubbornness and his incisive mind. He and the many committed comrades in TAC and FoTAC have informed me about an issue I inexplicably neglected while in Parliament. They have given me the opportunity to make amends for that failing.

Rachel Holmes was crucial in persuading me to continue writing, cajoling and encouraging when things were tough. She devoted time, at a very difficult moment in her life, to reading drafts and suggesting improvements. Most important of all, she eventually helped me understand that while identity is a useful construct, identity politics are a cul-de-sac for anyone with a commitment to equality and justice. Thank you.

Critically, Rachel introduced me to my agent, the wonderful Isobel Dixon. Isobel has inspired me with her belief in this book and managed to find it the perfect publishing home. My thanks to Isobel and to all at Jonathan Ball, especially Jeremy Boraine. Frances Perryer, my editor, was both diligent and creative and, more importantly, a pleasure to work with.

On the bumpy but fortuitous political road I have travelled it has been my privilege to know some remarkable human beings, even if only superficially. Amongst them I would like to thank Nelson Mandela, Tokyo Sexwale, Cyril Ramaphosa, Kgalema Motlanthe, Ahmed Kathrada, Mac Maharaj, Trevor Manuel, Sipho Mpahlwa and Jabu Moleketi for giving me the opportunity to serve.

Leon Cohen, Laloo Chiba, Pregs Govender, Melanie Verwoerd, Murphy Morobe, Janet Love, Audrey Coleman, the late Sheila Weinberg, Roland Hunter, Serake Leeuw, Cheryl Gillwald, Fatima

Chohan-Khota, Roddy Payne, Mark Phillips, Theuns Eloff and many others were enriching colleagues and friends during the transition and early years of democracy.

Richard Calland, Mark Gevisser, Alan Fine, Mungo Soggott, Sam Sole and others have acted as sounding boards, critics and friends in years past and hopefully for many to come.

Besides the many I am not able to name I am grateful to John Dunne, Markus Dettmer, Fredrik Laurin, Richard Young, Ann Feltham and the Campaign Against the Arms Trade, Sue Hawley, Joe Roeber and Marianne Camerer for information and assistance.

The main arms deal section, Chapter 13, is drawn primarily from my own experiences. In addition to the footnoted sources I have also drawn on unpublished material of Marianne Camerer and Gavin Woods. I thank them for making this available to me.

Nathan Geffen gave valuable time to share his unparalleled knowledge of HIV and AIDS and the struggle against denialism. Oliver Phillips reviewed the section on Zimbabwe with an insider's knowledge and a patriot's empathy. BF, AZ, CS, CM, CT, DK and BK provided me with a roof over my head during crucial years, support and friendship in a new and different environment.

I would never have finished this book were it not for the generosity of the Rockefeller Foundation and their Bellagio Study Centre where I spent a luxurious, thoughtful and incredibly productive four weeks in 2006. To Pilar Palacia and all the staff at Bellagio for creating such a conducive environment and to Jesus, Bishakka, Seemi, Sinclair, Raka, Fanny, Leonard, David and Cynthia for fun, friendship and wise counsel. Next year in Bellagio?

To Lance, a true friend since the day we were both unceremoniously ejected from a Shakespeare tutorial, who supervised the research diligently undertaken by Natascha Visser. My thanks to you both.

To the memory of Kevin Ferguson-Brown who demonstrated how to live an individual life in truth and who died tragically young, but happy.

My family bore the brunt of both the consequences of the events described in the book and my absences while transcribing them. My mother Erika, who like all good Jewish mothers believes I can do no wrong, also provided me with a continuous flow of relevant paper cuttings from South African newspapers after I had moved to London. My sister Lesley and her family provided support throughout and a base for us when in South Africa. I spent many wonderful hours at their house in Kommetjie writing, thinking and clearing my head in the Atlantic waves. My 'ma', Runi Khan, was a massive support not just to me but to Simone and the children throughout these times and continues to be so. Our 'baba', Viquar, was a source of wise counsel to us, informed always by his life-long humanism, and love and affection to the children.

Simone provided unwavering support and counsel during the events and coped with a young family single-handed during the drawn-out writing process. She was also an honest but sympathetic reader. More importantly, she is my best friend, my confidant and the love of my life. And for my Misha and Maya: too little not to complain profusely about my writing-enforced absences, but little enough to forgive instantly and take me away from it all.

And finally to the memory of my father, Ralph, whose sagest advice was that even when there is no money to be had one can always justify the purchase of another book.

Clearly any mistakes and all opinions in this book are my responsibility alone.

INTRODUCTION

Cape Town, mid-winter 1982. A little white mini trundles along Klipfontein Road. A dreary road, straight and monotonous like so many others on these Cape Flats. Behind us Table Mountain has disappeared beneath dark clouds, heavy with rain. We drive past the lower middle class white suburb of Retreat, through bedraggled, dilapidated Manenberg and Athlone. 'Coloured'[1] areas: grey and drab. The car's bonsai wheels bump along the rough road. At the back, the bread-bin boot lid is plastered with political declamations: End Conscription; I love Poland: Solidarnosc; South Africa needs Peace; Shawco; 'I Have a Dream'.

I was lucky, born a white boy in apartheid South Africa. Because of this accident of birth I was guaranteed a life of material comfort, of privilege, of few worries. I had just started my heavily subsidised higher education.

As a rather insecure first-year student at the University of Cape Town I had become involved with the university welfare agency, Shawco, whose Director for Education and Welfare, Mike Pothier, was taking me to Crossroads – a sprawling shanty town, home to illegal migrants from the Eastern Cape in search of work. The apartheid state, determined as only Calvinists can be to maintain the absurd edifice it had engineered, abused them daily. These families had seen their shanties bulldozed so often by the Bantu Administration Board that they could no longer afford to replace the corrugated strips and bits of plastic that were confiscated. Having no choice, they decided to create 'Bed City'. Maybe 20 families; sodden, bereft, stripped of shelter and dignity. Under the beds, their few possessions, in mulchy cardboard boxes. Children with rheumy noses, inadequate clothing, bare feet, running in the mud and the puddles.

I was only 10 kilometres from my warm, cosy cottage in 'white'

1

Wynberg, but I was on a different, inhospitable, inhuman planet. I was angry, scared, ashamed. How could this happen? What could I do?

Over the following months and years I did a little: helped dig a few pit latrines, taught black pupils extra lessons, cajoled students to help in crèches in Crossroads, doled out bread and soup to a few of the indigent and added ever more indignant stickers to the back of my car. In 1983 I succeeded Mike as Head of Education and Welfare at Shawco. By 1986 I was Student President of the Agency. However, within months of seeing 'Bed City' – months in which I aged as I saw more and more of the daily reality of apartheid – it became clear to me that these interventions, while they might provide a few moments of relief from hunger, from the numbing dumbness of Bantu education, made no real difference to the daily lives of millions of South Africans. What was needed was massive and fundamental change to the very structure of South African life – to its politics, its economics, its very psyche.

As I met more people in Crossroads, Manenberg, Nyanga, Mitchell's Plein, Gugulethu and Langa it was clear that many had realised this long before me. In the black community, welfare agencies like Shawco were tolerated for the temporary palliatives we supplied. But there was another real struggle, a struggle to liberate the minds and bodies of all South Africans. And even in the Western Cape, where liberation politics were more complex and contorted than anywhere else in South Africa, there was an unambiguous leader of this struggle, the African National Congress. Defiant graffiti – the ANC logo, 'Viva MK', 'Long live Nelson Mandela' – would occasionally daub the wet, vibracrete walls of the townships. People would talk furtively of Mandela, Tambo, Modise and Slovo.

*

Pretoria, 1 May 1994. I sit with Simone, my sari-clad Bengali wife, in the alcove of the Union Buildings, a newly elected parliamentary representative of the African National Congress, a guest at the inauguration of South Africa's first democratically elected President, Nelson Mandela. Fidel Castro and Hillary Clinton vie for centre stage. But today the world belongs to Madiba and to the millions of South

Africans who have overcome centuries of racially inspired subjugation, humiliation and trauma, who have emerged from the darkness of racial purity to the light of an African Renaissance.

Above the Herbert Baker-designed colonial edifice thunder the gun-metal grey defenders of the nation. Reviled by many for their role in illegal conflicts in Angola and Mozambique, on this momentous day they fly in obeisance to their new commander-in-chief, the President of the ANC, the President of South Africa. Nelson Mandela stands regal, noble, acknowledging the fly-past. Nothing could signify with more drama and emotion the extraordinary distance that South Africa has travelled to reach this remarkable day.

*

Turffontein, Johannesburg, 8 May 1996. Driving the mine-dump-dusty road from my constituency south of Johannesburg into the CBD I listen to Deputy President Thabo Mbeki's inspiring speech celebrating the adoption of South Africa's new constitution:

I owe my being to the Khoi and the San ...
I am formed by the migrants who left Europe to find a new home on our native land. Whatever their own actions, they remain still, part of me ...
I am an African.
I am born of the peoples of the continent of Africa.' [2]

It is a seminal moment in South Africa's developing democracy – and in my own sense of identity. Thabo's eloquent, heartfelt words fill me with pride, redouble my commitment to the party and the country.

*

Cape Town, August 2001. Seven-and-a-half years after that exultant inauguration I announce my resignation from Parliament, where I represented the ANC. As my reason I cite the ANC leadership's refusal to allow an unfettered, comprehensive investigation into a multi-billion rand arms deal that was tainted by allegations of high-level corruption.

This dreadful decision by the leadership and the subsequent deception and crushing of dissent marked the arrival of tawdry politics-as-normal in the ANC and South Africa; politics characterised by an autocratic leadership giving precedence to the interests of the political party and personal power over those of the country as a whole.

I had been compelled to choose between my loyalty to this extra-ordinary party and my constitutional responsibility to the country. On this occasion the two did not coincide. For me, the party was over.

*

From that day I have sought to understand what happened between my proudly throwing in my lot with the ANC and quitting the movement that I revered. This book charts that journey, both personal and political.

SECTION I
EARLY POLITICS

CHAPTER 1
A Dry White Season

it is a dry white season
dark leaves don't last, their brief lives dry out
and with a broken heart they dive down gently headed for the earth,
not even bleeding.
it is a dry white season brother,
only the trees know the pain as they still stand erect
dry like steel, their branches dry like wire,
indeed, it is a dry white season
but seasons come to pass.

'For Don M. – Banned'
Mongane Wally Serote

My journey began with a polyglot upbringing by an Austrian, Jewish mother who survived the racial hatred of World War II in occupied Vienna, and a South African father of Lithuanian descent. A peripatetic childhood spent in South Africa and Austria involved three 'semigrations' from South Africa when my liberal-minded father could not tolerate the asphyxiating insularity of apartheid but found, again and again, that he could live nowhere else but this tortured country on the southern tip of Africa.

My father bought a home for the first time in his life in his late fifties. Three days later he was dead. He was one of a never-ending parade of Jews who were by instinct and history rootless.

This rootlessness manifested in me as a wanderlust that has never dissipated. After a multitude of schools it persisted into early adulthood which I spent in Cape Town, Berkeley and Cambridge. Amidst the spires and chapels, economics books and cricket on the greens I met Simone, a highly politicised Bangladeshi. At the first meeting of our class Simone was reluctant to speak to me on the grounds of my being a white South African. Four years later we were married in the first-ever ceremony in the 700-year history of Cambridge's King's College Chapel in which neither bride nor groom was Anglican.

Perhaps my background is best reflected in the life and death of my maternal grandmother. She was born Jewish in the Austro-Hungarian Hapsburg Empire, married a Catholic and converted to Catholicism for reasons of self-preservation in late-1930s Vienna. She remained a devout practising Catholic after World War II but nevertheless insisted on being buried in an orthodox Jewish cemetery in Cape Town by a family who could not even muster the *minyan* of 10 Jewish men to say prayers.

This polymorphous history informs my thinking on notions of identity and belonging, and especially questions of Africanism, Eurocentricity, non-Jewish Judaism and 'otherness'. In a world of great divides between Muslim and Jew I am an agnostic cosmopolitan. Identity is at one level irrelevant and meaningless and at another crucially important.

*

Our semigrations were spent mainly in Vienna, the romantic city of Freud, Klimt and Bruno Kreisky, the Jewish leader of the Social Democratic Party which ruled Austria for much of the post-war period. The madness, brutality and evil insanity of apartheid was perhaps easier to discern when it was regularly contrasted with 1970s Austria, which was inclusive, fairly tolerant and enlightened.

While in Austria I missed South Africa terribly. However, back in Cape Town in mid-1976 I began to think there was something odd about my surroundings. I was 12 years old and attending a small, government-run primary school in Wynberg. Our class teacher was Mr Naude, a squat, well-built, crew-cutted man who spoke English with a thick, guttural Afrikaans accent. One morning in June he was called from our classroom to see the Headmaster and returned bright puce in the face and neck, the veins in his forehead bulging. Ordered out of the classroom, we joined the river of exiting children and were corralled into the school's only tennis court where, shouting manically, Mr Naude ordered us to sit down. He barked at us that we were being sent home as soon as it was safe as there was great danger afoot: there were black students in 'the location' causing trouble.

As he gesticulated his bottle green jacket rode up his paunchy midriff, exposing a holstered gun attached to his belt. We were far too excited to be scared but as I walked the couple of minutes to our house I wondered what had so exercised our teacher.

It was, as my parents told me later, the Soweto uprising in which black students, led by amongst others Murphy Morobe, rose up against an iniquitous education system. The fact that it was centred in far-away Johannesburg only made Mr Naude's terrified reaction seem more paranoid. But his was the response of many whites to what they saw as 'the marauding hordes' from whom they were protected by racial laws, separate group areas and a repressive police force and army.

A few years later, as a 15-year-old at high school, I was compelled, along with all of my white male schoolmates, to register for compulsory military service. We were told by the registering officer: 'They say that on the border [with Marxist Angola, against which a largely covert war was being fought] there is a communist behind every bush. It's not true. There're not enough bushes.' I realised after an abortive school cadet camp that, for reasons of cowardice as much as nascent, unformed political awareness, I could never serve in the South African Defence Force.

The move from the strictures of an all-male, whites-only government school to the University of Cape Town – 'Moscow on the Hill' to the authorities – was an enlightening one. My time at UCT was characterised by demonstrations forcibly broken up by police, frustration with well-intentioned but sometimes juvenile student politics and the usual gamut of police spies in student ranks. It also marked my awakening to real politics through Shawco's work amongst the impoverished communities on the outskirts of Cape Town. 'Bed City' was one of countless manifestations of the human misery and suffering wrought by apartheid.

In the townships and squatter settlements of the country resistance to apartheid was growing. This defiance led to the creation of the United Democratic Front (UDF), a thinly disguised, mass-based internal wing of the ANC that developed a remarkably open, non-racial and inclusive culture. As part of its strategy the UDF spawned a number of white left-wing organisations that were sympathetic to the ANC. I was peripherally involved in the End Conscription Campaign and the Five Freedoms Forum. This was our 1960s, socially and sexually carefree while politically committed, hopeful and idealistic.

My sense of the history and principles of the ANC intensified during this heady time. I developed a romantic picture of a values-driven, moral and quite dashing movement organised in underground structures within South Africa, in exile and at 'the university', as Robben Island was known.

Ten years after the Soweto uprising, in June 1986, an atrocity was perpetrated when the police and army, supported by reactionary warlords within the community, destroyed countless shacks – leaving 60 000 people homeless and killing 60 – in an attempt to quash the militant squatter settlement of Crossroads and move its inhabitants to Khayelitsha. As President of Shawco I was one of the coordinators of the relief operation for these destitute families. Together with my Shawco colleagues and the other relief agencies I was one of the few non-residents who had access to the area cordoned off by the security forces. We saw at first hand the devastation that had been wreaked.

Anton Richman,[1] one of the students working with us, was stranded in a church hall as the security forces unleashed an attack on it. A close friend, Lance van Sittert, and I jumped into a kombi and raced towards the building, which burst into flames as we approached. From the smoke-filled distance shots rang out – aimed, we thought, at us. I turned the kombi around and sped back to our base. Thankfully, Anton managed to escape, but at least a couple of local residents who were seeking refuge in the hall were not so fortunate. The incident brought home to us the brutality of late apartheid and the manner in which the community – organised by the ANC underground and the UDF – united in defiance and fought back. There were even occasional snipers from within the community firing at the security forces.

At the height of the Crossroads crisis I was asked to attend a meeting with the UDF leadership. I was taken to a small house in Nyanga East where I was introduced to a vivacious young woman and a slightly sinister looking man with a balding pate and longish hair straggling down on to his neck. They asked for details of what we had been doing in Crossroads and how we intended to proceed. Cheryl Carolus was warm towards us and full of praise for what we were doing. Trevor Manuel was more abrupt and slightly gruffer. He asked me to keep them informed of what we were up to and any important develop-ments in the relief operation. I was filled with awe and respect for these two activists who I knew had been battling the apartheid state on the streets of the townships since their teens.

For the duration of the crisis we were hosted and supported by a remarkable household. The Jacks, a stalwart ANC family, had devoted their lives to the overthrow of apartheid. Their house served as a physical, political and emotional base for us. The eldest son, Pro,[2] a member of the banned ANC, would guide us through the political dynamics of the area. Led by their indomitable mother, known to us as Ma Jack, together with sister Buyiswa, a fiery gender activist, and younger brother Xolo, they offered food and succour throughout those long weeks. By the end of the crisis Xolo had given up his studies and had developed what became a debilitating alcohol problem.

The violent flames raging from the destroyed Crossroads com-munity were visible from the centre of Cape Town just 10 kilometres away. But most white South Africans, including my own parents, refused to believe what was happening. On hearing that my col-leagues and I had been using our status as a welfare agency to take undercover journalists into the area, an uncle of mine admonished me and remarked: 'Just be grateful it's the *schwarzers* and not us.' It was a graphic reminder of how the vast majority of white South Africans had allowed themselves to be insulated from the reality of the country; how willing the white mind was to be numbed by igno-rance and avoidance.

During my involvement in these events the Defence Force took pleasure in informing me that I was about to be conscripted and would be sent back into Crossroads as an infantryman serving the apartheid state. I was teaching a course on Freud and psychoanalysis at the St Francis Adult Education Centre in Langa at the time, and when my star student, a woman teacher from the militant Gugulethu township, commented: 'Andrew, that was highly entertaining, but what relevance does it have for our lives?', I saw her point. It was time to move on.

CHAPTER 2

Stirrings of Change

I cherish my own freedom dearly, but I care even more for your freedom ...
I am not less life-loving than you are. But I cannot sell my birthright, nor
am I prepared to sell the birthright of the people to be free ...
Only free men can negotiate. Prisoners cannot enter into contracts ...
I cannot and will not give any undertaking at a time when I and you, the
people, are not free.
Your freedom and mine cannot be separated. I will return.

Statement rejecting a conditional offer of freedom from President PW Botha
Nelson Mandela, 10 February 1985

Two days before I was due to report for military service I left South
Africa for the University of California at Berkeley, sponsored – with
comic consequences – by the Rotary Foundation.

As we crossed the Bay Bridge from San Francisco into Berkeley my
elderly Rotary 'host father' drove past a car abandoned in the middle
of the bridge. 'Bloody niggers,' he intoned. 'Only a nigger would
leave his car there.' A few hours later, during dinner with a few
Rotarian guests, he ushered me into the kitchen: 'Andrew, I notice
you use the word 'adore' a great deal. Men don't say 'adore' here,
especially in the Bay area. People may get the wrong impression.'

Welcome to the world of Reagan and Thatcher, the rise of monetarism and its social consequences. This revolution was characterised
by a profound contradiction: its extreme free market reforms served
to undermine the very social conservatism, connoted by the apho-
rism 'family values', that was its supposed moral underpinning.

As I was about to address my very wealthy host club, Reagan supporters to a man, a senior member said to me: 'I am so glad you are
here to set right the lies that are told about your country.' After my
speech – entitled 'South Africa: Its People and Politics' – he was
somewhat less enamoured of me. I received a message from my

sponsoring club in South Africa reminding me that Rotary scholars were expected to desist from discussing politics.

Once in bohemian Berkeley (whose main square had been re-named Biko Plaza), I flirted with dependency theory and an Israeli student of Russian origin working on a PhD in Buddhist studies. I made contact with the liberation movement in exile and became involved in the Azanian South African Students Movement, led by Saths Cooper, a former leader of the Steve Biko-inspired Black Consciousness (BC) group, Azapo. I also befriended another former Azapo leader, Mlungisi Mervana. My engagement with them felt a little strange at first: I had been told that the BC movement was anti-white, but Saths, Mlungisi and others were never anything less than welcom-ing and great company. At times, however, I got the impression that the BC movement was stronger in California than in Crossroads.

Meanwhile, in the South Africa of the late 1980s, a contradictory dynamic of secret negotiations and simultaneously intensified repres-sion had been initiated by President PW Botha. Measures such as the assault on Crossroads were taking place in parallel with a covert approach to the jailed Nelson Mandela. Botha was, however, unable to make the political leap of freeing Mandela and others and instead created less powerful and thus meaningless political institutions for each of the Indian and 'coloured' population groups. Botha suffered a debilitating stroke in 1989 and was deposed in a silent coup from within the National Party.

My father died unexpectedly of a heart attack while I was at Berkeley. My journey home for his funeral, generously paid for by Rotary despite my political misdemeanours, took me via Tel Aviv where, in an unfriendly hotel, I passed an unsettled night ruminating on his unsuccessful attempts to create a bond between his children and the state of Israel. While he was a completely non-observant and I assumed non-believing Jew, he was deeply conscious of anti-Semitism and was unambiguously supportive of Israel.

His death also led me to consider the basis of his rootlessness. My parents moved house 29 times in 32 years of marriage. It probably didn't help that his domineering Lithuanian mother, who ran a 'frock shop' in Johannesburg, would move him from boarding school to boarding school as she heard from her society friends that yet another school was now the country's premier educational establishment. This impermanence was exacerbated by her habit of buying him gifts, most memorably a puppy and a bicycle, 'on appro' and returning them to the shop as soon as he had departed for whichever school was the current favourite.

After my father's funeral and the completion of my time at Berkeley I returned to South Africa briefly to set up a Public Affairs business. Called Interface Africa, it comprised myself and a colleague, Mohammed Salloojee, providing political and corporate social responsibility advice to companies and NGOs. We also assisted the ANC's nascent business wing, run by Peter Roussos. I embarked on an engrossing, sometimes surreal tour around the rural areas of the country, managing a music talent show. This brought me into contact with the burgeoning jazz scene in Johannesburg. I worked with the newly created non-racial musicians' association, SAMA, led by the People's Poet, Mzwakhi Mbuli, Johnny Clegg, Jennifer Ferguson and the formidable Queeneth Ndaba, all ANC-aligned musicians.

To continue avoiding the long arm of the draft I returned abroad in 1989 to study economics at Cambridge University, where I met my wife Simone, made contact with the ANC in exile and fell under the intellectual influence of Professor John Sender, a South African-born economist who was a follower of the little-known but brilliant and controversial political economist, Bill Warren.[1]

While I was at Cambridge the stirrings of change in South Africa intensified with FW de Klerk's ousting of Botha. Although regarded as conservative within the National Party, De Klerk had the foresight to realise that apartheid's days were numbered. He acted with courage and alacrity, stunning not only South Africa but many of his own party colleagues by unbanning the ANC and its allies and affiliates, and releasing political prisoners.

I watched Nelson Mandela walk free from Victor Verster prison on a small black and white television in my room in Cambridge. I was struck by how he emerged both regal and humble, this man whose only likeness the world had seen was almost 30 years out of date. It was the most significant moment of my and many South Africans' lives. I abandoned plans to research a PhD under John Sender and returned to South Africa, where I could now join the ANC legally. I wasn't sad to leave behind the suffocating conservatism and hypocrisy of Thatcher's Britain.

CHAPTER 3
Towards the New Jerusalem

Forward we shall march, forward we shall march
Forward we shall march ... to the people's government.

Liberation song popular amongst students in the 1980s

The World Trade Centre near Johannesburg's international airport
was an incongruous venue for the Conference for a Democratic
South Africa (Codesa) – the constitutional negotiations that would
determine an interim constitution and transition mechanism for
South Africa. A vast, warehouse-like structure, it lacked atmosphere
and character, which however were provided in abundance by the
participants and their often explosive encounters.

I was part of the Secretariat/facilitation team under the auspices
of the Consultative Business Movement (CBM), an organisation
funded by business but trusted by all sides to act as neutral interme-
diary – although the National Party attempted to have me removed
from the team as the negotiations started, complaining that I was too
close to the ANC.[1]

The role enabled me to get to know a number of political personalities, including Murphy Morobe, a leader of the 1976 uprising and
a thoughtful and engaging human being, Mo Shaik, the intelligence
operative who headed ANC security with an irrepressible sense of
humour, and Essop Pahad, ANC and South African Communist Party
(SACP) leader, whom I knew by fearsome reputation but who surprised me with a passionate discussion about English football as we
shared a bus ride to the airport. A witty, bright and captivating new
friend was Janet Love, who had spent 12 years underground inside
South Africa for the ANC. I had expected a dour, earnest comrade,
but we would often sit late into the night gossiping and laughing
about some of the wackier participants. Her boss, both underground

and in the negotiations, was Mac Maharaj. Gaunt, bespectacled and with a small Trotsky-style goatee, Mac had the sharpest mind of anyone I had met. Together with Fanie van der Merwe of the government's Constitutional Affairs Department, he laid out each day's proceedings, ironed out the difficulties that inevitably arose and determined the way forward for the following day. He and Fanie were the true unsung heroes of the South African transition.

Mac's intellectual dominance of his government counterpart reflected the supremacy of the ANC over the National Party in the negotiations. It was spellbinding to watch one impressive negotiator after another dominate his or her counterpart. The more public version of the Mac–Fanie duet was the Cyril–Roelf show: Cyril Ramaphosa, the erudite, savvy new ANC Secretary-General and his charming if slightly plodding counterpart, Roelf Meyer, the Minister for Constitutional Affairs.

It was only when things really went awry that the mighty elephants got involved. For instance, on a day of high drama, Nelson Mandela bitterly attacked FW de Klerk after the President had effectively blamed the ANC for what he described as black-on-black violence that was ravaging the townships. In contrast to his genial public persona, Mandela angry is a terrifying sight to behold. He rose to answer De Klerk with a steely glare. He (quite correctly) accused De Klerk's government of fomenting the violence that was threatening to undermine the negotiations and spoke scathingly of his counterpart, claiming he was unable to keep his word. He came within a whisker of calling De Klerk a blatant liar. After his controlled tirade, Mandela marched off the stage and seemingly out of the negotiations. It took months of frantic behind-the-scenes efforts to put the talks back on track.

Up to this point De Klerk had believed that he could remain a key player in South African politics, along with a motley collection of moderate black leaders. Now he realised that he had underestimated his opponent. The ANC's strength came from the quality of its participants, the organisation's strategic acumen and the knowledge that it was the voice of the vast majority of South Africans.

The negotiations also had their lighter moments. I recall the sight of the loquacious Kader Asmal, an ANC representative on the Commission to which I was attached, having to flee the amorous advances of an elderly IFP delegate. The same party's controversial

16

advisor, Mario Ambrosini, a smooth Italian-American lawyer, was deeply paranoid about pretty much everybody outside of his own party and some within it. One night after a session had concluded at around eleven o'clock he insisted that the IFP offices were being bugged and was only a little shame-faced when the 'independent' security group he brought in to sweep the offices found nothing.

Some of the smaller parties did their utmost to build their often non-existent profiles. Most prominent and long-winded among them was Amichand Rajbansi in one of the incarnations of his personal fief-doms that purported to be political parties. A prominently bewigged gentleman with a charming lack of self-irony, he would drive the Secretariat to distraction with his long discourses that interested no one.

The Commission I looked after comprised not only Kader Asmal but also the craggy and shrewd Minister of Correctional Services, Kobie Coetsee. Neither of them short of a word, they dominated the Working Group dealing with the creation of an environment for free political participation. However, they worked impressively together, making my job an easy one. Coetsee could be exacting, though. I took a weekend off to rush down to Cape Town for my mother's birthday. While enjoying the celebrations at a restaurant near her house I was called to the phone. Who on earth knew where I was? It was Coetsee, who had tracked me down to let me know that he was unhappy about a sentence in the day's minutes.

I also acted as informal aide to the Commonwealth Secretariat del-egation, whose secretary-general was the urbane Chief Emeka Anyaoku. I bonded with his Ghanaian political advisor, Moses Anafu, a huge man with a deep, booming voice, who had a good rapport with Thabo Mbeki. During a rather embarrassing lift ride with the two of them it became clear that Mbeki had a soft spot for Moses' niece.

The success of the negotiations was down to the skill of the nego-tiators, a readiness to compromise and unbelievably hard work. Sessions regularly finished close to midnight and would be followed by party briefings, strategy sessions and regular ANC–NP one-on-ones. Our team would often start again before seven in the morning. The notion that consensus was often reached by exhaustion was, on some occasions, not far from the truth.

*

It was perhaps strange that an organisation funded and driven by business was playing such an intimate role in so delicate a political process. This was not only because the CBM had employed a number of people who were extremely well regarded politically, but also because business in South Africa had played a unique role in the lead-up to the transition, with a number of senior businesspeople acting as key go-betweens.

The nexus between business and politics in any society is complex. In South Africa this was doubly so. Apartheid was seen initially to benefit the private sector through the provision of cheap, fairly compliant labour. However, as the benefits began to be outweighed by the disadvantages of international isolation, an ever more restive workforce and a stagnant economy, so the captains of industry became committed to a process of peaceful transition.

Despite participating in this important role I was struck by how poorly the corporate sector, with a few notable exceptions, understood the country's political dynamics. However, there is no doubt that it played a crucial role in facilitating change. It is even possible that a fairly shallow understanding of politics was advantageous in doing this.

One of the key processes that the CBM facilitated, in which I was engaged, brought together education activists and authorities in an attempt to give the former a role in education during the transition. The process was instructive both for the remarkable commitment of these activists and for the difficulty Minister of Education Sam de Beer had in coming to terms with the reality that his hold on the education system was collapsing. In meetings of the committee, the short, swarthy De Beer would often talk down to the activists as though this was the height of National Party rule, not its demise. The Minister's struggle, sometimes verging on outright denial, reflected the ruling party's assumption that they could control the transition in a manner that would enable them to continue as key political players. All the while, the ANC was undermining any authority the state still had through processes such as the Soweto Education Crisis Committee.

At the initiative of business in the area, I chaired the Vaal Reconstruction and Development Forum in the aftermath of the Boipatong massacre of 17 June 1992, in which IFP-supporting hostel dwellers, abetted by the state security forces, attacked ANC hostels, killing 45 people.

Before leaving for Cambridge I had worked briefly in this complex of nondescript, chemically polluted, politically conservative industrial towns and their linked, impoverished townships. My job was as a consultant attempting to bring change to a racially divided workplace. The white workforce were pushed and bullied into accepting a mixed canteen, but when it came to integrating the toilets all hell broke loose and management backed down. What struck me on returning to the area a few years later was the brutal efficiency of the local administration and the manner in which the security forces had become intertwined with local government in a practice that was common throughout the country and was provoking a great deal of the so-called 'black-on-black violence' by favouring the more 'moderate' IFP over the ANC. My time in the Vaal once again reminded me of the viciousness of the apartheid security forces. This daily brutality, so central to the divide and rule strategy that underpinned late apartheid, has contributed as much as the globalisation of crime to the excessive levels of violent crime that bedevil post-apartheid South Africa.

While chairing the forum I interacted extensively with the civic movement, an important player in extra-parliamentary politics. The civics in the area were led by two very impressive ANC-supporting activists, Mlungisi Hlongwane and Linda Mngomezulu, who went on to become President and General Secretary of the South African National Civic Organisation (Sanco). Their negotiating and organising skills were quickly apparent. When they became frustrated at the stalling tactics and general deception of the local administrator, who had a close working relationship with the notoriously brutish local security police, Mlungisi and Linda swung into action. They occupied the administrator's office and would not leave. For hours I attempted to negotiate a way out of the impasse, which I feared would turn violent. The civics held out until they had eked significant concessions out of the administration, including the replacement of the old administrator by a 'new Nat', Johan Killian. It was a lesson for me on the power of local activism.

Again at the behest of business I was involved in the creation of the Pretoria-Witwatersrand-Vereeniging (PWV) Economic and

Development Forum, a successful effort to bring together all economic stakeholders in South Africa's industrial heartland. As chair of the Forum I had regular contact with the ANC's regional leadership. They included Paul Mashatile, a remarkable, sanguine young leader of the SACP, Joan Fubbs, an incendiary, quixotic, brave activist, and Ben Turok, a maverick economist who had been one of the original Treason Trial accused along with Mandela.

My own position within these processes was a strange one. While my sympathies were unequivocally with the ANC-supporting structures, I had to act neutrally, which sometimes angered these organisations. It was a position I partly enjoyed, as I felt beholden to no one, while clear about my own beliefs. At the same time, I had to restrain my desire to be publicly associated with the ANC ... to belong to the forces of change, to be seen as a member of this extraordinary family.

*

As the first democratic elections approached, jockeying for position within the ANC intensified. Thabo Mbeki ruthlessly carved his way to the deputy presidency at the expense of the more popular Cyril Ramaphosa, Mandela's favourite. These political manoeuvres not only gave an early indication of the Machiavellian intrigue that would characterise Mbeki's presidency, but also brought into sharp relief the cultural and organisational differences that characterised the various components of the ANC: those who had operated politically inside South Africa through the UDF and its affiliates, those who had been on Robben Island, and those who had run the organisation in exile.

The UDF and its affiliates aimed to mobilise the broadest possible base of support against apartheid. It focused on massive community mobilisation in black areas while spreading its tentacles into white suburbs through smaller, targeted initiatives. Its culture was one of openness, discussion and tolerance of differing political and personal starting points. It was profoundly non-racial and inclusive in its outlook. Despite being quite chaotic and shambolic in its operations, the UDF was enormously effective.

The ANC on Robben Island was minutely organised, hierarchical, extraordinarily disciplined, close knit but also quite democratic within the obvious constraints. It was referred to as 'the University' because of the stress placed by the leadership on political and theoretical learning. As a consequence many of those who spent time on the island had a remarkable knowledge of ANC history and the ideological debates within the movement. They also tended to be open to ideas and discussion. The islanders stressed discipline and establishing a moral advantage over the warders and the prison system.

The movement in exile contained different formations, strands and groups. The life of those in the camps was very different from those in London and other leading cities. Exiles were constantly targeted by the South African security forces in the frontline states and European capitals,[2] while spies attempted to infiltrate the organisation at all levels. Unsurprisingly, therefore, the exiles were organised in a very hierarchical manner, with information tightly guarded and decision making centralised. Open debate was constrained and new arrivals treated with caution. The vanguardist, democratic centralist aspects of the organisation in exile betrayed Leninist roots, while an additional Stalinist dimension saw the party as paramount and loyalty as the crucial currency.

These different cultures and ways of operating were all required by the diverse contexts and realities in which parts of the organisation found themselves at different times. They were crucial to the success that enabled the ANC to strike the path and open the door of liberation. But as the various strands of the organisation came together in South Africa in the early nineties the differences became more apparent and led to tensions.

SECTION II
INSPIRATIONAL POLITICS

CHAPTER 4
Let Freedom Reign

Free at last! Free at last!
Thank God Almighty, we are free at last!

Martin Luther King, Jr

Formerly a remote Indian university town built to accommodate 800 000, Dhaka is now capital of independent Bangladesh and home to over 10 million people. Simone and I are here to continue the celebration of our marriage. A few days earlier, on 18 December 1993, we were married in the King's College Chapel in Cambridge. The ceremony in this grand but comforting place of worship, where I had spent many contemplative hours while a student, included readings in Bengali, Arabic and Hebrew, none of which I understood.

Leaving the plane at Dhaka airport I was overwhelmed by the sensation of being in a place unlike any I'd experienced before; by the sweet cinnamon smell, the pressing humidity, and the closeness of millions of people occupying every inch of space. Simone had coached me in the formality of 'salaam-ing' her grandmother, the family matriarch. In the close, sweating throng I was introduced to 'nanu', a small, regal lady with white hair, enveloped in a white sari. I sank to my knees and touched her feet. Introductions to numerous other family members followed. I touched the feet of those who were old enough to warrant a salaam. After a workout's worth of bending I glanced around for Simone, only to realise that she and the family were already in waiting cars while I had respectfully greeted countless bemused strangers.

At our Hollud ceremony Simone and I sat on a low platform swathed in traditional garb, as each guest filed past to feed us sweets and daub henna on our foreheads. My bald head would have turned a deep reddish brown were it not for the protection offered by the grand white and silver wedding turban I wore. As the children sang Bengali wedding songs gently mocking the groom, as is traditional – my baldness, pallor, obvious unsuitability for marriage – I wondered how many white Jews from the southern tip of Africa had been fêted in this way in the magical land of Tagore.

Between continuous receptions where Simone and I were served vast, steaming bowls of wedding fare, often including a whole roast chicken for each of us, ingloriously planted into a mountain of rice, I managed one evening to phone my office in Johannesburg. My colleague informed me that I had been included in a list of ANC parliamentary candidates published in the press the day before. I was elated.

*

The ANC process of selecting candidates for the first democratic election was wonderfully haphazard. The movement was still too disorganised to arrange an orderly, methodical procedure. The lists of candidates for the national Parliament and nine provincial legislatures comprised many of the former exiles and internal activists who had been prominent since the ANC's unbanning. But to broaden its appeal and affirm its inclusiveness the ANC approached a range of less obvious candidates. These included the highly politicised jazz singer Jennifer Ferguson, whom I had worked with in SAMA; Leon Cohen, the respected chairman of a leading manufacturing company, who was also prominent in the CBM; the former, allegedly corrupt Prime Minister of the 'independent' homeland of Transkei, Stella Sicgau, and the young army officer who had ousted her. A number of celebrity sportsmen, writers, academics and entertainers turned down the opportunity to become politicians.

I found myself at number 64 on the list for the PWV[1] Legislature as a consequence of being known to some in the ANC as an internal activist, albeit with a low profile, and more publicly in my role as a facilitator of reconciliation, development and education processes. Like Leon Cohen, I was seen as having some knowledge of economics and finance, skills in limited supply within the ANC at that time.

On our return to Johannesburg, after a honeymoon in Rajasthan and yet another wedding celebration with Simone's father in Abu

Dhabi, Simone and I held a party for friends and my new colleagues in the ANC. To the saxophone-drenched rhythms of the African Jazz Pioneers – a band famous in the fifties, deprived of opportunities to perform outside the townships for almost 40 years – we jived until the early hours of the morning, exulting in the joy of a new home and a new life.

As the business of preparing for the elections got under way I was welcomed into the formal ANC fold by the vast majority of my colleagues. One or two other white candidates were a little more sceptical. Ben Turok, the elderly, energetic former Treason trialist, suggested that as a white, educated candidate without a long struggle history I might be resented by my black colleagues. Ben's fear never came to pass.

At the time, the ANC in the PWV was led by a young, charismatic former Robben Islander, Tokyo Sexwale. Not particularly well known on his release, Sexwale had been elected chairperson of the ANC in the PWV in 1991. He really rose to prominence as a consequence of his evocative, statesmanlike response to the assassination of his close friend, the fiery SACP leader Chris Hani.[2] At the time of Hani's murder Tokyo was not just a close friend but also a near neighbour. So on that fateful morning of 10 April 1993 he was first on the scene, captured in iconic photographs weeping over the bloodied body of his friend and comrade. The funeral a few days later took place amidst tension and anxiety. Young township followers of Hani were threatening violent reaction to the murder. As the coffin was lowered into the earth a volley of gunfire broke out and intensified. Was this the moment at which the relatively peaceful transition would descend into anarchy?

Impressive in military fatigues, Sexwale reacted more quickly and purposefully than many of his more senior colleagues. He grabbed the microphone and bellowed: 'Cease fire, cease fire,' again and again with an authority that quelled the shooting. The media played and replayed the image of this commanding figure, confirming Tokyo as a leader of consequence amongst both fearful whites and the militant youth.

Sexwale was a dynamic election campaigner, not only a charismatic if sometimes long-winded speaker, but also possessed with the Clintonesque ability to make everyone he met feel that they were of singular importance. Mandela, by contrast, was a much less flashy but no less charismatic campaigner.

A distinctive aspect of the election campaign was the ANC's People's Forums, in which Mandela or other leaders of the movement would meet with a few hundred people at a time in a smallish venue and discuss the issues that faced the country with an honesty and pragmatism that is unique in today's spin-driven politics of image. At these forums Mandela spoke to an audience hungry for material change of the magnitude of the task facing a democratic government in South Africa. He stated the ANC's desire to redress the inequities of the past but explained that real, material change would be slow in coming and that people would need to be patient for many years to come. This candour was admirable but also a little disconcerting to someone like me who was rather low down on the list of candidates. While delighted that the nation was in such trustworthy hands I did silently pray for more tub-thumping performances to ensure my own political future.

Mandela doesn't do tub thumping. Even at the vast, exuberant rallies that the ANC held at stadia around the country he would be measured, calm, occasionally mischievous such as when launching into his famous, turkey-like Madiba shuffle. But there were others who thumped tubs up and down the country, such as Peter Mokaba, the firebrand leader of the ANC Youth League, who would promise to deliver the earth the day after the election was won.

*

Together with Graham Dewar, I was assigned the electoral district of Randburg, a sprawl of white suburbia in the northwest of Johannesburg. Our electoral office was run out of a small storeroom in the garden of our pink Melville house by Simone's brother Chamoun, a neurologist, and his doctor friend 'Viv' Patel, who were visiting from London. Despite their efforts to draw up methodical plans set out on large flip charts, we drove around haphazardly, meeting as many people as we could.

To find support for the ANC in predominantly white Randburg was a fairly rare occurrence, but so too was outright hostility. Instead many of the white voters I spoke to wanted to know why a white, educated South African would throw in his lot with the ANC. So, while house meetings we held up and down the district didn't garner the party many votes, they gave us an opportunity to talk about the non-racial philosophy at the core of the ANC, and the quality and – dare I say it – sheer likeability of many of the leaders of the movement whom sectors of the South African media had demonised for decades. These encounters, often passionate and rambunctious, enabled me to talk about the deep commitment I felt towards the ANC and the new democracy that was dawning. I was thrilled to have the opportunity to communicate my depth of feeling to a sometimes sceptical, often uninformed constituency.

*

On 25 April the euphoria of the campaign was violently interrupted by a bomb explosion just behind the ANC's Johannesburg offices. A fellow candidate, Susan Keane, who was on her way to a meeting we were all attending, was killed in the blast. Joan Fubbs, another candidate, who was in the car with Susan, was only lightly injured but deeply traumatised.

Despite the relatively benign reception we were receiving on the doorsteps of middle class white areas, Susan's tragic death was a reminder that there were some who violently opposed the advent of democracy in our country.

There were some 70 extreme white right-wing groups in South Africa in the pre-election period. Once their views would have been the mainstream of National Party thinking, but many of the unrepentant racists had moved into parliamentary opposition with the Conservative Party under Andries Treurnicht in 1982, or into varying degrees of extreme extra-parliamentary activity. Some of these groups were composed of nothing more than a few close family members and like-minded friends and neighbours, while others, such as the Afrikaanse Weerstandsbeweging (AWB), were more extensively organised.

The AWB met its effective end days before the election, when a ramshackle motorcade of Terreblanche's supporters stuttered to the rescue of one of the soon-to-be-extinct homelands, Bophuthatswana. Rather than welcoming their supposed saviours with open arms, the homeland soldiers turned their guns on them, killing four of the misguided adventurers. The media images of the dead AWB men in their shorts and long socks slumped against their vehicles destroyed any perception of the white right wing in South Africa as a serious force. What remained was the impression of a small group of men caught in a time warp, rendered pathetically impotent and irrelevant as the world around them changed.

Instead of a glorious march that might have presaged a violent election, the right wing's bathetic forage into Bophuthatswana increased the pressure on more moderate conservatives to go the parliamentary route as elections approached. And so it proved with the former Chief of the South African Defence Force, General Constand Viljoen, persuaded just days before the election to lead a slate of right-wing candidates on to the ballot. While their electoral impact was minimal, Viljoen's Freedom Front provided a respectable political home for the country's declining far-right wing.

Nevertheless, on the eve of the election some white South Africans panicked, hoarding supplies in anticipation of Armageddon come the voting. A number of doomsayers shamefacedly admitted to having an excess of baked beans, toilet paper and powdered milk in the calm aftermath of the poll.

Having persuaded the white right wing to exercise their democratic right through the ballot box, the ANC, NP and election authorities had another drama to deal with before voting got under way. The Inkatha Freedom Party, a predominantly Zulu movement based in the rural areas of KwaZulu-Natal and led by the enigmatic, prickly Chief Mangosuthu Buthelezi, initially decided to boycott the election. Buthelezi's capitulation at the very last minute required election officials to manually apply rapidly printed stickers on to every ballot paper the night before the vote.

*

April 27 will always be Freedom Day in South Africa. In 1994 it was a day of unbridled elation as a nation voted on equal terms for the first time. The three days of voting were virtually violence free, characterised instead by administrative chaos that saw people queuing for up to eight hours to cast their sacred ballots. The time spent in those snaking queues had an almost cathartic affect on the nation. It was an opportunity for those who had been kept apart for so long to stand together in rain and sunshine, to talk about waiting as equals, at least in one sense, for the first time.

My April 27th was a day of frenetic chaos, driving voters to polling stations, ensuring we had monitors at all of the stations and casting my vote. As a white South African I had always had the right to vote, but had never exercised it while the vast majority were excluded from doing so. Contributing to the ultimate democratic process for the first time was deeply moving. As I drew my two crosses on the long, thin ballot I couldn't help but be tearful for all the senseless suffering that had taken place to get to this point – for the privilege of reaping the benefits and for the future of a country I finally felt was mine.

Since that day I have never forgone an opportunity to cast a vote. Winning the right to vote in a democratic ballot is something that has been hard-fought-for almost wherever it is possible. It is the seminal act of citizenship, the act that states that even if I spoil my ballot in protest I am participating in the democratic process, a right millions of men and especially women were deprived of for centuries.

Much to the amusement of those close to me I continue to get excited by the night-before anticipation of voting, even in local elections in my current home in leafy northwest London. And every time I draw my X, I feel something of that initial pride, emotion and privilege that I experienced on 27 April 1994 as South Africa became a democracy.

*

The process of counting the votes was in some ways as exciting as the voting itself. As I scrambled around the counting stations the mountains of ballots lying on tables represented another important block in the edifice of democracy that we were building. I would receive reports from each station as the day progressed. I recall at one school the ANC-supporting economist, Maria Ramos, scuttling out every few hours to let me know how we were doing. To see someone whose true passion is macro-economic modelling so excited by the mundane task of counting the paper fragments of democracy exemplified the joyfulness of the process.

After a tortuous six-day wait for the final results and with a turnout estimated at almost 100 per cent, the ANC won just under 63 per cent of the vote. In Randburg we managed a creditable performance of 49 per cent of the vote, mainly due to domestic workers and the near-by ANC-supporting township of Alexandra.

My position on the ANC list of candidates for the PWV Provincial Legislature meant I was a quarter of a per cent short of winning a seat. The elation of the election process and outcome was tinged with the anxiety of knowing that I had given up my job to stand as a candidate and might now be unemployed. However, a number of candidates ahead of me decided not to take up their positions, usually because they had been offered senior civil service or political advisory roles, and I was sworn in as an ANC Member of the Provincial Legislature days before the inauguration of President Nelson Mandela.

I now had an opportunity to reflect on my first few months as a for-mal cog in the ANC machinery. In the early stages of the campaign I had felt like something of an impostor amongst my fellow candidates, many of whom had sacrificed so much in pursuit of the freedom that was being realised. Having been materially – if not morally or psycho-logically – advantaged by apartheid, who was I to be benefiting in this way from its demise? But as campaigning intensified so I felt more and more a part of this welcoming political family. My pride at now being a public representative of the movement that had spearheaded the fight against injustice and oppression knew no bounds.

This delight reached its apex with the inauguration of Nelson Mandela as South Africa's first democratic President. The symbolism of the might of the South African military giving the country's first black president a 21-gun salute and an Air Force fly-past brought tears to all but the most cynical or racist eyes. The outgoing First Lady was tearful, but we felt that Marike de Klerk wept for her loss rather than the elation that reverberated around the hill.

Tens of thousands of liberated South Africans danced on the lawns of the Union Buildings to the exultant sounds of the nation's foremost trumpeter, Hugh Masekela. Mandela's ideal of 'a democratic and free society in which all live together in harmony with equal opportunities' – the ideal for which he was so close to being executed 30 years before – seemed close to being achieved in this remarkable land.

CHAPTER 5
Place of Gold

Jo'burg City, I salute you;
When I run out, or roar in a bus to you,
I leave behind me, my love,
My comic houses, my dongas and my ever-whirling dust ...

'City Johannesburg'
Mongane Wally Serote

In the immediate afterglow of the election we turned our attention
to the task of running the country's powerhouse province. A key role
would obviously be the management of budgets and the economy.
Leon Cohen and I had been expecting to engage with Jessie Duarte,
a delightful, diminutive woman of huge personality, who was ear-
marked to be the first Member of the Executive Council (MEC) for
Finance and Economic Affairs in the PWV. However, a few days
before Tokyo Sexwale was due to announce his provincial Cabinet, he
was persuaded to change his mind. Supposedly senior members of
the police force objected to Sexwale's intended choice as MEC for
Safety and Security, Jabu Moleketi. Moleketi, while only in his mid-
thirties, was a senior leader of the SACP and had been one of the
ANC's most successful underground commanders, infiltrating the
country regularly for over a decade without being caught. To avoid
antagonising the police force leadership, who needed to be won
over if the battle against spiralling crime was to be won, Sexwale
swapped Jessie and Jabu's portfolios. So Moleketi, trained in military
studies at Moscow University, was to be Finance and Economics
Minister in the country's economic heartland. 'Too red for the
police but OK for the economy' was how one businessman described
the appointment to me.

Moleketi asked to meet with Leon and me on the morning the
announcement was to be made. For a late riser like me the starting

33

time of 7.15 am was intimidating, but this being the less-than-punctu-al ANC I expected nothing much to happen before 8 am. When I arrived at the office in downtown Johannesburg just after 7.30 Jabu was ready and impatient, having already been to gym. A good-look-ing, slight man with a twinkle in his one good eye (he had lost the other in a grenade blast), he concealed his irritation and was charm-ing and friendly. What was immediately apparent was his sharp mind and astute political brain. Here was a leader of the highest quality, and a lovely human being to boot, whose studious exterior hid an impish sense of humour. Jabu asked us to work with him in establish-ing a provincial Finance and Economic Affairs Department.

Leon Cohen brought experience, calm and gravitas to this fledg-ling team. One of the sponsors of the CBM, Leon had run PG Bison, a manufacturer of furniture and other household items, for many years. His commitment to the ANC and South Africa was such that he was willing to give up this comfortable corporate life to participate in building a new provincial government. Warm, fair-minded and unim-peachably honest, Leon was a source of enormous comfort and encouragement as we addressed the challenge of establishing a com-pletely new provincial department that would be responsible for the country's second biggest budget, after national government's, and would also have to determine policy and legislation on matters as diverse as gambling and horse-racing, consumer rights, tourism and economic growth.

Our first legislative home was in a tatty exhibition centre on the outskirts of Johannesburg in an arena aptly entitled 'the bullring'. Soon after I had arrived at the Legislature, a shy, almost coy man with a round, smiling face approached me, held my hand gently in both of his and said in a quiet voice: 'Comrade Andrew, I am Comrade Bob, it is a pleasure to have you here.' Bob Mabaso was a senior mem-ber of the provincial Communist Party and would go on to lead the Party in the province. He struck me as one of the kindest, most sin-cere people I had met in politics.

In stark contrast to Bob's humility loomed the massive ego of Robert McBride. I was intent on liking him, if only because of the complex trauma he had endured on Death Row for his part in the bombing of a beach-side pub in Durban (purportedly but not clearly under orders from the ANC). However, he was petulant, almost

34

child-like: much of what he said seemed designed to create discord and focus attention on Robert McBride. He soon moved on to national Parliament, then rapidly to the Department of Foreign Affairs, and finally to the police services of a local authority. In all of these roles his controversial behaviour was seldom out of the news.

Sheila Weinberg was perhaps the least likely politician of us all, despite being the youngest white woman detained and sentenced under apartheid in the 1950s. She detested the backbiting, bickering and grandstanding that were a part of the political process. A warm and gentle soul, she would sit on the back benches of the Legislature knitting intently. Sheila inherited from her noteworthy parents an acute sense of right and wrong and was moved to indignation only in the face of injustice.

Unlike Sheila, Ignatius Jacobs thrived on the brutal cut and thrust of even provincial politics. A fiercely intelligent firebrand who would eventually become the provincial Education Minister, Ignatius was typical of young activists who had grown up in the violent and dangerous world of township politics, in his case the coloured area of Riverlea. His passion and energy were enviable and inspiring, his focus and aggression intimidating.

Trish Hanekom had endured a torrid period in detention that seemed to have given her a steely resolve and discipline, as well as an almost permanent earnestness. Married to the affable Minister of Land Affairs and Agriculture, Derek Hanekom, she was probably the most committed, hardest-working person I have known, pushing her small, slender frame to the verge of collapse on an almost daily basis.

Across the benches, representing the National Party was a group of generally mediocre talents: former national politicians who hadn't made the grade, ex-township administrators, including Johan Killian from the Vaal, and the occasional young party member who, under apartheid, would have been assured of a sparkling career as part of the ruling elite despite a lack of discernible talent. Among them was Annelise van Wyk, a gaunt woman, already middle-aged in her late twenties. Annelise had been one of Trish's prison warders and had also allegedly worked at the prison in which another ANC member of the Legislature, Nomvula Mokonyane, was tortured during her apartheid-era detention.

I found sitting in the same Legislature as someone like Annelise infuriating. But Jabu, Trish and Nomvula handled it with equanimity. Whenever I raised the injustice of it, they patiently reminded me that it was precisely because of reconciliation with people like Annelise that South Africa had achieved its largely non-violent transition to democracy.

*

In our early days in the Legislature a veteran of the struggle, now in his seventies, doffed his hat to me and said 'morning, baas'. I was embarrassed and shamed. This instinctive subservience in an elderly liberation figure illustrated how deep racial power relations in South Africa ran. As a white person in the ANC, with experience and training outside the organisation, I was always treated with a degree of deference. The set of performance criteria applied to Leon and me differed somewhat from that applied to other whites, such as Trish, Joan Fubbs or Mary Metcalfe, who had been intimately involved in the ANC for far longer. This special treatment was a mixed blessing. At times of endlessly tedious caucus sessions or when mundane political tasks were being handed out we could often escape without a murmur from the whips.

Together with this special status was an unstated view that it was inappropriate for whites, who had had the benefit of superior education and work experience outside of politics, to hold too many senior positions in government. Intellectually I supported this view with a passion. It was essential that the majority who had been excluded from opportunities for hundreds of years should dominate the running of the new democracy. It was only in this way that the state would reflect the needs of this excluded majority and build the foundations of a more equal, non-racial society. There may have been times when I was a little resentful, believing that I would not be recognised for the contribution I could make, or that I might not be able to fully use my skills, but if I was honest with myself, I would see in someone like Jabu not only a growing level of technical skill that would very quickly surpass my own, but also a political insight and astuteness that I neither possessed nor developed in any meaningful way.

I certainly didn't feel underutilised in the first 18 months of democracy. I was thrust uncomplaining into an exhilarating, chaotic maelstrom of activity. First came the finalisation of legislative committees and their chairpersons. The provincial leadership had decided to create a Finance and Economics Committee with Leon as its chair, and a Public Accounts Committee, which I was to lead. At the time I had little understanding of what a Public Accounts Committee did or its crucial importance in the accountability chain. All I knew was that in parliaments around the world these committees were chaired by the opposition. Showing a modicum of political acumen, I persuaded Leon that we should split his committee into a Finance Committee and a separate Economic Affairs Committee, with myself chairing the latter. The Public Accounts Committee could then be chaired by the opposition. The leadership agreed to this arrangement.

My committee covered all economic matters for which the provinces had legislative powers. ANC members of the committee included Sheila Weinberg, Joan Fubbs and Mohammed Dangor. Mohammed, brother of Jessie Duarte and the novelist and activist Achmat Dangor, was a real political operator. His chubby, dishevelled exterior belied a sharp, Machiavellian streak that meant he was constantly involved in political intrigue in the province or nationally. The opposition Democratic Party was represented by Brian Goodall, a former national MP well versed in economics. The National Party representative was Patricia Lion-Cachet. The daughter of a former Cabinet Minister, she had a rather self-important air. Her primary interest was in maintaining state support for a tourism organisation on whose board she served and which enabled her to travel the world.

The Committee worked well together. The legislative experience of Brian and Patricia was complemented by a political focus and energy from the ANC component. Differences arose between us on the extent to which we transformed the various economic structures we had inherited. The NP argued vociferously for the maintenance of the status quo, with the DP not far behind them.

I found myself in a political and intellectual dilemma. I fully endorsed the need for transformation, but was wary of completely obliterating the experience and administrative competence that had been built up in pre-existing structures. The social milieu and material reality of the predominantly white opposition parties was closer to my own background than that of my ANC comrades. I could to some extent relate socially to Brian, Patricia and their colleagues, but not politically. My political convictions and social reality thus lay at obtuse angles, something I was not uncomfortable with.

At the same time as running our committees Leon and I, together with Jabu and a secretary, comprised the new Finance and Economic Affairs Department. We attended all meetings with economic stakeholders in the region and represented the province in interaction with the relevant national departments. While this elision of the legislative, executive and administrative functions was probably unconstitutional, it was the only way we could maximise the very limited financial and economic capacity of the ANC in the early years.

The creation of a provincial tourism authority was one venture in which my background as a facilitator proved invaluable. It took months of haggling to bring together the diverse interest groups in the province, and to develop a coherent vision and strategy for promoting this aesthetically challenged region to the rest of the country and the international community. To get people who had dominated the province's tourism structures for years, like Patricia and others, to cede power and give access to small black tourism entrepreneurs was no easy matter. Turf wars, disagreements and jealousies came to a head at a massive tourism indaba we organised. After a powerful speech by Jabu about how we would put aside our differences and forge a unified tourism structure for the province, the 120 delegates proceeded to defend their own territory with me scribbling the key points of their disagreements on to flipcharts. While they enjoyed tea Jabu and I surveyed this wreckage of non-cooperation, drew out the points of value and coalesced a common tourism strategy and structure for the province. We presented this back to the disparate audience and felt relieved to observe their eventual acceptance of a unified way of doing things.

The creation of consumer rights legislation and a consumer rights body for the province, championed by Jabu and driven by Sheila Weinberg, proved similarly satisfying. It also reflected the global economic shift in power that monetarism had engendered away from producers and towards consumers.

The scarcity of human resources and our unconstitutional dual role meant that Leon and I were involved in every stage of the governmental process, from formulating policy with Jabu, drafting legislation as his advisors, to getting it through the Legislature in our capacity as committee chairpersons and then implementing it as members of the Department. This multiplicity of roles served my short attention span well. It was exhausting, chaotic, but enormously enjoyable and fulfilling – a unique opportunity to build something from nothing.

Working with Jabu was gratifying and enjoyable. I was constantly amazed by his political acuity and learned an enormous amount from him. We also had some wonderful social occasions with Jabu and his impressive wife, Geraldine, at that time a rising star in national government. On one of the few occasions we all managed to get a night off, Geraldine and Jabu had dinner with us at our small, pink house in bustling Melville. Geraldine spoke intently of their harrowing experiences in exile and the challenges facing government, while Jabu, no mean theorist himself, still managed to insinuate levity into the evening with hysterical anecdotes about some of his more bizarre escapades underground. I felt humbled by these two exceptional people who had already led such brave lives.

*

Running through all of the policy making and legislative processes was a massive public participation initiative. In drafting policy we would attempt to meet with as many interested people and groups as possible – in fact, legislation could not be passed without being preceded by formal public hearings which were advertised throughout the province.

This commendable effort to involve South Africans in the law-making process, which mirrored what was happening nationally and in all of the provinces, was bedevilled by the disparity in voice of the people of the country. Every hearing would be dominated by business, labour and other organised interest groups, with very few individuals or small community groups having the resources or even access to the invitations to participate. Jabu, before leaving the province to become the country's Deputy Minister of Finance, attempted to address this by creating government one-stop service centres in a number of townships around the province to dispense advice, information and assistance to those excluded individuals and groups.

Through my involvement in all stages of these various processes I was well positioned to reflect on how different South Africans were coming to terms with the new order. The fraught domain of gambling legislation was a veritable jackpot for these observations.

Gambling had a sleazy history in South Africa. Banned by the puritanical National Party in white South Africa, it was allowed in the so-called independent homelands. By one of apartheid's many failures of logic it was immoral for South Africans to gamble on our own soil, but acceptable in these desolate, uneconomic sham states which relied on the likes of the gaudy Sun City to generate any revenue. How we student lefties loved Steve van der Sandt for his rollicking 'I ain't gonna play Sun City', while Frank Sinatra, Liza Minnelli, Rod Stewart, Elton John and many others took the apartheid-sanctioned Kerzner shekel.

As repressive legislation was eased in the early nineties, thousands of illegal casinos flourished around the country, especially in Johannesburg. Provincial governments had the twin tasks of closing down these illegal operators and creating a framework for a controlled, regulated gambling industry. Within weeks of the election, before we had even had an opportunity to think through our policy on this difficult area, we were invited to a meeting by the Sun King, the man behind Sun City, gambling tycoon Sol Kerzner.

Jabu, Leon and I made our way to Kerzner's offices and were greeted in a bizarre East Rand/Las Vegas drawl by a swarthy, squat man with a bull-like neck. Kerzner had assembled about 17 of his acolytes along one side of a long, thin table. The three of us gingerly assumed our seats on the opposite side. Dispensing quickly with pleasantries, Kerzner began an address that amounted broadly to: 'Mr Minister [pronounced "Mynstr"], I've got a deal for you. You give me a licence for a mega-casino on the Vaal River and I'll give you excellent revenue without fail. No need for an extensive gambling board, officials or the like. Later we can float the thing on a US exchange and the Province will make a few billion from that. And what do ["whadda"] I need from you? Just an understanding that it makes no sense to have any other casinos in the Transvaal and the Orange Free State.'

Jabu, Leon and I were not just sceptical but insulted. Kerzner assumed that the new government would be much like the homeland leaders he had dealt with in the past.

40

This wasn't our only interesting encounter on the subject. As we worked to develop gambling legislation for the province, every proverbial worm emerged from the woodwork. A tall, charming casino operator from Ghana, regal in flowing magenta robes, swept in to see Jabu and me. Jabu voiced our concerns about the negative social consequences of having casinos in impoverished areas. The Ghanaian attempted to put our minds at rest. 'Don't worry, Mr Minister,' he said, 'in the poorest parts of Accra, even when they have no money, they will steal some to come and play in my casinos. You will generate revenue from even the poorest.'

A portly, bling-bedecked gentleman from the former Soviet republic of Georgia arrived with three bodyguards and a letter of support from President Eduard Shevardnadze. After asking me whether I could arrange for the Reserve Bank to supply him with gold bullion and drop in a casino licence on the side, he enquired whether I would like my million dollar fee to be deposited in Switzerland or somewhere else more convenient. I was, naively, outraged. On another occasion a local gaming magnate asked with great understanding and compassion whether I had any personal financial difficulties. I retorted that I did but that they were none of his business. I was beginning to realise the importance of public accountability and transparency in political life.

The horse-racing fraternity were desperate – either for government protection when their monopoly on legal gambling ended, or for gaming licences in compensation. They went out of their way to be hospitable. I was invited to address the annual banquet of one of the leading horse-racing clubs near Johannesburg. As I didn't possess black tie regalia, Simone and I decided to attend in traditional Bangladeshi dress, but emerging at the top of the escalator on to the marbled mezzanine level, we witnessed a 300-strong, all-white crowd stunned into silence. Was it the fact that my wife was not white that shocked them, or that I was wearing a Nehru jacket and churidah pants? The club's president and his wife hurried to introduce themselves. By way of small talk his wife, sporting a necklace in the shape of a tie made entirely of diamonds, asked whether the choker Simone was wearing had any 'deep significance or meaning'. A few moments later one of the guests remarked that Simone spoke remarkably good English. Simone replied: 'I spoke pretty good English even before I went to Cambridge.'

41

The process of public hearings on the Gambling Bill was difficult, with most presentations taking the form of pre-emptive bids for licences. I only lost my cool once, when a group of highly regarded academics gave a few of us a private presentation on why there should be only one licence in the province, a line not dissimilar to the argument Sol Kerzner had made. On further questioning it transpired that their research was being paid for quite generously by Sun International, one of Kerzner's companies.

After over 40 public submissions the committee, with the help of excellent legal advisers, drafted a solid and fair piece of regulatory legislation, which led to the shutting down of many of the illegal gambling operations in the province. The casino bosses and their employees were outraged. At one point about 250 laid-off employees protested outside the Premier's Houghton home, blocking access to the property. I was sent to negotiate with them and explain why we needed to regulate the industry. They eventually abandoned their protest, but I had become the new object of their wrath. The next day *The Citizen* newspaper ran an article claiming that many of the illegal casino operators had been forced to open brothels as an alternative business. Somehow they mixed up the paragraphs about these new business interests and the fact that I was the person drafting the legislation, so the article read:

> Representatives of the gambling industry will meet today with the chairman of the Gauteng Economic Affairs Committee, Mr. Andrew Feinstein, to discuss the granting of licences.
>
> In 10 days he will open a massage parlour with saunas and an escort agency – the shop premises he occupies are big enough.[1]

With the exception of my own putative career as a brothel owner, for which *The Citizen* had to print a large apology, the provincial department achieved notable successes with the creation of an Economic Development Agency and a Provincial Consumer Watchdog. However, engagement with governance at this level had its frustrations. Key amongst them was the way some committed people changed when they came into government service. One incident mirrors a fairly generalised, if not all-encompassing experience.

It became apparent that we required support in developing the provincial tourism structure. We interviewed a range of impressive candidates. One stood out. She was a young woman known to some of us for her selfless, committed work as an activist prior to 1994. She had completed a diploma course in tourism and was extremely keen to join. We hired her immediately.

Two weeks after she had started work I asked her to represent the Department at an important meeting of a number of the tourism role players in the province. She was excited to do so and we spent some time together preparing for the meeting. The day after, I asked her how the meeting had gone. She replied: 'I didn't go, you didn't tell me it only started at 4.30. I finish work at about that time.'

For an activist who had willingly worked until all hours of the night in the service of the struggle, walking into a government office had a sadly enervating effect. What is it that engenders such languor: exhaustion after many years of struggle, a sense of entitlement, the public service framework? It is a question I return to whenever confronted by inefficient bureaucracies wherever they are in the world.

*

During 1995 the Legislature moved from the convention centre on the outskirts of Soweto to the old, colonial City Hall in the centre of the Johannesburg CBD. A beautiful Victorian building replete with characterful wooden floors and exquisite cornices, it was tastefully renovated and restored for our use. The move was not simply a matter of convenience or pleasure, however: it was also an attempt to staunch the flow of established businesses out of the CBD. Rising crime rates, the proliferation of unregulated pavement hawking and anarchic taxi ranks had caused corporate offices to relocate to the more sedate suburbs. Unlike the corporate decision makers I loved the CBD, a real African metropolis, and enjoyed both my morning walk from the parking garage to the Legislature and my regular stroll between our building and the nearby Executive offices where the Premier was now ensconced in a penthouse suite with its own glassed press briefing room.

Tokyo was extremely popular in the province. He loved the theatre of politics, and as Premier, behind the lectern in his penthouse facing a pack of journalists, he had if anything become more flamboyant and larger-than-life. As Mark Gevisser so poignantly noted: 'There is no South African politician as self-conscious about leadership and public image'[2] (although, to his credit, Tokyo's first official car as Premier was a modest VW Jetta).

The first time I confronted Tokyo was around the re-naming of the province. 'PWV' hardly reflected the diversity or power of the country's economic heartland, nor was it likely to set the pulse racing amongst potential investors or visitors. Of the hundreds of proposals made by the public it came down to a choice between two options, both meaning 'Place of Gold'. Egoli, the Nguni word, was much favoured by Tokyo. The fact that it was also the name of the country's leading TV soap opera only added to its allure for the telegenic Premier. A group of us in the caucus, under the pushy leadership of Ignatius Jacobs, preferred the Sotho word, Gauteng. We felt it had more gravitas while being less showy. I was tasked with presenting our arguments to the ANC caucus.

Our weekly caucus meetings tended to be long-winded, stultifying affairs dealing with the minutiae of the legislative, political and administrative functioning of the party in the Legislature. In the tradition of the ANC, most people wanted to have a say on almost every issue, and weak chairing in the early years allowed this. The meetings were occasionally enlivened by factional antagonisms between Tokyo's supporters and those of his hapless deputy, Mathole Motshekga.

Though exciting sessions were the rare exception, people felt quite passionate about the naming issue, so as we congregated for our weekly meeting on 24 November 1994 there was a buzz of anticipation in the long, narrow caucus room. Tokyo spoke first. Charismatic as always, he argued for a name that reflected our status and glamour, that was easy to pronounce and recognisable. I had done some research into our preferred Sotho name and spoke with emotion about how the name was used by the first miners in the area to denote not just the promise of riches but also the struggles they endured underground. The work was dangerous, their lives difficult, separated from their families and squashed into single sex hostels. Invoking Hugh Masekela's 'Stimela', a haunting anthem to the life of migrant workers, I argued that the use of Gauteng better reflected the real experience of those miners whose back-breaking endeavours and hardship had been the foundation of the wealth of today's Gauteng. Caucus supported us overwhelmingly.

I hadn't yet got to know Tokyo that well, but he gave me a big hug at the end of the meeting and whispered to me: 'I prefer Egoli, but who can compete with such passion and learning.' His graciousness and affability in defeat said a great deal about the man.

*

The ANC's economic policy development had been contested terrain since the mid-1980s, and the debate was still divided between those who continued to support significant state intervention in the economy and those who had moved to a reluctant but determined embrace of the basic tenets of monetarism and a reduced role for the state. When we came into government in 1994, the adage that runs through politics – 'it's about the economy, stupid' – certainly applied. There is little doubt that next to reconciliation, the deracialisation and energising of a moribund economy were paramount.

The ANC mainstream, including probably two-thirds of the senior leadership, was committed to continuing the National Party's orthodox policies, resulting in the appointment of a private sector banker, Chris Liebenberg, as the first post-apartheid Finance Minister.[3] In reaction to this orthodoxy the Congress of South African Trade Unions (Cosatu) and the UDF championed the Reconstruction and Development Programme (RDP). Supported by a group of progressive international economists – the Macroeconomic Research Group (Merg), which included my former Cambridge professor, John Sender – they propagated a more expansionist approach to fiscal and monetary policy, with a focus on growth and employment rather than minimising inflation. The RDP was intended to be people-driven and envisaged a massive national public works programme to facilitate employment and reduce inequalities.

At this time of rampant neo-liberalism, Merg had the feel of a gathering of international renegades who had identified South Africa as a bastion of hope in a world of economic conformity. Their zeal was best represented by Neva Seidman-Makgetla, a strident economist with a nasal twang from years in exile in America, who was determined to vanquish capitalism and its excesses.

45

A national RDP Office was created, with Jay Naidoo, formerly Cosatu General Secretary, as the responsible Cabinet Minister. Jay, a smooth operator with somewhat satanic good looks, clad in a designer collection of Nehru jackets, was inspirational but lacked the administrative nous to turn his soaring sentiment into delivery. In Gauteng, Ben Turok was the province's RDP supremo. He would extol the virtues of the *ujamaa* experiment in post-colonial Tanzania and his own role in what he referred to as 'true African socialism'. In practice, Julius Nyerere's policy, while well intentioned, had been a tragic failure.[4] Ben's pugnacious personal style didn't necessarily help the RDP initiative in the province, but its ultimate demise was due more to defeat in a political-ideological battle than to personality issues.

Jabu, with his mix of astute ideology and technocratic pragmatism, voiced in the language of the struggle, dominated economic policy thinking in the province. He demonstrated his support for the more orthodox framework in practice by delivering close to balanced budgets or surpluses for every year in which he controlled the purse-strings. This was achieved through the creation of a formidable Treasury team comprising Leon, a calmly energetic accountant called Paddy Maharaj, and the newly recruited Head of Finance and Economics, Roland Hunter.

Roland was an impressive figure. While undertaking his compulsory military service during the apartheid years he had passed on confidential Defence Force documents to the ANC. He was caught and served four years in jail. During this time he studied finance and economics with great intensity. He emerged from detention not only an accomplished economist but a wise, humble and selfless human being. Through his role in Gauteng and later as Finance Chief of the Johannesburg Metropolitan government Roland made a massive behind-the-scenes contribution to the fiscal success of the new South Africa.

An interesting dimension of these early years of government was the fractious relationship between the provinces and central government, and particularly Trevor Manuel's Department of Trade and Industry and ourselves in Gauteng. I endured countless meetings in drab government buildings in Pretoria where long-serving bureaucrats would lecture us in a world-weary manner on why they couldn't yet hand over devolved powers to the provinces. Their resistance was

to transferring structures as parochial as provincial Liquor Boards –
hardly the stuff of quixotic campaigns. On some occasions at meetings between himself and his provincial counterparts Manuel would
admonish his civil servants and instruct them to relinquish control.
But on matters of real significance he would hold firm, on one occasion causing a sharp and unpleasant exchange between us on the
matter of trade promotion initiatives. Trevor, a street-wise, sharp
operator, thrived on conflict and the assertion of his considerable
political power.

These tensions were not just about the ennui of the old bureaucrats, many of whom resented the new order in its entirety, but were
caused by differences in the ANC itself over the weak federalism that
had been agreed as a political compromise in the pre-1994 negotiations. In principle, the ANC was opposed to any form of federalism.
By creating provinces with their own legislatures, executives and
administrations, it was inevitable that those serving in these structures would quickly develop a vested interest in enhancing their own
power. This created a new dynamic in the ANC that was indicative of
the early impact that power and patronage were to have on the
organisation.[5]

*

As the provincial administration grew in size and confidence, so the
need for Leon and me to play a role in the Finance and Economic
Affairs Department diminished. The senior appointees in the administration were far more able administrators and advisors than we part-
timers could ever be. Leon felt that his role had run its course and
returned to business, having made an indelible impact on the structures of government in Gauteng. I lost a wise colleague and confidant, but gained a committee. In the weeks before his departure,
Leon, Jabu and I engineered a merger of the two committees, with
me as the Chair of the combined Finance and Economics Committee. Having argued for their separation after the election in 1994,
when it suited me, I was not averse to arguing the opposite for similar reasons. At about the same time, Tokyo asked me to become his
economic advisor. So I had an enhanced committee load and another
unconstitutional role with the Executive.

Working with Tokyo was more taxing than my experience with Jabu. Whereas Jabu had quickly mastered the detail of finance and economics, including undertaking a Master's degree by correspondence through the University of London, Tokyo with his wider brief had less time for financial and economic matters. I was, therefore, engaged in extensive speech-writing and constant attendance at meetings, briefings and trade events. But what helped was that Tokyo always had an instinctive entrepreneurship which has seen him become one of South Africa's most successful businessmen over the past few years.

Working for him was exciting, exhausting and occasionally exasperating. For instance, on our first visit to the World Economic Forum in Davos, Tokyo was nervous about talking to a group of senior businessmen, so he was thoughtful, measured and inspiring. He earned many plaudits from the assembled grandees. Imbued with confidence, we headed for Washington DC, where he gave a more extemporaneous speech, using figures out of context, so that rather than saying that Gauteng accounts for almost 36 per cent of South Africa's GDP, he instead ended with the flourish that 'Gauteng was responsible for 36 per cent.' He couldn't understand why his audience looked bemused rather than appreciative, as they had in Davos.

Tokyo had about him a commanding air, as befitted his larger-than-life personality, but which belied the limited powers and authority of a provincial premier. He was an inspiring figurehead and created a real identity for the new province and its government. He drove the reconciliation agenda of his mentor, Mandela (and also did the best impressions of Madiba I have ever seen), played the media brilliantly, was charismatic and engaging. But he wasn't always interested in the detail of governance. He would sometimes let vexing, important issues meander on without resolution, such as the non-performance, lethargy and rumoured corruption of his deputy, Mathole Motshekga.[6] But in spite of this, as Gevisser argues, he presided over one of the cleaner and more efficient provincial governments.

Gevisser has provided the most apt summation of Sexwale. 'Like [Bill] Clinton he is a man of substance, a man with more policies and ideas than his head has room for; but like Clinton too, though, he is inconsistent and capricious. He is more White House than Shell House,[7] a snazzy, jazzy American politician trapped in the body of a comrade who must at all times be accountable and collective rather than individualist and inspirational. Therein lies his power, but also the potential seeds of his failure.'[8]

His 'failure' in political terms, which has led to great personal financial success, was primarily due to the fact that at the time of the battle to succeed Mandela within the ANC two people saw Tokyo as a potential threat to Thabo Mbeki: Tokyo and Thabo. I experienced at first hand how Thabo took every opportunity to undermine Tokyo, and the personal enmity that existed between them. One evening, while talking through a speech with Tokyo at his house, a call came through from the then Deputy President. I could see from Tokyo's expression that he was enraged by the conversation. At its conclusion he said to me that Thabo was trying to force him out of politics by spreading false rumours about him within the movement. Tokyo's anger was visceral.[9]

Closer to Mandela than Mbeki, Tokyo was always his own man, even on Robben Island. That is perhaps one of the reasons I so enjoyed working for him – and why the final chapter on his role in South African public life has not yet been written.

CHAPTER 6
A Window on the World

I come of those … who taught me that we could
both be at home and be foreign.

'I am an African'
Thabo Mbeki

In my capacity as Tokyo's economic advisor I travelled extensively on behalf of the ANC and government, travels that revealed as much about the ANC as about the destinations.

As Jabu Moleketi and I settled into our Business Class seats on Cathay Pacific bound for Hong Kong, just a few months after taking office, Jabu leaned over to me and said quietly, only half jokingly: 'We have an understanding in the movement that nothing we do outside the country is mentioned on our return.' I was intrigued but didn't yet know him well enough to pursue the conversation.

Our trip had been arranged by Peter Mokaba, Chair of Parliament's Tourism Committee, under the auspices of his National Tourism Forum (NTF). We were to meet a group of Chinese businessmen who, Peter said, wanted to build something called 'The Window on the World' in Gauteng. The 'Window' in southern China was a gargantuan theme park featuring large-scale replicas of the seven wonders of the world.

Viewed from the air the runway at Hong Kong's airport seemed as narrow as a finger biscuit, surrounded on three sides by sea. As we descended I noticed a small plane being winched from the sea next to the runway. It did not bode well. Immediately on touching down we escaped the stifling humidity by jumping into the stretch limo that our hosts had arranged. Peter, a big bear of a man with a ready smile that belied his reputation as a Youth League firebrand, sat comfortably in the plush leather couch at one end of the vast car. Beautifully attired, as always, in a polo shirt and smart sports jacket, he looked very much at home. We were whizzed to the Grand Hyatt, owned by our hosts, and installed in luxury suites. Peter occupied the lavish penthouse.

We showered, changed and were back in the limo, headed for – horrors – a karaoke bar. Although it was after ten pm, Hong Kong was busier and buzzier than central Johannesburg on a Monday morning. Arriving at the somewhat seedy venue, we were ushered into a smallish private room with a screen taking up the far wall. I was nervous about making a complete prat of myself in front of Jabu, Peter and the new arrivals, our hosts and someone I was introduced to only as Neo, who ran the NTF on Peter's behalf. Jabu and I sat down and whispered to each other about our lack of musical prowess. He at least had the prospect of alcohol to lubricate his performance; I've been a teetotaller since a bad head injury in a high-school rugby game.

A glamorous middle-aged hostess moved us apart so that there was a free seat between each of us. A few moments later a line of beautiful young Chinese women filed in and occupied these seats. The music started up. It was marginally less embarrassing to belt out a stream of Abba, Tina Turner and Michael Jackson songs than to respond to the inane questions purred into my ear by the gorgeous young woman gently stroking the inside of my thigh. At some point before dawn we returned to our hotel, Jabu and I sensible enough to do so unaccompanied.

The next day the purpose of the trip became clearer as we were shown into a meeting room in the hotel. Judging by the haze of smoke hanging over the table, Peter, Neo and our hosts had been in lengthy, intense conversation. It was soon apparent that our hosts wanted a casino licence in Gauteng, and that Peter had portrayed us as the men to deliver it. I explained the legislation we were in the early stages of drafting and the application process we envisaged through an independent Gambling and Horse-racing Board. We were plied with questions about the number of licences, the criteria for granting them and how soon they could have one. We explained that it would not be a political decision. Our hosts pressed on, promising that once they had their licence the new Window on the World would attract hundreds of thousands of tourists to Gauteng (pronouncing it, like most of the world, 'Howteng').

Jabu and I slipped out of the meeting as quickly as we could. After changing out of our suits we met up in reception, planning to join the throng of shoppers outside. Peter came rushing down from the meeting. He was panicked, desperate: 'Listen, comrades, we've got to keep these guys interested, they're worried now that they might not get a casino.' Jabu diplomatically responded: 'Comrade Peter, that's not our concern. They must apply like everybody else.' Exasperated, Peter shot back: 'These guys give us half a million a year. We can't piss them off. Come back into the meeting. Just make it sound as though they're going to get one.' I was way out of my league here, but Jabu was quietly adamant. We left Peter steaming and wandered out into the oppressive humidity.

I figured that Peter had been receiving money from our hosts for a while through the NTF, on the assumption that he was likely to be the first Tourism Minister post-1994, a line he had used on a range of tourism-linked people in South Africa. When that didn't come to pass he had then presented us as the guys who were going to dish out the licences. It later transpired that Peter was paying himself $71 000 a year from the NTF, in addition to his ANC salary.[1] In my naiveté I was battling with the notion that this 'lion of the struggle' was clearly using his position as an MP, the Chair of Parliament's tourism committee, to raise money for what was, in effect, a front organisation for himself. I asked Jabu what we should do. He said I should leave it to him.

I was concerned, but sure Jabu would deal with it through the appropriate ANC mechanisms. It was only years later, when I was on the national Parliament's Public Accounts Committee and the NTF appeared in an unflattering light in a Report of the Auditor-General's Office, that I spoke about my experience of Peter and his organisation.

Of no use to Peter, Jabu and I journeyed on to Tianjin, an industrial city 120 km from Beijing. This grey, dirty, concrete conurbation was enlivened by the tens of thousands of cyclists who swarmed its every street. There was, however, none of the noise, jollity or buzz of Hong Kong. Instead people seemed quiet, sullen. We were treated to a sumptuous dinner around a circular table by the leader of the Communist Party in the region. Throughout the meal toasts circulated round the table, our glasses immediately refilled before each new salutation. I piled my still full glasses under the table while *gan bei'ing* (clinking glasses) with mineral water. After about a dozen rounds our host, looking the worse for wear, slumped in his chair, slowly slipping towards the floor. A couple of minders emerged, lifted him under his arms and half dragged him out of the dining room. Dinner was over.

The next day we flew out of Hong Kong. We never did get to see the Window on the World.

*

I made a somewhat surreal excursion to Poland with SACP head Blade Nzimande and a leading party intellectual, Raymond Suttner. They asked me to join them at an inter-governmental conference with the centre-right government in Warsaw.

The old part of Warsaw is quaint, if touristy. The rest struck me as soulless, commercialising at an extremely rapid rate. I was struck by the number of sex shops littering the streets, a strange manifestation of political, social and economic liberalisation. We visited a smoky jazz club filled with a vibrant young intellectual audience listening to high-quality bebop. However, my visit to a small nondescript memorial to the Jewish Ghetto left me with the sense that this was a city that was a long way from coming to terms with its horrifically anti-Semitic past.

The conference itself was bizarre. Our hosts were effectively High Tories, swapping the stultifying madness of the control and command communist regime for a naked, obscene wild-west capitalism. The lack of any regulation or control over the new entrepreneurial forces was understandable as a reaction to an enterprise-free period under such stifling Soviet control, but traumatic social and political consequences seemed inevitable. There was thus ideological distance between us and our hosts, which was exacerbated by Raymond's suggestion in his opening remarks that the Poles should not be only negative about the legacy of communism in their country, but value the fact that the system had bequeathed them inheritances such as education and a social system which abandoned no one. The impact was funereal, as if our hosts had suggested to us we should not be totally negative about the effects of apartheid. At least the infrastructure was good and the economy sound, they might have said. While there might be grains of truth in these observations, a couple of years into democracy, with traumatised populations still dealing with the consequences of oppression, deprivation and tyranny, was not the time to engage in the debates.

Raymond's less than sensitive remarks were surprising, coming from someone so thoughtful. They did, however, reflect something of the inflexible, doctrinaire history of the South African Communist Party. While the Party had been instrumental in the adoption of a non-racial rather than purely Africanist outlook on the part of the ANC, it was one of the last Communist Parties in the world to reject Stalinism, only catching up with Khrushchev in the 1970s and only becoming critical of the USSR in the late 1980s.[2]

*

Our longest trip abroad was one of our most eventful and successful. In 1995 Tokyo and Jabu led a delegation of businesspeople on an investment promotion tour of East Asia, where we experienced at first hand the impressive state-led growth strategies of Malaysia, South Korea, Singapore, Hong Kong and China. These strategies had seen the region develop from the economic basket case of the late 1950s to the success story of the late twentieth century, achieving exceptionally high rates of economic growth with a massive reduction in poverty and among the smallest inequality gaps in the world.

In lush Kuala Lumpur we heard how the ethnic riots of 1969 had led to the Bumiputra campaign, which ensured the indigenous majority was given a meaningful stake in the economy dominated up to that point by the Chinese and Indians. While undoubtedly success-ful, it was also clear that this empowerment approach had resulted in extensive nepotism, conflicts of interest and corruption. A bene-ficiary of the system, Dato Samsuddin, who had invested heavily in South Africa, joined us in KL. Besides his lavish lifestyle he had also acquired a wife in Johannesburg, the former Playboy centrefold becoming the Datin Samsuddin, much to the consternation of her husband's mentor, the Malaysian Prime Minister, and Samsuddin's devoutly Muslim family. The collapse of Samsuddin's business empire a few years later (followed by the breakdown of his marriage) was a painful example of how badly wrong an empowerment system can go when it is based on little more than cronyism.

Korea was both fascinating and frightening. Ordered, almost militaristic, the vast blocks of flats where workers lived next to their pristine, technologically advanced factories were unsettling. Here was the ultimate entanglement of politics and business. Every aspect of urban citizens' lives was governed by the company they worked for. The location and size of your apartment in the towering company block was determined by your status in the hierarchy within the firm. So your position on the shop floor was replicated when you went home. This inability to escape the social order of work at any point in the day or night struck me as a sacrifice too far for the phenomenal growth rates that Korea has experienced for decades. What was interesting in the South African context was the insight that this economic miracle was built on an extensive land reform process in the late 1950s, and an almost pathological focus on education.

After a day in the traffic jams of Seoul, where we witnessed a student demonstration that resembled an army marching exercise more than an exuberant outpouring of youthful resistance, we headed for the nearby region of Kyonggi, our soon-to-be sister province. For all three days of our visit we were shadowed by the anxious, sweating Mr Kim, Head of Protocol for the province. Our hosts outdid themselves in their hospitality. However, only formal speeches and signing ceremonies included translations, and even then it was a fraught exercise. At one event the translator, whose language skills were restricted to Korean and Japanese, locked himself into the translation booth to prevent an English-speaking official replacing him. We continued the incomprehensible formalities while the two officials screamed and shouted at each other through the glass. The dispute only came to an end when the English-speaker did himself serious injury in an attempt to batter down the locked door.

The lack of translators meant that for our one social dinner we sat at a long, narrow table with the 20 Kyonggi representatives along one side, all smoking and knocking back small glasses of a vicious transparent spirit. We were arranged along the other side facing our hosts and bemused not only by the unintelligible conversation but also by the array of unidentifiable but delicious dishes that were being grilled in front of us. At this event Mr Kim lost his decorum thanks to a good few bottles of the said spirit. His raucous conversation and passionate but lamentable singing were made more hilarious given his earlier formality. However, the next morning at seven he was as rigid and stressed as ever, ushering us into buses for a most embarrassing visit. Our hosts insisted on taking us to a war memorial for South Africans who had died fighting for South Korea against their communist North Korean foe. Tokyo was asked to don white gloves and lay a wreath at the foot of the ugly concrete swoop, atop which sat a grey jet fighter with the livery of the old South African air force. Jabu was livid, telling us pointedly that he had eaten North Korean rations while in exile in ANC camps in southern Africa.

For Jabu and myself, our return to Hong Kong and China was more productive than our previous visit. We met with an array of business people and financial journalists in Hong Kong before heading for Beijing. Our carrier for the short flight was Dragon Air, which had put our whole party in Economy Class. We sat on the tarmac at the airport for over two hours in sweltering heat. Where many political leaders might have been deeply aggrieved, Tokyo entertained everyone with stories of his exploits as a trainee pilot. His tales of how much could go wrong with a plane only served to make me more nervous when we were finally airborne.

On our eventual arrival in Beijing we experienced a reversal of the usual social order. Those of us from government were transported in luxury limousines with police outriders, while the businessmen were sardined into a very hot tin bus. Clearly the Party was in control here. I think we were also being rewarded for Tokyo being the first South African Premier to travel to Beijing without visiting Taipei.

Our state hotel was basic and sparse. It was novel to have a 'concierge' behind a desk on each floor noting our individual comings and goings in a little pad. We had dinner in the cavernous Great Hall of the People, where the Chair of the Communist Party gave a speech exclusively about corruption, lacking even a vague reference to South Africa. It turned out that the Prefect of Beijing was under corruption-related house arrest. I believe he was later executed. During our stay in Korea the Prefect of Kyonggi Province had been sacked for corruption. Retribution for corrupt officials seemed to be following in our slipstream.

*

The following year we made a political pilgrimage to Cuba via the USA. Tokyo had been invited to deliver the Du Bois Lecture at the New School for Social Research in New York City. We decided to take along a delegation of politicians and businesspeople from Gauteng. Tokyo was in his element. I finished the Du Bois speech about three minutes before he was due on stage, but he was unfazed, delivering it with aplomb, ad-libbing about his time on the Island and his relationship with Mandela with theatrical flair. He was hugely impressive.

We met with political and business leaders in New York, Washington DC, Orange County and San Francisco. We were entertained at the home of the South African Consul-General in Los Angeles, a sumptuous mansion atop a hill overlooking the urban sprawl. I reckoned the cost of this pile was in excess of the annual budgets of most of South Africa's provinces. Our announcement that we were travelling on to Cuba caused something of a political stir and elicited an outraged response from the *Wall Street Journal.* As we were about to leave San Francisco we were delayed by passport officials who expressed concern about our onward itinerary. Eventually a representative from the South African consulate persuaded them to let us continue our journey.

Cuba at the time was creaking under severe economic strain. Russia had stopped paying a subsidised price for the island's sugar, and the morally dubious US embargo was really biting. On arrival in Havana we sat in splendid isolation for two hours in a small airport waiting room, until eventually Tokyo asked me to find out what was going on. An embarrassed protocol official explained to me that our luggage had been lost and they were trying to locate it before having to tell us. Tokyo was OK; he travelled with his luggage on board. I suggested we proceed without ours.

A motorcade swept us through the beautiful, crumbling ruins of old Havana, past 'fifties automobiles abandoned in the middle of the road for lack of fuel. We arrived at a serene diplomatic compound in rolling gardens that contrasted sharply with the squalor we had just witnessed. Once inside I was desperate for the loo. I rushed to the nearest of the ornate ceramic toilets only for it to collapse beneath me. I tried another. As I lowered myself onto the bowl in relief an attendant knocked at the door and muttered in broken English: 'No work, no work.' Third time lucky. We had equally limited success contacting our embassy. The phones worked only intermittently. Our meals consisted of rice and black beans, twice a day, every day. This was a nation in crisis.

Most of the delegation received their luggage later that day. I wasn't so lucky, and spent the rest of the visit swathed in one of Tokyo's track suits. Not only was it about five sizes too big for me, but it was also patterned from head to toe in the vibrant colours of South Africa's new flag. As a consequence I was spared the ordeal of listening to Raul Castro, brother of the more famous Fidel and chief of the military, welcome us in a two-hour speech that evening. Not to be outdone, Tokyo replied in a snip of a speech at an hour or so. When I heard about this from my colleagues, I fondly caressed my outlandish attire. However, my brash outfit didn't prevent me exploring the small, cobbled streets of old Havana and eating at a water-side restaurant allegedly frequented by Hemingway.

Havana left myriad contradictory images. The faded 'seventies clothes and the beautifully maintained 'fifties cars gave the appearance of a city in a time warp. The women lining the streets outside the international hotels in anticipation of dollar-bearing clients; the doctors and engineers working as barmen – earning from an evening's tips what they would in a month in their professions – were a constant reminder of the current economic difficulties. All the while the clusters of gyrating people around bands of musicians playing under the ubiquitous portraits of Fidel and Che got on with enjoying life regardless.

For many of my colleagues Cuba was a political idyll. I felt more ambivalent. On the one hand was the aura of the romantic revolutionaries who had overcome Batista's venal playground for wealthy Americans and had built remarkable health and education systems; gregarious people, sustained by Latin rhythms, always smiling, living a difficult life to the full. On the other hand was the knowledge of human rights abuses, economic mismanagement, homophobia and the contrast between the relative luxury in which the political elite lived and the poverty of ordinary Cubans. I left, however, feeling enormous affection for this complex island.

*

Given this jet-setting around the globe it may seem surprising that we managed to get anything done in our constituencies at home. But we did. My first constituency was a melange of suburbs just south of the Johannesburg CBD, including La Rochelle, Turffontein, Rosettenville and Booysens. Historically the area had been home to the white working class. Politically it was dominated by the neo-Nazi AWB. During the period I was there it started to transform rapidly into a black middle-class locality. The dynamics of this change were not always easy to manage. The ANC office in the constituency, staffed by black comrades, was initially visited almost exclusively by Africans and coloureds seeking help, advice, sometimes just someone to talk to. Our first white visitor was an elderly man of small build, greasy hair and chalky pallor who asked specifically to see me. As soon as he had sat down in my little office he leaned towards me and whispered: '*Jislaaik*, it must be difficult working with all of *them*,' cocking his thumb back towards the reception area. 'I wanted to speak to you because only a white man will understand my problem.' I had a strong desire to kick him out of the office. Instead I responded: 'I really enjoy working with my colleagues and I'm sure one of them could help you too.' This caricature of a racist then told me about his inane problem, which I was able to sort out fairly easily, if reluctantly.

It was difficult to deal with overt racism. I was often confronted with the view that apartheid was necessary because 'different' people are unable to live together and the policy intended separate but equal development in place of the melting-pot anarchy of much of the world. Confronting it head-on would have been more courageous and honest. Instead I took the route of trying to explain that all people are equal and that each community comprised good, bad and indifferent people. I found myself using my own experience of being married to Simone to explain how harmoniously different 'groups' could live together. This was a little disingenuous, as I never perceived Simone as Asian and Muslim as against white and Jewish. Rather we were just two like-minded people who fell in love.

At first I shared the constituency office with Gertrude Shope. By now in her seventies, Ma Shope had led the ANC Women's Section for 20 years in exile, and the Women's League for a period on her return to South Africa in 1991. She was a hero of the struggle and a delight to work with. Mothering and protective, she would offer good advice, often in the comfort of her own nearby home. She worked extensively with domestic workers in the area and was a welcoming, familiar face when I moved to the national Parliament.

Together we got involved in the schools in the area, witnessing at first hand the difficulties and triumphs of deracialising the education system. One of our most heart-warming days in the constituency was when we presented a South African flag that had flown over Parliament to a local, recently deracialised school. Standing in front of the patchwork of eager young faces singing the stirring *Nkosi Sikelel' iAfrika* brought tears to our eyes. I imagined Ma was crying with joy at what freedom had achieved as well as sadness at the memory of over 50 years of hardship and struggle.

The small informal settlement of Elias Motsoaledi, just next to the Baragwanath Hospital in Soweto, was appended to our constituency. We spent many hours in meetings with this courageous community, which, having fended off countless attempts at removal by the apartheid authorities, was now determined to gain the right to remain on this land permanently and to upgrade the site. Eventually Ma Shope and I were guests at a joyful celebration to mark the granting of title to the community. This was achieved through the efforts of the community leadership, the provincial Minister for Land Affairs and the national Minister, Trish Hanekom's husband, Derek. It was my introduction to the crucial and complex issue of land reform.

An equally pressing issue was the crime wave sweeping the country, and especially Gauteng. Soon after I arrived in Johannesburg South a group of shopkeepers came to see me to explain that they would have to close their shops if they continued to be held up with the current alarming regularity. One of them had a distinctive and familiar accent. It transpired that he was a recent arrival from Sylhet in Bangladesh, the ancestral home of my father-in-law. Our newfound kinship did not make his situation any easier. In less than three months in the country he had been held up at gunpoint on four occasions and was scared and desperate. Interacting with the police was not an enjoyable experience. The limited levels of co-operation and their open disdain for the new community policing initiatives in the country were demotivating and frustrating. When the police informed us that they couldn't respond to all the emergency calls because their vehicles were often off the road being repaired we managed to raise money from local businesspeople to buy a couple of small motorbikes that improved their response time.

I came face-to-face with corruption in the force when a constituent asked me to follow up a charge he had laid against a wealthy landowner in the area. After days of getting no co-operation over the phone I went to the police station and demanded to see the docket. The duty sergeant took me out to a damp garage in which hundreds of thousands of dockets were being stored. He trawled through the dank cardboard files for about 10 minutes before saying: 'Sorry, sir, the docket must be missing, which is why the case hasn't been followed up.'

The chaos and corruption of the policing service during the transition obviously contributed to the extreme levels of violent crime that benighted the new South Africa. However, there were other reasons. South Africa had always been a violent society. Much of this violence had been restricted to the 'non-white' areas of the country, a significant amount of it perpetrated by the state in maintaining the apartheid system. With the abolition of racially defined Group Areas, crime spilled across the country. A police force that had been used primarily as a political tool was no match for the international criminal gangs that poured into South Africa as our borders opened up. Crime is also unsurprising in an economy with a formal unemployment rate of around 30 per cent. But most of all, apartheid was maintained with a ferocious brutality. Such brutality breeds only more brutality

*

On 8 May 1996 at about midday I was driving back into the CBD of Johannesburg from a constituency surgery. Listening to Radio South Africa I was captivated by an astonishing speech from the national Parliament on the occasion of the adoption of South Africa's new constitution.

I owe my being to the Khoi and the San …
I am formed by the migrants who left Europe to find a new home
    on our native land. Whatever their own actions, they remain
    still, part of me.
In my veins courses the blood of the Malay slaves who came from
    the East …

I assumed I was listening to Cyril Ramaphosa, the chairperson of the Constitutional Assembly. I pulled the car over to the side of the road to be able to focus on what was one of the most profound and lyrical speeches I had heard.

I soon realised that the speaker was actually Thabo Mbeki. The speech captured the complexity of identity in a racially and ethnically diverse nation and articulated many of my own feelings about both the diversity of my heritage and my deep and passionate commitment to this complicated land.

> ... I am the grandchild who lays fresh flowers on the Boer graves at St Helena and the Bahamas, who sees in the mind's eye and suffers the suffering of a simple peasant folk, death, concentration camps, destroyed homesteads, a dream in ruins.
>
> I am the child of Nongqause. I am he who made it possible to trade in the world markets in diamonds, in gold, in the same food for which my stomach yearns.
>
> I come of those who were transported from India and China, whose being resided in the fact, solely, that they were able to provide physical labour, who taught me that we could both be at home and be foreign, who taught me that human existence itself demanded that freedom was a necessary condition for that human existence.
>
> Being part of all these people, and in the knowledge that none dare contest that assertion, I shall claim that – I am an African.

This poetic oration, celebrating the progressive and unique nature of the new constitution that had been negotiated over the preceding two years, encapsulated what is best about Thabo Mbeki: his erudition and learning, his seemingly cosmopolitan world view and a lifetime's devotion to the building of a free South Africa.

> I am an African.
> I am born of the peoples of the continent of Africa.
> The pain of the violent conflict that afflicts the peoples of Liberia, Somalia, the Sudan, Burundi and Algeria is a pain I also bear.
> The dismal shame of poverty, suffering and human degradation of my continent is a blight that we share.

The blight on our happiness that derives from this and from our
drift to the periphery of human affairs leaves us in a persistent
shadow of despair.

This is a savage road to which nobody should be condemned.

This thing that we have done today, in this small corner of a great
continent that has contributed so decisively to the evolution of
humanity says that Africa reaffirms that she is continuing her
rise from the ashes...[3]

However, the speech also highlighted Mbeki's problematic practice
of using his erudition to obfuscate a deeper, often less palatable intention. Re-reading the speech a few years later, it became apparent
that it had presaged the start of a shift from the ANC's non-racism to
a complex and less inclusive Africanism.

*

The inspiration sparked by the speech and my own frustration with
the limitations of provincial legislative powers led me to start thinking about a move from the dusty mine dumps of Johannesburg. The
momentum of the move gathered inexorable pace and early in 1997
I raised the possibility with Tokyo while we were en route yet again to
Davos. He readily agreed. I was almost taken aback, but understood
his enthusiasm when a few months later he announced his departure
from politics.

One evening in the shadow of Mont Blanc Tokyo took me with
him to see Mandela. The President had just arrived for his speech the
next day and invited us into his small bedroom where he was sitting
in yellow pyjamas. Tokyo told him that they could use my finance and
economics skills in Cape Town. 'Good, good,' said Madiba in his distinctive tones: 'You make the necessary arrangements.'

CHAPTER 7
Cape Town Calling

All day above the city, two seas, the far sand-flats
where Africa begins in earnest, the mountain overshadows.

'The Mountain'
Stephen Watson

Cape Town, my strange home town, at once aesthetically breathtaking and seared by the omnipresent contrast between the super wealthy along its exquisite coastline and the desperately impoverished strewn across its flat, windswept interior; its strange, convoluted left-wing politics; its uneasy, sometimes fractious diversity, with Jew and Muslim living skull cap by skull cap, the Cape Town Holocaust Centre a few streets away from the museum that memorialises the forced destruction of the non-racial community of District Six in the early 1960s.

I remember as a nine-year-old accompanying my mother to the People's Space Theatre, where she worked as a puppeteer. The Space was an oasis of normality in a desert of insanity, a place where black and white were illegally united as performer and audience for the few years of its survival. This is where I first saw the world-renowned Abdullah Ibrahim performing his Afro-Malay jazz that resonated with the cadences of the non-racial District Six, the teeming ghetto of his upbringing.

Abdullah's music, which reflects so many aspects of South Africa – the tragedy of apartheid, the pain of exile, the spirit of resilience and revolt, the joy of return and the elation of liberation – has been a constant in my life wherever I am in the world. I hear the opening bars of his anthem 'Manenberg – where it's happening' and I'm back on the windswept Cape Flats or Signal Hill, past the kramat, gazing out to the vista of Robben Island surrounded by an eternity of ocean.

*

The parliamentary precinct nestles in the shadow of Table Mountain. Long, narrow and cobbled, it includes the original, ornate building of the Governor's Legislative Council (now the Upper House), the Old Assembly Wing, more functional but still beautiful, the tacked-on Tricameral Chamber, the Office of the Presidency in Tuynhuys with its picturesque garden, and the British High Commission to remind us of our colonial history.

I was sworn in as a Member of Parliament on 27 January 1997, replacing Marcel Golding, a former trade unionist who had left Parliament to focus on running one of the new union investment trusts. My physical seat in the Chamber was formerly occupied by Bantu Holomisa, who had been expelled from the ANC and was about to form a new, rival political party. Alongside me sat Johnny de Lange, the ebullient Chair of the Justice Committee and long-standing activist; Brian Bunting, an elderly, erudite veteran of the Communist Party, and Rob Davies, the studious chair of the Trade and Industry Committee, who, in exile, had lectured in Mozambique with Ruth First.

The national Parliament under the ANC was the epicentre of the new South Africa, the characters giving life and vibrancy to the Parliamentary buildings. I particularly enjoyed Steve Tshwete, the larger-than-life Minister for Sport, whose glasses always tinted darkly when he entered the Chamber, giving a sense of Isaac-Hayes-cool as he ambled slowly towards his seat, accompanied by a deep, elongated rumble of 'Steeeeve' from the ANC benches; the Speaker, Frene Ginwala, an imposing, sari-clad dominatrix, and, a few seats in front of me, Winnie Mandela, who occasionally graced Parliament with her aloof presence.

World leaders flocked to address Parliament and to be in the presence of the man-myth, Nelson Mandela. An impressive, fresh-faced Tony Blair, flushed with the excitement of the Third Way, was followed by an exhausted, gaunt, post-Monica Bill Clinton, and an ageing, ill but defiant Yasser Arafat – whose mere presence caused a walk-out by at least one Jewish member of the opposition.

One of my first parliamentary speeches was during a debate on the budget. No sooner had I started speaking than a member began muttering, ever louder, '*Jou kommunis*' ('You communist'). Since he was clearly basing his assumption not on the orthodox economics I was discussing but rather on the fact that I am white, Jewish and a member of the ANC (and, therefore, *obviously* a communist), the rotund, pink-faced Willem Odendaal was attacked in turn by my ANC colleagues, one of whom, Gill Marcus, insisted that his remarks were anti-Semitic and that he be ejected from the Chamber. The disruption provided me with a wonderful opportunity – in an otherwise arid debate – to speak of the importance of diversity and the ethnocentric narrow-mindedness of some of my new colleagues. Much to Odendaal's chagrin I also managed to praise the SACP (while stating that I was not a member) for its significant contribution to the non-racial politics of the ANC, and lauded the contribution of Chris Hani, Joe Slovo and Bram Fischer, among others, to the liberation of South Africa. I realised I was going to enjoy Parliament.

*

I devoted myself to the work of the Finance and the Public Accounts Committees. My involvement with the former focused primarily on economic policy and specifically government's orthodox economic framework, the Growth, Equality and Redistribution strategy (GEAR). I was supportive of this controversial approach, which was criticised by the trade union and SACP allies of the ANC for being overly influenced by the Washington consensus of the World Bank and the IMF. I argued that as a small, open economy South Africa had little choice but to engage with the global economy largely on its terms.

Economic policy in the first decade of democracy in South Africa can be seen as a constant tug-of-war between the need for social and material justice on the one hand and gaining the acceptance of the global economic power brokers on the other. Historically, the growth of the South African economy has been limited by a combination of perpetual balance-of-payments difficulties, relatively high inflation, political pressures during the apartheid years, high interest rates and supply-side deficiencies. Furthermore, the internationalisation of the world economy and its attendant volatility posed particularly acute economic and political challenges for a country that had been more insular than most during the second half of the last century.

GEAR was the centrepiece of government economic strategy. It was premised on the mainstream assumption of the early 1990s that strong economic growth was characterised not by import substitution within a closed economy and expansionary spending by the state but by policies which promoted high domestic savings and foreign direct investment, low inflation and free international trade. In addition, investment in human capital and productive infrastructure, rather than publicly financed consumption, was seen as critical to sustainable economic growth.

During this period many political parties of the left and centre-left adopted the view that, in the prevailing global circumstances where investment and financial flows can be switched on or off, quite literally, at the press of a button, economic stabilisation and liberalisation were important prerequisites for the achievement of progressive social objectives. This shift in thinking was largely informed by the stagflation and boom/bust experience of many Latin American countries in the 1980s, known as macroeconomic populism.[1] GEAR was drawn up with these disastrous experiences in mind. Its key premise was that the most effective mechanism for the meeting of basic needs, the deracialisation of the economy and the eradication of massive inherited structural inequalities was through rapid sustainable growth, job creation and targeted social spending on the poorest of the poor.

The long-term vision of GEAR was a virtuous cycle of prosperity within which the South African economy would be open to competitive international pressures and foreign investment which would bring with it technology and foreign exchange. Higher productivity through technology and better training and a competitive exchange rate would improve the competitiveness of manufactured exports. Together with a more flexible but stable labour market, these measures were expected to lead to increased, more sustainable job creation and a healthier balance of payments. Reduced government dissaving[2] and positive net capital inflows would increase the level of savings available for productive investment, lowering the cost of capital and the level of inflation in the economy.

Opposition to this blueprint within the ANC alliance was vociferous, especially in the SACP and Cosatu. This opposition was given intellectual substance by the work of Merg. In broad terms they proposed a more inwardly focused strategy of increased government spending through borrowing to increase domestic demand, meet basic needs and increase employment. They also proposed a significantly more progressive tax regime, some political influence over the South African Reserve Bank, a more gradual reduction in protection for the domestic economy, improved domestic savings rather than reliance on external capital flows, the maintenance of the existing high levels of public service jobs, and a halt to privatisation and public–private partnerships in municipal service delivery.[3]

On my arrival in Parliament the ANC soon dispatched me to argue the case for GEAR in forums ranging from a heated debate with Cosatu economists in the Western Cape to a workshop for local ANC members in rural Kokstad in the Natal Midlands. I revelled in these exchanges, attempting to show why the strategy was the correct way forward and how it differed from the classic prescripts of the Washington consensus. For me the crucial issue was how the surplus funds generated by lower debt and reduced dissaving would be utilised to address the country's obvious social needs.

To the credit of Thabo Mbeki and Trevor Manuel, they took a massive political risk in pursuit of readmission to the international club of nations. GEAR certainly stabilised very ropey public finances, significantly increased government revenues and social spending, improved the country's balance-of-payments position, ensured a more predictable currency environment, kept inflation at historically low levels and increased growth levels. Whether a less restrictive fiscal policy would have created greater employment while not undermining international confidence is a moot point. On the other hand, a more expansionist policy might have seen South Africa neglected, even ostracised, by the global economy with the consequent populist disasters that afflicted Latin America.

Economic performance in 2005 and 2006 managed to break through the 4 per cent growth threshold with low inflation, low interest rates and some evidence of small increases in formal employment. 2007 offers the prospect of growth of around 6 per cent and growing employment, albeit not at the levels required. Poverty between 2002 and 2006 also declined strongly.[4] This may be the beginning of significant economic progress. If so, the foundations set in place by GEAR will be seen to have been crucial to this success. If not, those of us who supported the fairly orthodox approach will have to acknowledge its failure and the massive human cost it incurred, especially in terms of unemployment and its consequences.

Two key reasons for the poor employment record of the South African economy since 1994 are the failure of labour-intensive public works schemes and labour market rigidities. The public works schemes have never got off the ground in a meaningful way, in spite of being a key element of the overall strategy. This has been due to a combination of poor public sector management of the scheme and possibly a lack of real political will. The scheme stood in contrast to the more orthodox prescriptions of GEAR and, therefore, commanded less attention from Deputy President Mbeki and Minister of Finance Manuel.

Another factor was the nature of labour market legislation enacted by the ANC. Key to GEAR's employment-creation targets was a fairly flexible labour market environment. The majority of the South African workforce is relatively unskilled. Under apartheid there had been massive abuse of employees, including almost slave-like wages in certain industries, excessive working hours, poor working conditions, limited training and much more. That this needed to be redressed urgently was a given. However, the labour market framework introduced by Labour Minister Tito Mboweni was more appropriate for a European-style, advanced social democratic economy. The job protection and conditions of service provisions were simply too onerous for a small, relatively uncompetitive, developing economy. This led to a scenario where companies in South Africa were loath to employ unskilled workers, the very people who most needed jobs.

The seeming contradiction of an orthodox economic policy being hamstrung by rigid labour market regulation has two related explanations. One is the possibility that Mboweni and Mbeki were not powerful enough to take on the trade unions and effectively compromised for the sake of political harmony. Another, not dissimilar, is that a characteristic of Mbeki's political style is to seek balance, in this case the orthodox economic policy that was deeply unpopular within the alliance, with European-style social democratic labour legislation that was popular with our political allies but simply inappropriate in the South African context.

What the debates around labour market policy also reflected was an on-going clash between Trevor Manuel and Tito Mboweni for supremacy in ANC economic policy making. This is a personal battle that predates the ANC's ascension to government and continues to this day.

The process whereby the ANC came to change its approach to economic policy from the avowedly socialist to the orthodox monetarist was a key time in the South African transition. From conferences as early as 1986 the failures of macroeconomic populism were brought to the attention of key ANC economic thinkers. Engagement with corporate leaders, academics and policymakers had profound impact on the economic thinking of some of the leadership. This included interaction with people of influence from the former Soviet bloc, which was stagnating economically, and China, which was in the early stages of its Party-led market reforms. However, many on the left of the organisation remained distrustful of global orthodoxies. This led to the use of obfuscatory language by the leadership in order to sell the policy framework – for instance, 'the restructuring of state assets' meant, in effect, privatisation.

The movement's historic language of revolution was utilised to make palatable an ostensibly neo-liberal approach to the economy. So the idea of a significant role for the private sector was presented as 'the National Democratic Revolution and the state presiding over it coexist with private capital at the same time as they reconfigure the relationship of sectors of society to private and other forms of capital'.[5] I was torn between the view that it was essential to obfuscate in order to ensure support for the strategy and the more palatable belief that through extensive, honest discussion we could persuade the majority of people in the ANC of the validity of following the chosen economic course. I was, therefore, troubled by the top ANC leadership's view that the strategy was non-negotiable.

The Finance Committee in Parliament was chaired at the time by Sipho Mpahlwa, now Minister of Trade and Industry. A pleasant, bright, hardworking but not well-organised MP, Sipho was studying for a postgraduate economics and finance degree while running one of Parliament's most important committees – a quite astonishing feat. Sipho asked me to chair a sub-committee on the important Public Finance Management Act (PFMA), a detailed framework for the management and control of public money. After numerous late-night sessions running into the early hours of the morning, we considered renaming the Bill the Woods-Momoniat Memorial Bill – after Gavin Woods, a fastidious member of the Finance Committee who queried every comma and full stop in the legislation, and Ismael Momoniat, a bright, energetic Treasury civil servant who was willing to debate every micro-detail with Gavin until there was clarity on the best way forward.

In my capacity as Chair I jousted regularly with Trevor Manuel, attempting to persuade him to make changes to the Bill. Trevor's natural combative streak had intensified on becoming Finance Minister. His appointment was initially received very negatively by domestic and international markets. He had no formal economic training or experience and was seen as something of an impetuous firebrand. Ten years on, he is the world's longest serving and among the most competent incumbents. I quickly learned a strategy to engage with him that involved adopting a position on a minor matter that I knew he would disagree with. This would invariably precipitate an explosive response and instant rejection. I could then raise a substantive issue, which – having blown off steam – he would invariably debate meaningfully, and agree on a productive resolution.

The final product, Act No. 1 of 1999, is a fine piece of legislation embedding accountability in the financial systems of the State. Gavin Woods, Ismael Momoniat and his boss, Maria Ramos, deserve enormous credit, as does its political sponsor, Trevor Manuel.

*

The Standing Committee on Public Accounts (Scopa) was an early monument to South Africa's new democracy. Before 1994 it had been just another tool in the hands of the apartheid government, acquiescing to its masters' commands. In the democratic era the ANC ensured it was chaired by the opposition and that it made non-partisan decisions on the propriety or otherwise of financial spending.

The ANC component of the Committee was chaired by Barbara Hogan. A pugnacious, thorough and fearless MP, Barbara had devoted her life to the ANC. She was the country's longest-serving white woman political detainee under apartheid. The ANC group on the Committee was single-minded in the implementation of its constitutional responsibility to review the public spending of the state and to recommend to Parliament whether to authorise it. Refusal meant the money had to be recovered from the individuals responsible for its spending.

Two ex-Robben Islanders were at the forefront of this work. Laloo Chiba and Billy Nair appeared older than they were as a consequence of the physical effects of years of torture and hard labour. Laloo had a head of curly white hair atop a thin, wiry body. Constantly desperate for a smoke, he combined fine political instincts with a wry sense of humour and a consideration for others that came from years of sacrifice to a cause. Billy, short, feisty, sometimes acerbic, eventually needed the aid of crutches to walk but never lost his energy. It was a privilege to learn about the often uncomfortable processes of accountability from these stalwarts of the struggle.

In my first term in Parliament the Committee dealt with a number of matters embarrassing to the ANC. On all of these contentious issues we were supported and protected by Chief Whip Max Sisulu and, where necessary, the President himself.

One of the first incidences of serious financial misappropriation I was involved in considering concerned the Independent Broadcasting Authority (IBA). A number of the councillors on the IBA engaged in cavalier spending of government money. This included travelling First Class to the 1996 Olympic Games and taking a whole posse of friends to hear Pavarotti sing. When asked why they were attending these events at state expense, we received a reply along the lines of: 'Our brief is communications. These were major communications events.' They regularly booked themselves suites at Johannesburg's leading Carlton Hotel, even though they lived in Johannesburg. On occasion, they even used their government credit cards to buy groceries.

Scopa's public hearing on the matter was a real eye-opener for me. I was impressed, almost intimidated, by the way in which the ANC members dominated proceedings with incisive, relevant questions and would not accept imprecise or vague answers. Mingled with the awe I felt was some apprehension. I had personal links to two of the councillors appearing before us. Peter de Klerk was an old friend of my late father from the advertising industry and Lyndall Shope-Mafole was the daughter of Ma Gertrude Shope, the MP with whom I shared my constituency.

I walked into the next meeting of the Gauteng MPs' caucus with trepidation, nervous about how Ma would treat me. She came bustling into the room soon after me. Rather than take up her usual seat she sat down next to me and whispered into my ear: 'You just carry on doing your job.'

On the basis of the hearing and our subsequent Report to Parliament, the councillors were forced to resign their prestigious positions with their reputations tarnished. A few weeks later, at our constituency office, Ma told me that it had been a tough time for the family. However, her warmth towards me never faltered.

The next major issue to confront Scopa was a matter related to HIV and AIDS. As part of its rather inadequate response to the pandemic, the Department of Health had issued a tender for AIDS education initiatives among young people using music and/or theatre. Actor and producer Mbongeni Ngema, who had shot to fame with a vibrant, life-affirming musical, 'Sarafina', devised 'Sarafina II' to meet the Health Department's tender. It was chosen in preference to a proposal from an emerging opera company. 'Sarafina II' was a disaster from the word go. First, a budget that started at just under R1 million ballooned to R14 million. The AIDS content was minimal and the play was only performed a handful of times, with kids charged for entry on one occasion. With the inflated budget, Ngema had built himself a state-of-the-art studio at his KwaZulu-Natal home and bought a luxury Mercedes bus in which to transport his cast. We were inclined to advise Parliament not to authorise the spending, meaning in practical terms that as much as possible of the spent money would have to be recouped and that the civil servant responsible for approving the expenditure would face grave repercussions.

Before our scheduled public hearing, Chief Whip Max Sisulu arranged for a few of us from the Committee to meet with the Health Minister, Nkosazana Dlamini-Zuma. Nkosazana is a tough woman with few social graces, and I was quite intimidated by this seemingly angry and unapproachable Minister, who was aggressively unhappy with the approach we were proposing. Barbara explained the reasons for our position and the Chief Whip made clear that he supported our decision. After a quite tetchy discussion, in which both Barbara and Max held firm, the Minister backed down and conceded that we must go ahead and do what we felt was necessary.

After a brutal public hearing with the Committee, the ANC-aligned Director-General of Health was fired, possibly as a scapegoat to protect the Minister. Half of the misappropriated money was recovered from Ngema by the Special Investigative Unit of Judge Willem Heath. Scopa's involvement in 'Sarafina II' will be remembered as an exemplary case of Parliamentary accountability working effectively to the benefit of the taxpayer.

One of our other long-standing enquiries was of a different nature altogether. It concerned Winnie Mandela, that most enigmatic of South Africa's political legends. My sense of Winnie is best described as a montage of inspiring and tragic images: the beautiful young wife left to face life on her own soon after her marriage; the brave anti-apartheid fighter representing her incarcerated husband with charisma and courage; the downward spiral of excess in the dusty Free State township of Brandfort to which she was restricted. I recall uncomfortably her ill-judged remarks about winning freedom through tyres and matches, an endorsement of the practice of burning informers alive, and the violent excesses of her awful band of thugs known as the Winnie Mandela Football Club.

As I revisit the iconic picture of Winnie and Nelson leaving Pollsmoor Prison hand-in-hand I cannot forget her endurance of constant harassment and intimidation. But I also recall the pain of seeing my friend, Murphy Morobe, shunned because he dared say publicly what so many felt about her unaccountable behaviour. From the back benches I observed, with a combination of awe and cynicism, her occasional bewigged, noble presence in Parliament, and again felt empathy as on 16 June 2001, a clearly irritated Thabo Mbeki pushed Winnie away from him and knocked her cap off when she tried to hug him on arriving late at a Youth Day rally in Soweto. In 2003 I once again balked at her pathetic justification when she was found guilty of defrauding loan applicants' accounts for a funeral fund.

Winnie divided opinion even within the ANC, so the arrival of an Auditor-General's Report involving her was bound to cause excitement and tension on the Public Accounts Committee. The Report referred to the facts that while briefly a Deputy Minister in her ex-husband's government she had travelled abroad without the requisite approval of the Presidency, and that she continued to use a government vehicle –

badly damaged in one or more accidents – after being dismissed from the Executive.

The opposition parties were determined to use the Report as yet another stick with which to beat Winnie. The ANC Study Group on the Committee was divided. Do we push ahead with the matter in our customary spirit of non-partisanship, or do we seek political guidance and play for time? We debated the matter backwards and forwards, people passionately arguing their perspective. Eventually, after considerable agonising, we agreed to press on with the matter, reaffirming the principle that we would deal with every issue dispassionately, regardless of who was involved.

The matter dragged on for many months. Eventually we required a legal opinion on some aspect of the case so, as a Committee, referred it to the State Law Advisor. He informed us that the matter had prescribed – the time for dealing with it in law had passed. The opposition were incensed. In the ANC we were quietly relieved. We had taken the appropriate position but now did not have to subject Winnie to any further embarrassment.

*

I was relishing Parliamentary life. I thrived on the cut-and-thrust and theatre of debates in the Chamber, the exercising of oversight and accountability in committee work and the impassioned caucus discussions. I continued to enjoy constituency work, although I could have done without the weekly commuting, as my constituency had remained Johannesburg South at the ANC's insistence when I moved to national Parliament.

However, the demons of our past continued to intrude on our flourishing present. During 1997 I observed a chilling session of the Truth and Reconciliation Commission which took place in Cape Town involving my fellow MP, Tony Yengeni. Yengeni had been commander of an MK cell in the Western Cape before his capture by security forces. His interrogator, Jeffrey Benzien, was a typical member of the security force, a mediocre man prone to violence. In the hearing Benzien spoke fairly fluently of how he eventually extracted information from Yengeni. He was asked to demonstrate the method. He had a man kneel down on all fours. Benzien then mounted him and placed a wet bag over his head and rode the man, denying him air while preventing any resistance with his powerful thighs. Benzien, of short, stout, hairy body, was breathing heavily, pink faced. He dismounted and answered questions in a flat voice, ironically short of breath:

MR YENGENI: But were there any, was there any physical condition that would make you to release the bag on the part of the person who is tortured?

MR BENZIEN: On occasions people have I presume, and I say presume, lost consciousness, they would go slack and every time that was done, I would release the bag.

MR YENGENI: How did I react and respond to you at the bag?

MR BENZIEN: I think you can bear with me that individually I cannot say how you reacted, I know that after the method was applied, you did take us to the house of Jennifer Schreiner where we took out a lot of limpet mines, hand grenades and firearms. In other words, your reaction as far as I understand it was, you told us where your weaponry was.[6]

The camera panned to Yengeni, the proud, arrogant chair of Parliament's Defence Committee. Tony was drawn in on himself, weeping, reliving the humiliation, the betrayal wrenched from him by this inhumane torture.

This episode brought home how traumatic the catharsis of the TRC was proving. But it was also a reminder of how important it was to develop a shared, unexpurgated record of what had been done in the name of a demented ideology of racial superiority, as we took the next steps to building a society in which all were equal.

*

Those next steps were to be marshalled by Thabo Mbeki, who in early 1998 became President of the ANC, a year before he was due to succeed Nelson Mandela as the country's president. While Deputy President he had already been responsible for a great deal of the day-to-day running of government, displaying a technocrat's competence interspersed with a few disconcerting moments. Amongst the latter was his leadership within the ANC of an ill-judged attempt to prevent publication of the Truth and Reconciliation Commission's final report. The Report, to some extent, equated the misdemeanours of some ANC members in exile with the indefensible actions of the apartheid forces. While this was inappropriate and annoying, the attempt to muzzle the Commission was a massive political blunder, as it undermined the cathartic impact that the TRC was continuing to have on the country. It also seemed to parallel the National Party's very defensive efforts to prevent publication of the same Report for its perceived bias against the apartheid government. This ill-advised action seemed to show the hand of someone whose commitment to and understanding of reconciliation fell short of Mandela's.

Was this misjudgement an exception to the character of an otherwise competent and principled politician? Or was it a sign of things to come? Despite this concern, the term of the first democratic Parliament ended on a personal high. I was invited to speak in the debate on President Mandela's final State of the Nation address.

Like most people I was in awe of the man-myth. He had an almost superhuman capacity for forgiveness and the most incredible personal warmth. It astonished me how, even after I had sat through a number of ANC caucuses, meetings and parliamentary sessions with him present I still found that whenever he was in a room he brought a unique, enveloping aura to the space, a feeling of security and of comfort.

Part of Madiba's extraordinary charm is his ability to humble himself through humour, so that while you know you are in the presence of greatness the knowledge doesn't overawe or paralyse. Soon after arriving at the national Parliament I received a message to attend the President's office. On my short walk across the cobbled pathway to Tuynhuys I nervously tried to work out what political misdemeanour I might have committed to warrant this summons. I arrived at his Secretary's desk to find a small parcel wrapped in newspaper. The secretary informed me that it was a bottle of homemade guava jelly that Simone's grandmother had insisted the President deliver to me when she had met him on his recent state visit to Bangladesh. When I next saw the President in caucus I sheepishly went up to him at the end of the meeting to thank him. 'Now you know why I went to Bangladesh,' he replied with a broad grin.

In addition to his capacity for forgiveness and reconciliation, what has marked Mandela out is his ability to remain a statesman rather than degenerating into a mere party politician. I suppose it was easier coming to the Presidency so late in life. But he has succeeded where so many liberation leaders around the world have failed: Nehru in India, Sheikh Mujib in Bangladesh, Nkhruma, Kenyatta and Kaunda in Africa. Mandela's ability to ensure that the interests of the nation preceded those of the party is what, I believe, has elevated him to the pantheon of greatness.

Not that he is without faults. His occasional populism, which led him, for instance, to suggest to a group of Youth League members that the voting age should be reduced to 14, must be seen as a weakness. He also has a characteristic that is both good and bad: his astounding loyalty to people who might not deserve it. Examples are Stella Sigcau and Joe Modise, both Ministers whom he refused to remove from office despite the fact that they were almost universally perceived as incompetent and enveloped in allegations of corruption, Muammar Gadaffi and the Saudi Royal family, whom he would not criticise because of their support for the liberation struggle, and a few dodgy businessmen who had been generous to the ANC after Mandela's release. Such loyalty in a friend would be commendable, in a politician it is a weakness.

The debate on the State of the Nation concluded, Mandela walked out with me to meet Simone and our then three-month-old son, Misha. He stopped an astonished passing tourist and asked her to take a photo of him with Misha. As she was doing so he remarked to Simone that this little boy would be angry with her in a few years' time, 'for forcing me to be photographed being held by this ugly old man'. As if.

SECTION III
IDENTITY POLITICS

CHAPTER 8
An African Arises

I am an African.
I am born of the peoples of the continent of Africa.

'I am an African'
Thabo Mbeki

South Africa's second democratic election, unsurprisingly, lacked the emotional exaltation of 1994's liberation poll. With people entrenched in positions of power, the stakes were higher for the 1999 ballot, and jockeying for position was intense. I was not immune to the temptations of incumbency. In parliamentary speeches I found myself departing from closely reasoned argument and adopting more strident political tones in an effort to ensure a safe position on the ANC's list of candidates.

This list process within the ANC was the site of untold political strife. In theory the process involved each of the ANC branches nominating candidates to the regional party structure. Regional conferences, comprising representatives from each branch, would then finalise the regional list of candidates to the Provincial Legislature and national Parliament. These were submitted to a Provincial List Conference, made up of representatives of all the branches in the province and the ANC's constituent organisations (i.e. the Youth and Women's Leagues). The provincial lists were finally submitted to a National List Conference.

This unwieldy and cumbersome process was profoundly democratic. However, after the National List Conference the national leadership then deliberated on the final lists for submission to the Electoral Commission. At this point the process lost its democratic character and fell hostage to the whims and internecine battles of the leadership of the ANC.

In my own case, the less democratic conclusion to the process was probably beneficial. I was not widely known within ANC branches, but the leadership would have pushed me up the list, citing my technical competence and experience in Parliament. When the lists were published I found myself at number 110 on the national list. Given that in the outgoing legislature the ANC had 260-odd MPs, my safe return to Parliament was assured. Others were less fortunate. My friend Cheryl Gillwald was left off the lists altogether. In the fierce struggle for supremacy between two warring factions in the Free State Province, Cheryl had been lost in the crossfire as a consequence of not being aligned to either side. She somehow slipped off the national radar as well. Barbara Hogan sent Cheryl's CV to the leadership and campaigned for the omission to be corrected. At the last minute Cheryl was returned to the list, and to everyone's pleasure (and her own surprise) was made a Deputy Minister after the election.

I was involved in campaigning in both Cape Town and Johannesburg. In the media campaign for the Gauteng elections I persuaded my colleagues to adopt Tony Blair's 'Tough on Crime, Tough on the Causes of Crime' slogan. My championing of the slogan reflected my admiration for the New Labour project and particularly the balance of state and individual initiative contained in the 'rights and responsibilities' rhetoric. However, somewhat like the New Labour project, Gauteng's use of the crime slogan was a one-off electioneering gambit, backed by neither forethought nor policy intent.

One of the key architects of New Labour, Peter Mandelson, announced in London that he was heading for South Africa to help the ANC campaign. This was in the wake of his first dismissal from Blair's Cabinet as a consequence of failing to declare a loan to purchase a property that he received from a fellow Cabinet member who was, in turn, under investigation by Mandelson's Trade and Industry Department. This obsession with ever grander homes is a recurring theme with the New Labour elite and illustrates, again, how the holders of political power develop ideas of grandeur regardless of their political background. On Mandelson's arrival in South Africa it was clear that he had consulted no one in the ANC, and he was sent packing.

My campaigning prior to the ending of the last Parliament had been blissfully interrupted by the arrival of our first child, a boy, whose polyglot parentage is reflected in his name: Mishanth Shamail Choudhury Feinstein. A fitting mix of cultural references for a 'Juslim'. With the support of Chief Whip Max Sisulu, I became, I think, the first male MP in South Africa's history to take paternity leave. The ANC were warm and enveloping of our new little family. Lindiwe Sisulu, at the time the Deputy Minister of Home Affairs, took great interest in their well-being and never lost an opportunity to ask after the 'little tsotsi'. Politics took a back seat for the first time in over 12 years, to the extent that I was almost oblivious to the vicious list battle raging within the party.

The 1999 election was successful at a number of levels. It was a consolidation of South Africa's nascent democracy in that people generally felt they had a stake in the political process.[1] The election was, to a large degree, free and fair. Administratively it was far more efficient than the 1994 poll and the ANC recorded just over 66 per cent of the vote, an increase of 3 per cent on the 1994 poll. It is estimated that 86 per cent of eligible voters cast their ballots. Un-surprisingly, analysts found that voting was still closely linked to race, reinforcing that South Africa, after five years of democracy, remained a highly race-conscious society.

In the aftermath of the successful election the topic of state funding of party campaigns featured in occasional opinion pieces. It was not an issue of major concern at the time, but a few of us nevertheless wondered where the ANC had managed to raise the millions we used to run a fairly sophisticated campaign. We knew that Bill Clinton's electoral guru, Stanley Greenberg, and his asso-ciates had been involved in the election effort and assumed they hadn't come cheap.

*

Thabo Mbeki's inauguration at the Union Buildings in Pretoria was, predictably, not as moving as Mandela's, but special for Simone and me with six-month-old Misha on my shoulders throughout the cere-mony. The atmosphere among the ANC invitees was celebratory. I particularly enjoyed getting to know a fellow MP whose hotel room was near ours. Ntsiki Mashimbye was a young former MK cadre who served on Parliament's Defence Committee. Good looking and sociable, he reflected the optimism of a new generation of leaders as we moved from the Mandela era into the age of Thabo Mbeki.

Despite whisperings about Mbeki's Machiavellian tendencies there was great optimism as he began his first term with clear goals and targets in all the obvious areas of need (save for HIV and AIDS). He announced that non-performing Ministers would not survive, but then appointed Mandela's blind spot, Stella Sigcau, rather than a number of more talented people in the ANC's ranks. One elderly fellow ANC MP wondered aloud whether Stella had some sort of maternal hold over the younger Thabo, or whether he was just in awe of the Xhosa princess. Some of the President's appointments were commendable, however, including Kader Asmal as Minister for Education and Phumzile Mlambo-Ngcuka as Minister for Mineral and Energy Affairs. His appointment of Jacob Zuma as Deputy President was something of a surprise. Zuma, a Zulu in the predominantly Xhosa movement, had been ANC Head of Intelligence in exile and after 1994 head of the party in KwaZulu-Natal and that province's MEC for Economic Affairs. He was only recruited for the post when Mangosuthu Buthelezi turned it down. JZ, as he was widely known, was generally perceived as a good Deputy who wouldn't harbour ambitions for the top position.

Sadly, some who did not see eye-to-eye with Thabo decided to leave politics. Prominent among these was Mac Maharaj, the behind-the-scenes mastermind of the World Trade Centre negotiations and a well-respected Transport Minister in Mandela's administration.

Restored to the backbenches, Barbara Hogan and I felt buoyant as Mbeki delivered a first State of the Nation address that outlined the promising shape of the economy and the potential for meaningful material progress for all South Africans. Here was the technocrat the country required after the visionary reconciliation of the Mandela years.

Even the appointment as Chief Whip of the not-much-liked Tony Yengeni, MP for an area that included the impoverished squatter camp of Crossroads, didn't dampen our initial enthusiasm. A stocky, handsome man of immense arrogance, Yengeni appeared in ads for Hugo Boss suits and talked often of the joys of driving his luxury 4x4 Mercedes. However, the transfer from Max Sisulu to Yengeni was to prove a key political turning point for the ANC in Parliament.

84

Yengeni set himself up as the centre of discipline and the dispenser of patronage. He laid down the political line. Meaningful discussion in caucus began to dissipate.

I continued working in the Finance Committee and was appointed to head the ANC component of the Public Accounts Committee, now chaired by the Inkatha Freedom Party's Gavin Woods, who appeared quietly determined and punctilious. The Committee continued its important non-partisan work with gusto, driven by an extremely strong ANC component consisting of the veteran Robben Islanders and committed, talented younger activists.

Sipho Mpahlwa became the Deputy Minister of Finance, with Barbara Hogan chairing the Finance Committee, which became an even more stimulating forum. Barbara spearheaded initiatives to overhaul the budget process. The old mechanistic and secretive process of finalising budgets was a leftover from World War II. In its place came a three-year medium-term expenditure framework, an extensive process of consultation through public hearings and, at least in the initial years, vibrant and productive parliamentary debate. These changes were of crucial importance to the governance of the South African state and are a testament to the work of Barbara, Trevor Manuel and Maria Ramos, who as head of the Treasury took a fairly typical, plodding government department and turned it into a dynamic unit at the cutting edge of current global thinking on financial management. A key sticking point in reforming this process was the issue of allowing Parliament to amend Money Bills – laws that impact expenditure. The Executive would not countenance the legislature impinging on their spending and taxation decisions.

The limits of our independence and influence were made clear on the issue of inflation targeting. On the Finance Committee, we had argued unanimously that this policy was unsuitable for South African conditions, but then we were called to a meeting with Trevor Manuel and the President in Mbeki's imposing Tuynhuys offices. Gathered around an ornate table waiting for the 'big bosses', we felt diminutive and cowed. The President arrived with Trevor and Sipho. After a few moments of pleasantries Mbeki made it clear that inflation targeting had been agreed on by Cabinet, and that as loyal members of the ANC we would therefore accept it as being in the best interests of the country. Barbara and I tried to splutter a few of the reasons for our reservations, but the President repeated the loaded phrase 'the leadership has decided'. We accepted defeat and filed out of the building with a handshake from the pleasant-again President.

The policy of inflation targeting was shown to be inappropriate in its early years, with targets missed year after year, rendering it all but useless. It is arguable that over time the target inspired confidence in the country's commitment to fiscal discipline, and it was probably because of the ambiguity of the economic arguments that we didn't see it as a life-and-death-issue. But we were taught a lesson in the political process under Mbeki through the unfortunate mantra of 'the leadership knows best'.

This was my first experience of the party leadership undermining the parliamentary system. It left me feeling diminished both personally and in my role as an MP. In terms of South Africa's admirable constitution, the Legislature is intended to hold the Executive to account. As the Executive tends to comprise most of the senior members of the party, the unworkable reality is a group of junior politicians trying to hold their superiors to account. This is only possible to do effectively if you have no fear of losing your seat as an MP. Under South Africa's proportional representation system a dissenting voice is easily removed from the party lists at the next election – if not before.

Concerned by this weakness in the accountability cycle and inspired by our work on the PFMA, I started making speeches about accountability and financial integrity on public platforms and to government departments. The most rewarding of these was to the Health Department, which I had attacked in the wake of the 'Sarafina II' debacle. The Department's Director-General was courageous in asking me to address about 150 senior managers, which I did by talking about 'Sarafina' and why the Committee acted as we did, then reciting my credo on financial management: 'The misuse or misappropriation of public money is the most heinous of crimes as it abuses the trust placed in public servants and elected representatives to utilise this money for the benefit of all the people of our country.' After outlining the new PFMA and the workings of the Public Accounts Committee I received a great ovation followed by penetrating questions. Key among these was whether the senior leadership of the ANC supported what I was talking about. I answered confidently that they did.

As I gave more of these talks and wrote articles for a variety of newspapers and publications, I started to become known in government and the media as the ANC's 'Mr Clean', a title first coined by the *Sunday Independent.* Publicly, the title was a little embarrassing; privately I was quite proud of it.

*

In the period after his inauguration the President spent significant amounts of time outside the country. He had appointed the former Health Minister, Nkosazana Dlamini-Zuma, as Minister of Foreign Affairs. Smart and feisty, Dlamini-Zuma (soon to be an ex-wife of the Deputy President, Jacob Zuma), was not known for her social skills and so seemed a strange choice for the job. South Africa's first democratic Minister of Foreign Affairs had been the dozy Alfred Nzo, who was known to sleep through meetings. Nkosazana was a step up, but hardly an inspired choice. It was felt that Mbeki wanted a novice in the role so that he could dominate foreign affairs, arguably one of his political strengths.

The President's absences from the country led to the view that he was becoming somewhat detached from the daily realities facing most South Africans. In a budget speech remarkable for his ignorance of or insensitivity to this perception, Mbeki spoke about his last eight weeks of travel and to the collective astonishment of MPs followed this up with the itinerary of his forthcoming escapades abroad for the next few months.[2]

He also began to speak far more about a divided nation of wealthy whites and impoverished Africans.[3] While true, this was in contrast to the nation-building reconciliation of Mandela and jarred a frail consensus in South Africa. His notion of African-ness, expressed in such an inclusive manner in his 'I am an African' speech, was metamorphosing into a more exclusivist, pan-African vision that troubled many who had been brought up in the ANC's non-racial, nationalist and values-driven ethos. That seminal speech had spoken of an African Renaissance:

The African Renaissance is upon us. As we peer through the looking glass darkly, this may not be obvious. Africa reaffirms that she
is continuing her rise from the ashes. Whatever the setbacks of the
moment, nothing can stop us now! Whatever the difficulties,
Africa shall be at peace! However improbable it may sound to the
sceptics, Africa will prosper![4]

Mbeki's notion of an African Renaissance was developed further over
the next few years. In a speech to a conference aimed at attracting
capital to Africa, he spoke of the creation of '...genuine and stable
democracies in Africa, in which the systems of governance will flourish because they derive their authority and legitimacy from the will of
the people.'[5] A year later he added: 'Africa has no need for petty
gangsters who would be our governors by theft of elective positions,
as a result of holding fraudulent elections, or by purchasing positions
of authority through bribery and corruption.'[6]

Mbeki's economic vision for the African Renaissance speaks not
only to the eradication of corruption and the building of transparency
and accountability, but also to a process of economic reform involving the encouragement of the private sector, the reduction of state
ownership of the economy and the attraction of foreign investment
and debt relief. This 'GEAR for Africa', to be achieved as an endo-
genous African process driven by and dependent on the people of
the continent, envisages a crucial role for a home-grown African business sector.[7]

By 2001 Mbeki was ready to take this broad outline further
through the creation of the New Partnership for Africa's Development (NEPAD). With the support of Senegal's Abdoulaye Wade,
Nigeria's Olusegun Obasanjo and Algeria's Abdelaziz Bouteflika,
Mbeki launched NEPAD as a policy framework. It posited the need
for local reforms to advance development, including peace and
security, good corporate and political governance, a new focus on
public finance management and regional cooperation and integra-
tion. A peer review mechanism was proposed to monitor good governance, respect for human rights, democracy and sound economic
policy. It also envisaged the creation of an environment conducive to
investment by protecting property rights, guaranteeing the rule of
law and providing a social and economic infrastructure. The goals set

included an African growth rate of 7 per cent a year for 15 years, halving poverty by 2015, reducing infant mortality by 66 per cent and maternal mortality rates by 25 per cent, and providing schooling for every eligible child.[8]

The plan has not been a great success. In one of a number of attacks on NEPAD, one of its founding fathers, Senegalese President Abdoulaye Wade, has described it as a waste of money that has achieved nothing.[9] ANC allies and critics on the left have described it as a fuzzy distraction from key domestic priorities, and criticised its adherence to the Washington consensus. Many of the reforming ideas of NEPAD have enormous merit; however, the project has undoubtedly shifted attention from the historic mission of the ANC as a nationalist movement towards a broader African focus.

*

While the President was extolling the virtues of democracy for the continent, at home the role of the legislature was being quietly undermined. In addition to the problems created by a proportional representation system under a party leadership that demands loyalty and is quick to dispense patronage, a series of poor decisions by incumbents of important parliamentary offices effectively ceded power to the party at the expense of Parliament. These two factors removed the backbone of the ANC backbench in spite of our constitutional responsibility for holding the Executive to account.

The leaders with the greatest responsibility to fight for the primacy of Parliament were the Speaker, Frene Ginwala, and Deputy Speaker, Baleka Mbete. Their wimpishness in the face of Executive authority was clear to see in what became known as the Maduna affair.

Penuell Maduna had been one of the least impressive of the ANC legal representatives at the Codesa negotiations. This had not prevented his appointment as Minister for Mineral and Energy Affairs. In mid-1997, in reply to a question in Parliament, Maduna had accused the Auditor-General of hiding the receipts of an oil transaction by the state oil agency. Unfortunately for the Minister, the position of Auditor-General, so crucial to the accountability process, is protected from unwarranted attack by the constitution and the rules of Parliament. Even after it was shown that the allegation was

completely baseless and caused by Maduna's inability to read a financial statement in which there had been an accounting write-off, he
refused to withdraw his remarks. This was an opportunity for the
Speaker to stand up to the Executive and make clear that being a
member of Cabinet did not give you the authority to break the rules
of Parliament and the constitution. Instead, the ANC caucused about
the best way to deal with the issue.

An ad hoc committee was set up which was chaired by an acqui-
escent young Whip, Andries Nel. I was unwisely appointed to the
committee. It was clear from the outset that the ANC would do
whatever it took to exonerate Maduna. The Public Protector's
report into the issue, which was not favourable to the Minister, was
rubbished by the ANC members of the committee. The Minister
himself appeared before us with legal counsel. I got involved in a
contretemps with his counsel during the meeting as he clearly had
no understanding of the rules governing the Office of the Auditor-
General. After the meeting had finished, Kesi Naidoo and I continued to have an ill-tempered exchange in which I told him that I
thought his approach was disrespectful of Parliament. Unfortunately a single TV camera was still in the room and it recorded our
argument. Despite the support my tirade generated from those who
saw it on TV, the ANC used a variety of stalling mechanisms to
prolong the investigation for months and months and then finally
concluded with a weak report which effectively exonerated the
Minister. The Speaker's support for the cynical approach of the
party ahead of the interests of Parliament was shameful and stood in
contrast to her spirited defence of the institution during the first
few years of democracy.

*

The subservience of the ANC backbench and the weakness of the
Presiding Officers, taken together with a fairly feeble opposition,
began to undermine the vibrancy that had characterised the first
democratic parliament.

In terms of opposition, the liberal Democratic Party (DP) had
veered to the right to win greater support, almost exclusively from
conservative whites. In 2000 they took this a step further, forming the

Democratic Alliance (DA) with the National Party. Led by an astute lawyer, Tony Leon, the party gained votes but was reviled by most black South Africans who saw the DP/DA as the defenders of white privilege at the expense of real change. Leon himself was a very clever politician – but at a time when cleverness was not the key requirement. What was needed was a critical opposition, but one which displayed a sensitive understanding of the country's past and an awareness of the still unequal nature of the present. Leon's unwillingness to find a credible black leader in his stead was a fatal flaw that undermined his party's prospects. In his recent memoirs, long-time party member and former leader Colin Eglin expresses his unhappiness about Leon's leadership style: specifically his advocacy of the death penalty and the abrasive, squabbling quality of his relations with President Thabo Mbeki. Eglin was also strongly opposed to Leon's 'Fight back' election slogan, which suggested the DA hadn't bought into the new South Africa.[10]

Leon's inability to support endeavours essential to overcome the massive inherited inequalities of apartheid was brought home to me in a paper released by the DA in his name.[11] In it he equates affirmative action with the early Nazi legislation of 1930s Germany. I was outraged and confronted Tony with the article. He made light of it, saying he would reread the paper and come back to me. He never did. This strategic inability to distinguish the issues that were crucial to the majority of South Africans from the incidental was a key reason the DP/DA was a largely irrelevant opposition at a time when South Africa desperately needed a critical, viable and credible voice in Parliament to keep the ANC on its toes.

As the second Parliament began work the NP was in disarray.[12] When democracy dawned in South Africa the party of apartheid was staffed by people of limited talent. I recall on my arrival in Parliament a vexing meeting of the Finance Committee in which a senior NP member, who had been a Cabinet Minister prior to 1994, asked a question, received a perfectly good answer, and asked the same question again, indicating that he had not understood the answer. After he had repeated his question a third time I turned to Cheryl Gillwald and whispered: 'That is no rocket scientist.' 'Unfortunately,' she replied, 'he is a nuclear physicist by training!' The Party's unintended lesson for history is that in a society where all are not allowed to

91

compete equally, the privileged grouping will rapidly become mediocre through that lack of competition.

In addition to the NP, a smattering of personalities formed minuscule opposition entities ranging from the far-right wing to deeply autarchic socialists. While seemingly irrelevant in the cut and thrust of parliamentary politics, the presence of these groups was crucial to continued buy-in to parliamentary politics by the vast majority of South Africans across racial, political and economic divides. And therein lies the one advantage of the pure proportional representation system: it ensures that any grouping with a modicum of support in the country is able to gain representation in Parliament.

However, the quality of that Parliament was in the balance.

CHAPTER 9
On Being Jewish

For my mother and father, who survived Auschwitz,
Judaism meant bearing witness,
raging against injustice and refusing silence.
It meant compassion [and] tolerance.

'A Jewish Plea'
Sara Roy

South African Parliament, *Hansard*, 26 May 2000:
Madam Deputy Speaker
On the 22nd of January 1943 my mother and her parents received, at their home in Nazi-occupied Vienna, this letter from her 84-year-old Grandfather.
It reads in part:

My dearest children
I have received your letter and thank you for your best wishes on my journey, to which I am not at all looking forward. May God have mercy on the Jews and send us the long hoped for peace.
I pray daily that our dear God will protect you all and give you peace.
In my thoughts I embrace you and kiss you. May you all stay well.
Adieu, adieu, adieu.
Your father.

This was the last contact Samuel Pick had with his family. My great grandfather's journey to which he referred was undertaken squashed into a cattle-truck, on a train bound for Theresienstadt, a Nazi concentration camp, from where he never returned.

In addition to her grandfather, more than twenty members of my mother's immediate family died in Nazi death camps, mainly Auschwitz.

This is the opening of a speech I gave in Parliament in May 2000 to mark International Holocaust Remembrance Month. With the support of the ANC Chief Whip, Tony Yengeni, it was, as far as I could establish, the first time the Holocaust had ever been discussed formally in the South African Parliament. This was unsurprising, given that all of South Africa's apartheid Prime Ministers, with the exception of FW de Klerk, were perceived to be Nazi sympathisers. BJ Vorster was even interned for activities with the pro-Nazi Ossewa Brandwag.

I had somehow spent two dry-eyed weeks preparing the speech through long conversations with my mother, who survived the war in Vienna hidden in a cellar for three and a half years. But on reading my great grandfather's letter in the hushed House of Assembly I felt overwhelmed and delivered the rest of the speech with choked voice and in tears:

> By the end of the Second World War the Nazis had murdered two out of every three European Jews. Six million men, women and children whose only 'crime' was to be born Jewish.
>
> All this, and much more, was undertaken in the name of an ideology of racial purity, driven by irrational prejudice and deep-seated hatred of 'the other'. This was an ideology to which millions of educated, sophisticated people subscribed. Civilised people who actively participated in, or, with a few exceptions, didn't raise a finger against mass murder on a scale the world never believed possible.
>
> What is, perhaps, as tragic about the Holocaust for our generation is that the post-war period has been characterised by a number of other genocides, not of the same scale, but borne of similar notions of difference and racial, ethnic, religious or class superiority. I refer here to the gulags of Stalinist Russia, the killing fields of Cambodia, the mass slaughters of central Africa and the bloody ethnic cleansings of the former Yugoslavia.
>
> How can we claim to be a civilised world while this madness continues?
>
> In this month of Holocaust remembrance, during this year when 46 countries met in a forum on the Holocaust in Stockholm, and at a time when racism and xenophobia are again rearing their heads close to home and in faraway lands, let us ensure that the

Holocaust will always hold universal meaning which transcends race, religion or nationality.

This meaning is derived from the Holocaust's demonstration of what the ultimate conclusion of racism, prejudice, anti-Semitism and xenophobia can be, especially when those attitudes are legitimised by the State. For while discrimination does not always lead to genocide, it does invariably precede it.

The Holocaust further provides a context for exploring the dangers of remaining silent, apathetic and indifferent in the face of the oppression or victimisation of others.

The Holocaust has a special resonance in South Africa, given our tragic history scarred so deeply by an ideology of racial superiority.

There are clear parallels between the policies imposed on the Jews by the Nazis between 1933 and 1939 and those imposed on the majority of South Africans during the apartheid era.

The Nuremberg laws which defined Jews as inferior and prohibited Jewish and non-Jewish marriage or sexual relations echo apartheid's 'Population Registration Act', 'the Immorality Act' and the 'Mixed Marriages Act'. Racial segregation in schools, job reservation, prohibitions against the use of public facilities and amenities, separate beaches and benches are all too familiar in our own not so distant history.

Pictures of Jews having their noses measured merge in our consciousness with Africans having pencils inserted in their hair. The slain victims of the Kristallnacht pogrom elide with the massacred women of Sharpeville or the slain children of Soweto.

However, significant and important differences also emerge when we realize that from 1939 the Nazis embarked on the intentional mass murder of all the Jews of Europe.

Whereas in South Africa demographic reality and economic necessity meant that, while the black majority was dehumanised in every aspect of life, extermination was not in the interests of the ruling minority.

But, despite these differences the similarity of ideology and mind-set and the common nature of deep psychological trauma, suggests that, in addressing our legacy and residue of the evils of racism, prejudice, abuse of power, apathy and indifference we can

95

draw on the universal lessons of the Holocaust encapsulated in the inalienable importance of tolerance, mutual understanding, justice and the celebration of diversity.

Let us, therefore, ... encourage the study of and education about the historical and moral dimensions of the Holocaust and honour those who stood against it.

Let us do this as we continue to teach each other about our own tragic past, as we honour the heroes who stood firm against the tidal wave of racial oppression that engulfed our beloved country for so long, as we strive materially, psychologically and politically to overcome the wounds of the past.

Let us thus commit ourselves to use our collective memory, from far and near, to plant the seeds of a better future amidst the soil of a bitter past. Let us reaffirm our common aspiration for mutual understanding and justice. Let us share a common responsibility to fight the evils of genocide, ethnic cleansing, racism, prejudice, anti-Semitism and xenophobia which still scar so much of humanity.

As South Africans let us focus on what unites us rather than what divides us. As Jew and Muslim, white and black, Christian and agnostic, rich and poor, let us focus on our similarities rather than our differences in building a nation in which greed, selfishness and status are replaced by service, sacrifice and commitment.

Motivated by our common heritage of suffering and pain, let us build a nation, a continent and a world of which we can all be justly proud. ...

Thank you.

The reaction of my ANC colleagues, a few of whom knew nothing about the Holocaust, was encapsulated by Bheki Mkhize, who approached my mother and other survivors present in the public gallery after the speech and gently uttered: 'I'm sorry for what they did to you. I am sorry,' in a manner that typified the remarkable humanity and compassion of so many individuals involved in the ANC's struggle – the key to the relatively bloodless resolution of the South African conflict.

*

On entering Parliament after the triumphant 1999 election I was allocated the Cape Town constituency of Sea Point and Camps Bay, a wealthy area with the highest concentration of Jews in the country.

The Jewish community in South Africa is, like any grouping, diverse and complex. On matters political the community had a small minority involved in the liberation struggle, while a grouping was openly committed to the apartheid state, and the majority remained detached bystanders.

A number of Jewish South Africans of Eastern European origin were key players in the founding and on-going development of the SACP and in the building of the ANC. Joe Slovo, liberation hero and Communist Party stalwart, was a key driver of the non-racism of the movement as the first white member of the ANC's National Executive Committee (NEC). Ruth First, committed journalist, political economist, philosopher and activist, was killed by a letter bomb sent to her in exile in Mozambique. Rusty Bernstein was one of the key authors of the Freedom Charter. Gill Marcus, selfless, impatient, unbelievably hardworking and dedicated, was an ANC Trojan in London from the early 1970s. Gill was the first chairperson of the post-1994 election Finance Committee in Parliament. She set the benchmark for accountability, standing up to the Executive and defending the constitutional role of Parliament. Then as Deputy Minister of Finance she revolutionised the Revenue Service, ensuring increasing revenues every year, and brought order to the crucial Public Investment Commission. After falling out with the tight-knit pair of Trevor Manuel and Maria Ramos, Gill was appointed Deputy Governor of the Reserve Bank, another role she filled with intellect, dedication and innovation. She has recently been named Chairperson of Absa Bank, a challenging and powerful role that reflects her competence and standing.

As Immanuel Suttner points out, the majority of South African Jewish activists describe themselves as non-Jewish Jews. Displaying an ambivalence towards the religion they were born into, or being self-proclaimed atheists, they nevertheless identify their Jewish cultural upbringing as having played a role in their activism. He suggests that 'their awareness of the historical dehumanization of the Jews was the experiential ground in which blossomed the conviction that no one else should be dehumanized.'[1]

The feeling of solidarity with the oppressed of South Africa was movingly evoked in Rose Zwi's 1990 novella *The Umbrella Tree*. An elderly Jewish woman addresses a group of her elderly black compatriots and tells them: 'We were the blacks of Europe ... like you are the Jews of Africa.'[2]

While Jews were over-represented in the ranks of the struggle, the majority of South Africa's Jews acquiesced in apartheid, as did the vast majority of white South Africans. In 1953, apartheid Prime Minister DF Malan returned from a visit to Israel full of admiration for the 'Jewish people'. Within the apartheid system Jews, as whites, were to have a rightful and welcome place. And for the most part Jews accommodated themselves to the racial order, content to abide by the Jewish Board of Deputies' apolitical and quiescent stance vis-à-vis apartheid. The rabbinate, with few exceptions, refused to speak out on moral and political issues.[3]

The most telling example of this connivance with apartheid was the case of Percy Yutar, the Jewish state attorney who prosecuted the Rivonia trialists, calling for the death penalty against Mandela. Although failing in his endeavours to see Mandela hanged, Yutar's efforts were rewarded by his appointment as Attorney-General first of the Orange Free State and then the Transvaal. At this time, as James Campbell recalls,[4] Jewish anti-apartheid activists were routinely shunned by the community, while Yutar was elected President of Johannesburg's largest Orthodox synagogue and described by Jewish leaders as 'a credit to the community' and a symbol of Jews' contribution to their adopted homeland.

Was my uncle's response to my involvement in the Crossroads crisis – that I should 'just be grateful it's the *schwarzers* and not us' – an example of a people, stigmatised on racial grounds, themselves becoming racist when the opportunity arose? Or was the Jewish community, after centuries of trauma, just looking for a quiet life? If that was the case, was it necessary to side with the racists for self-preservation, as some did?

The centuries of oppression, persecution and suffering that the Jews have endured should surely make one hyper-sensitive to the suffering of others, finding any form of racism, homophobia, stigmatisation, persecution or discrimination on the basis of 'difference' unforgivable. Although my life is lived as a secular humanist, I am proud of being Jewish, of belonging to a people who have endured untold trauma and degradation and have yet managed to contribute so profoundly to many areas of positive human endeavour: the arts and sciences, education and politics, the academy and humanitarianism. The names of Freud and Einstein, Menuhin and Barenboim, Marx and Luxemborg, Levi and Arendt, Bellow and Sontag give me a little more pride, irrational as it is, because of some distant ethnic bond.

I feel strongly that the long history of Jewish suffering and persecution should instil in Jews a deep humanism and an intolerance of injustice and discrimination. I consequently felt anger at most of the Jewish community's passivity during apartheid.

The mainstream of South African Jewry is a very tightly knit, insular community. It boasts amongst the lowest marrying out rate in the diaspora. Nowhere else do so many Jews go to Jewish schools.[5] The community is also overwhelmingly Zionist and donates enormous sums of money to Israel.[6] Unsurprisingly, therefore, as Cyril Harris noted, the community is very conservative on Israel.[7] I feel ambivalence towards the Jewish state. While understanding the motivating force of Zionism after centuries of persecution, I am deeply troubled by the ethnic cleansing that was required to create Israel.[8] This brutal dispossession of Palestinians and the decades-long thwarting of the Palestinian quest for self-determination are to my mind indefensible even in the shadow of the most horrendous genocide of our age.

The almost ubiquitous Zionism of the South African Jewish community creates an environment in which criticism of Israel is sometimes fallaciously and dangerously equated with anti-Semitism. As a consequence I never felt able to discuss these matters openly with my Jewish constituents. I believe it is possible to be in favour of Palestinian self-determination, but condemn suicide bombings; to be in favour of Israel's right to exist but still ask what is the most democratic form that existence ought to take.[9]

Ideally, Jews and Palestinians should be able to live together in a democratic, economically viable state. If, under present circumstances, that is not possible, the two-state solution only becomes workable if Israel enables such a state to thrive economically and socially. The current occupation of the Palestinian territories, the regular destruction of homes, the cordoning off and economic strangulation, to say nothing of the profound divisions among Palestinians, make even the two-state solution seem a far-off chimera.

As Sara Roy, the daughter of Holocaust survivors and a researcher at Harvard University, says:

> in the post-Holocaust world, Jewish memory has faltered – even failed – in one critical respect: it has excluded the reality of Palestinian suffering and Jewish culpability therein. As a people we have been unable to link the creation of Israel with the displacement of the Palestinians. We have been unwilling to see, let alone remember, that finding our place meant the loss of theirs.[10]

Irena Klepfisz, a writer and child survivor of the Warsaw ghetto, whose father spirited her and her mother out of the ghetto and then himself died in the subsequent uprising, precisely captures how the memory of suffering should inform our response to current trauma:

> I have concluded that one way to pay tribute to those we loved who struggled, resisted and died is to hold onto their vision and their fierce outrage at the destruction of the ordinary life of their people. It is this outrage we need to keep alive in our daily life and apply it to all situations, whether they involve Jews or non-Jews. It is this outrage we must use to fuel our actions and vision whenever we see signs of the disruptions of common life: the hysteria of a mother grieving for the teenager who has been shot; a family stunned in front of a vandalized or demolished home; a family separated, displaced; arbitrary and unjust laws that demand the closing and opening of shops and schools; humiliation of a people whose culture is alien and deemed inferior; a people left homeless without citizenship; a people living under military rule. Because of our experience, we recognize these evils as obstacles to peace. At these moments of recognition, we remember the past, feel the outrage that inspired the Jews of the Warsaw Ghetto and allow it to guide us in present struggles.[11]

This could refer not only to the occupied territories but also to Stalin's Russia, apartheid South Africa, Mugabe's Zimbabwe, and many more.

*

My Judaism is not lived through the synagogue or through religious belief. But rather it informs a determination to fight injustice, inequality and oppression, to practise a tolerant cosmopolitanism that not just recognises, but embraces difference and seeks out commonality with others.

The extreme suffering caused by the politics of hatred, deceit and denial has caused me to consciously seek to further openness, honesty and accountability in my politics. I suppose, in some way, it is through my commitment to South Africa, to non-racism, integrity, honesty and morality in governance that I attempt to pay tribute to my mother's family, which was decimated by the horror of Nazism, and to those South Africans killed by the brutality of apartheid.

CHAPTER 10
Home At Last?

... if anyone, anywhere, anytime,
feels fully 'at home',
they are not paying attention.

Bram Fischer and the Question of Identity
Stephen Clingman

Sea Point abuts the Cape Town docks, where my father's parents, fleeing the pogroms of Lithuania, arrived at the beginning of the last century. They had bought passage to New York but were dumped in Cape Town instead, on a land that they experienced as alien and hostile. By contrast, during those heady days in the late 1990s, this little corner of Cape Town felt more like home than I had ever experienced. As the MP for the area I found myself having to fulfil all sorts of formal obligations. One involved launching a multi-million rand yacht that had been built in the local harbour for a wealthy businessman. Standing at the side of the sleek vessel I glanced up at Table Mountain and wondered what my paternal grandparents must have made of this flat-topped sandstone mass as they peered anxiously through the sea-spray for a sight of the Statue of Liberty from their rusting, cramped ship.

Sea Point contains half a dozen synagogues, most of them Orthodox. The biggest of them was led at the time by Rabbi Jack Steinhorn. A self-assured New Yorker, Steinhorn was outspoken on matters of both religious practice and politics. He would allow us to use the shul hall for ANC meetings and arranged multi-party debates on issues of importance. I used the synagogue itself for my first public ANC meeting in the area. It felt wonderfully incongruous but somehow appropriate to be addressing a multi-racial, multi-faith audience on the rights of sex workers, the need to allow domestic workers to remain in their accommodation, and voting for the ANC,

102

while surrounded by the paraphernalia of Jewish religious observance. I was saddened to hear that a few years after my departure from politics the rabbi was forced out of the synagogue by more doctrinaire members of the congregation.

I shared the constituency office with the Speaker of Parliament, Frene Ginwala. She had little time available for the area but made a few high-profile appearances around election time. I now interacted with the ANC Western Cape Office, and particularly Max Ozinsky and Cameron Dugmore, two key activists in the province who had been prominent in campus politics at UCT. They remained as intense and earnest as they had been in their student days, but their commitment and energy were laudable. I became friendly with Tasneem Essop, a bubbly, hyperactive, dryly cynical comrade who was involved in accountability issues in the Western Cape Legislature and then, deservedly, was appointed a provincial Minister.

The ANC in the Western Cape was split into two main factions: the Africanists, led by the General Secretary of the Province, Mcebesi Skwatcha, and James Ngculu, a fellow national MP, and a non-racial grouping around the provincial leader, Ebrahim Rasool. Their battles, as much about control of the province as ideological differences or race, continue to blight the ANC in the Western Cape to this day.

In my small ANC office just off Sea Point's Main Road I received myriad requests for help, mirroring how residents of the area were coming to terms with a changing society. In a request redolent of my grandparents' experience I was asked to assist in preventing the deportation of a Ukrainian Jewish family who had fled anti-Semitism. A middle-class Jewish divorcee beseeched me to help her son who had landed up in Pollsmoor Prison for fraud. The thought of her 'Jewish boy' hurled into the anarchy and violence of the prison system was just too much for her to bear. The best I could do was ensure that he received his medication and as much of his mother's cooking as possible. Another constituent informed me that since her daughter's engagement she had dreamed of staging the wedding in Parliament, 'the site of Mandela's democracy'. I couldn't organise the legislative precinct, but managed to arrange for her daughter to be married at Parliament's nearby recreational estate.

Of more importance for people's daily survival were numerous efforts to resolve problems of pension payments, an attempted intervention in extortion rackets run by local thugs, compelling slumlords to repair crumbling properties, addressing verbal or physical abuse meted out by private security operators, resolving disputes between landlords and tenants, exerting pressure to ensure local school admission for black children who didn't speak much English, gaining notice pay for sacked domestics, some of whom had been working for their employers for decades, and helping people facing criminal charges with access to Legal Aid.

On one occasion a constituent called me to her block of flats on Sea Point's quite dangerous Main Road at around ten o' clock one night. She insisted I kneel behind the door and peer through the letter flap. Convinced I was being set up for ridicule, I was shocked to witness the goings on at a crack house across the corridor. Drugs were exchanged for huge wads of money; a harem of women arrived, signalling the start of a loud and raucous party. We called the police station but were told that no vehicles were available.

On occasion I was astonished at the alacrity with which people reacted to representations. An elderly couple who lived around the corner from my office complained that an alleyway running alongside their flat was used for all manner of drug-related sexual and ablutionary activity which had disturbed their sleep for years. I wrote to Woolworths, who owned the alleyway, and within weeks it was fenced off and cleaned up. The grateful constituents brought culinary treats to the office for months afterwards.

*

Sea Point is predominantly flatland, with tall, often ugly, apartment blocks built from the beachfront all the way up the gentle slope of Signal Hill. Many of the inhabitants of these blocks were fearful of the change taking place around them. Historically each of the flats included a small 'maid's room' for occupation by the live-in domestic worker. The local ANC branch comprised many of these workers. Within days of arriving in the constituency in May 1999 I received representations from dozens of domestic workers who were being evicted and from employers who complained that their 'maids' or 'boys' were refusing to leave their rooms.

One was an elderly arthritic caretaker who was told, after 40 years of service, that he was no longer needed and would have to vacate his room. A dignified small black woman who had left her children in the Eastern Cape to serve her 'madam and master' for 25 years was given three weeks' notice to move out. When she refused, the water was cut off and the toilet locked. She pleaded with her employer to allow her to stay. 'Don't complain to me, go and ask Mandela for a house,' came the response.

My interventions had mixed success. There were a few blocks that simply refused to budge, closing down the rooms with no compunction. In others, negotiations with management boards or agents led to compromise. In the case of one block, an ANC stalwart in the area, who had lived in the flats for decades, managed to persuade his board not only to keep the rooms open but also to upgrade them. Meyer Kaplan, a garrulous, white-haired 75-year-old, was an active member of the Lubavicher congregation in Sea Point. On my first visit to his shul I was unsettled by the dozens of men shrouded in prayer shawls rocking backwards and forwards as they studied Torah. However, I warmed to the congregation when I saw that after each service they opened the shul to the many homeless from the surrounding area and offered them food. Every night would find Meyer making his way down to the menacingly dark, littered Main Road to deliver sandwiches to the children living rough on the streets. He spoke with pride of his relationships with ANC leaders in the townships of the Eastern Cape while he was growing up. A real mensch, Meyer was an example of how one's faith could be realised daily in practical, humane ways.

Meyer exposed himself to some danger during his late-night missions, as Sea Point was a focal point for the criminal gangs that swarmed into South Africa as it opened up to the world. Running drugs, women, cars and extortion rackets, the Chinese, Nigerian, Russian and local gangs battled for supremacy, regularly leaving bodies in their wake. In the first nine months I worked in the area there were eight bomb explosions in two 'American' restaurants, a number of gay clubs and a refuse bin primed with a second bomb to explode as the police arrived on the scene. It was impossible to know whether responsibility lay with anti-American/anti-Jewish extremists, drug lords involved in a fierce turf battle, or homophobic right-wingers. The inadequacy of the criminal justice system, the consequences of

105

transition in what had been a highly politicised police force, and the economic marginalisation of hundreds of thousands of young black men all played into the gangsters' hands.

Efforts to address violent crime were channelled through a local community policing forum on which Meyer served. Its members had a range of personal and political agendas that were sometimes obstructive, as was the ambivalent attitude of some of the police leadership, but on the whole it was a valiant attempt to improve a desperate situation. Meeting on 9 February 2000 at the local police station, the forum chair, a driven Jewish lady with greying hair was withering in her criticism. The station commander, Superintendent van der Toorn, had been very suspicious of me when I arrived in the area, but we eventually developed a good relationship of mutual respect. He reported that crime figures for December 1999 were down from 595 to 454 incidents year-on-year, and that the whole of 1999 saw 6 200 incidents in the area, down from 6 600 the year before. Only Cape Town city and Mitchell's Plein experienced more crime than Sea Point in the metropolitan area of Greater Cape Town. He reported on the rape of a prostitute by a man using the name of a policeman. Was it the policeman or someone trying to frame him? Like so many other cases, we were never able to establish the truth.

The issue of prostitution along Main Road in Sea Point and Green Point highlighted the clash of a new liberated society with its authoritarian antecedent. A number of sex workers came to the constituency office requesting protection from their often violent, drug-pushing pimps. A leading chiropractor whose practice opened out on to Main Road phoned the office and shouted abuse at me about the way in which the country's morals had declined. I calmed him down by agreeing to visit him. He showed me the used condoms lying under the bushes in the garden and pointed out the corners on which women paraded for most of the day and night. He wanted the police to arrest them, repeatedly, until they went elsewhere. Continuing inaction would leave him no choice but to shoot at the women to chase them away, he said. I felt that the only way to address the issue was to legalise sex work in specific controlled areas, thereby dealing with the safety and health of the sex workers, improving the neighbourhood environment outside of the red light zone, and hopefully undermining the pimps. Although often discussed, no real solution was implemented and Main Road remains dangerous for those who work and live on the street.

*

The adjoining constituency of Bo-Kaap was predominantly Muslim, a hillside of small, multi-coloured houses with a plethora of little general dealers and eight mosques, oozing the sounds, aromas and vitality of the city's Malay community.

Ariel Sharon's provocative visit to the Al Aqsa mosque in Jerusalem in September 2000 triggered the second *intifada* in the occupied territories and heightened tensions between the Muslim and Jewish communities even in this southernmost city in Africa. The MP for Bo-Kaap at the time was Salie Manie, a veteran of trade union and community struggles in the Western Cape. He and I decided to attempt to lower the rising tension by appearing together a couple of times on a local Muslim radio station. I made it clear that not all Jews supported the incendiary actions of the Israeli government. Stressing the importance of tolerance, I told of my personal discovery when falling in love with Simone of how similar Jewish and Muslim cultures are. I related the story of Simone's mother visiting us in Johannesburg and the two of them being asked by a Muslim shop owner what they were doing in South Africa. On hearing that Simone was married to a local, the proprietor asked whether her husband was 'from the community'. When she replied that I was Jewish, he disappeared into the back of his shop, much to Simone and Runi's consternation. He re-emerged carrying a beautiful, leather-bound book. 'Here, this is for you and your husband. The Koran. Because we are all brothers and sisters.'

Simone and I participated in similar conversations at meetings of the Union of Jewish Women (UJW), local shuls and Rotary Clubs. It's unclear whether these interventions had any ameliorating effect on communal tensions. However, a number of participants at a UJW meeting expressed concern about how we planned to raise our children given our religious/cultural differences – a few remained sceptical that we could possibly provide a moral basis for their upbringing.

107

A couple of years before, Misha had been the focus of a journalist friend's attention when the celebration of the fiftieth anniversary of the founding of the state of Israel took place in Cape Town's Town Hall, with the Call of Islam demonstrating outside. My friend wondered what Misha would do if invited to such an event in the future: attend, protest outside or, like his father, be cowardly and remain at home.

*

In the first half of the twentieth century, Jews, Muslims and others lived convivially not only in District Six but also in a small community in Tramway Road, Sea Point. Mainly employees of the city's public transport company, the community was close-knit and vibrant. In 1959 the non-white members of the community were brutally dragged from their homes and dumped on the wasteland that would become the 'coloured' township of Bonteheuwel. One person died in the move and two others were so deeply traumatised that they died soon after.

The removed community held together through 40 years of anguish and dislocation, determined to return one day to Tramway Road. On a July morning in 2000 a tall, thin, greying figure of great dignity, accompanied by an earnest middle-aged woman, came into my Sea Point office armed with maps, documents, press cuttings and photographs. Leonard Lopes and Elizabeth Davison informed me that I had constituents who lived far away in Bonteheuwel. They took me through the history of Tramway Road and the difficulties they were having trying to get a land claim through the slow and bureaucratic Land Claims Commission in the Western Cape. Elizabeth, who had worked at the Commission and was assisting the claimants *pro bono*, explained the convoluted process and why it was being hamstrung.

Leonard invited me to attend a meeting of the Resident's Committee a few days later. Sitting around the lounge of his small Bonteheuwel home was a group of determined, angry people. We spoke for hours, after which I was ready to help them in any way I could. And so began a series of seemingly endless meetings with the Commission – which was in a state of administrative chaos, the City

Council, the claimants and the local residents surrounding the park that had been established on the land formerly occupied by the community.

The claimants were a disparate group. Some were politically committed, others disaffected with the old and new South Africa; many were religious. There were some real characters, most notably the self-proclaimed Princess Diana of Tramway Road, a vivacious, demonstrative middle-aged lady. And there were one or two who seemed to be less than trustworthy. About a third of them had moved on in their lives and didn't want to return to Sea Point, but wanted financial compensation, as allowed for in the legislation. The others were determined to win back their land and recreate the community of Tramway Road.

My contribution was limited to efforts to iron out difficulties between the claimants and the Commission by involving the Minister for Land Affairs. The Minister was a redoubtable young woman, Thoko Didiza. Energetic, smart and indefatigable, Thoko was back in her office four days after giving birth to her fifth child. Whenever there was an obstacle in the way of settlement Thoko would intervene to maintain progress. The City of Cape Town and particularly a very effective council employee, Dave Daniels, were a pleasure to deal with. Eventually after a year of meetings, negotiations and consultations the people of Tramway Road received their land back in August of 2001. They met to celebrate at the desolate park that had once been home. I was privileged to be asked to join them.

The story of Tramway Road continues, in that the community is still not living back on the land. They have not yet been able to raise enough money for the modest development they desire. The economic reality of the new South Africa has hit them hard, and theirs is an unfinished house.

*

The Sea Point and Camps Bay branches of the ANC were hardly the political hub of the movement. Notwithstanding this relative insignificance, branch life was a combination of exhausting commitment and enthusiasm on the one hand and dirty tricks aimed at the achievement of political control on the other.

Both branches were dominated by local domestic workers and, quite appropriately, their issues and concerns. My Sea Point office was run by a formidable former domestic, Florence Gwadela. A tireless worker come election time, Florence had a relaxed, somewhat chaotic approach to day-to-day matters. She was also very resistant to any threat to her power base, so the arrival of Lorna Levy, an ANC veteran and former Labour councillor during exile in the UK, was hardly welcome. The two tough, uncompromising women saw eye-to-eye on virtually nothing, leading to Lorna's eventual drift away from the branch.

Camps Bay, by contrast, was dominated by a young Afrikaner, Pieter Venter, who himself had political ambitions. He worked for a while in the ANC's parliamentary media office before resigning over President Mbeki's support for Robert Mugabe. While the protest was commendable, our respect for him was somewhat diminished as he became a Democratic Alliance council candidate within hours of his departure. Pieter's limited history with the ANC or democratic organisations generally was evident in the autocratic way in which he ran the branch, inhibiting the real talent and ability of his eventual successor, Sylvia Ntsaluba. The domestic workers attracted to the branch tended to be a small group of fairly passive ladies who were content for Pieter to take the lead on every issue.

Both branches undertook excellent work on behalf of the area's domestic workers, but the Atlantic Suburbs, one of the wealthiest belts of coastal land in the country, were never going to be natural ANC territory. We only marginally increased support outside of our captive constituency in local elections, despite public meetings, regular tables at shopping malls, and numerous articles in the local media. Other initiatives included increasing environmental awareness by cleaning up the beaches, and providing assistance to street children. The branches ran a well-intentioned adult education school in the evenings in Sea Point. However, on my arrival I heard assorted grumblings about the scheme, and on closer inspection it became apparent that control of the project and its Education Department funding lay at the heart of most of the tensions in and between the branches. With the help of the Department we managed to restart the Centre with a new Board of Governors.

The constituency, a source of both frustration and invigoration, also provided occasional moments of humour. An aged Bulgarian émigré whom I tried to help gain permanent residence in the country enthusiastically joined the Camps Bay branch. Dimitri Sabev had been an office-bearer in his country's communist hierarchy. He had written and self-published a 10-volume tome on the history of communism and believed we should seek to establish a Stalinist hegemony along the Atlantic seaboard of Cape Town.

At his first branch meeting he spoke interminably in a heavy Eastern European accent of the revolutionary challenges facing us, and his commitment to walking with us in our struggle to liberate the Atlantic seaboard. This rendered the mainly domestic worker audience either catatonic or collapsed in fits of giggles. Meanwhile, outside the church hall the palm trees swayed and the waves lapped gently on the white sand of Camps Bay beach.

*

The ecumenically named Kwame Anthony Appiah[1] writes of cosmopolitanism comprising two ideals, sometimes conflicting: universal concern, and respect for difference. I am fascinated both by the differences we exhibit and the commonalities we share. While our differences are enriching, our commonalities provide the basis on which to understand and appreciate them. In a sense mine is an iPod culture, shuffling between Abdullah Ibrahim one minute and Dexter Gordon the next; Bob Dylan followed by Tinarewin's blues of the Sahara; Sibongile Khumalo and Renata Tibaldi; Hugh Masekela and Hank Mobley – and finding ultimate expression in the music of Nitin Sawhney, an artist whose palette draws from Indian classical, modern jazz, Afro-beat, hip hop, Latin, flamenco and Western classical, to create music as a 'place with no barriers'.

I feel a degree of comfort with Isaac Deutscher's concept of the non-Jewish Jew, who 'dwells on the borderlines of various civilizations, religions and national cultures ... where the most diverse cultural influences cross and fertilize each other. They live on the margins ... of their respective nations. Each of them is in society and yet not in it, of it and yet not of it.'[2]

My constituency's multiculturalism, its daily contrast of new and old worlds, Muslim radio stations and Lubavicher shuls, was a source of inspiration – in a strange way, a source of pride. For I am an amalgam of my past and my present: white, Jewish, agnostic; South African, Austrian, Bengali, British, Lithuanian; father, son, husband. I feel no need to choose which of these identities is strongest, but proudly acknowledge their currents in the stream of what constitutes my identity together with the values and principles that I hold dear.

*

Parliament was the ideal job for me, requiring a superficial knowledge of many things, while mastering few. I relished the constituency work, being able to intervene on behalf of people with real problems that were so contrasting, often clashing. I enjoyed being a minor local celebrity, speaking at community events from school prize-givings to meetings of wonderfully optimistic revolutionaries; preventing the eviction of a homeless person from a disused shed, launching luxury super yachts. It was rewarding to be recognised in the constituency, and my political and philanthropic urges were more than satisfied by having impact on local issues. I thrived on the theatre of parliamentary debates and questioning experts in committees, on 'politics as show business for the ugly'.[3] I felt I was making a small contribution in this incredible process of building a new nation.

I revelled in the licence this role gave me to straddle a diversity of communities and perspectives. When with ANC colleagues I would argue the corner of business, when with the business community and sceptical whites I would do anything to persuade them of the positives of the ANC. When with the Muslim community I would trumpet the virtues of the Jews, when with the Jewish community I would speak of the achievements of Islam.

Our Georgian home was within walking distance from Parliament in a little lane of similar houses that had been built for members of the British Governor's Advisory Council, the original legislators. There, nestling in the shadow of the majestic Table Mountain, with my young family, a platform to perform and a nation to build, it was a wonderful life. But, while I was content within a complex, almost indefinable identity, the identity of the ANC was inexorably shifting away from the values that are so intrinsic to my sense of self.

SECTION IV
POLITICS AS NORMAL

CHAPTER 11

Comrade Bob and 'the dogs and pigs'

The concept of 'truth'... has inculcated the necessary element of humility
[into politics]. When this check upon pride is removed, a further step is taken on
the road towards a certain kind of madness – the intoxication of power.

A History of Western Philosophy
Bertrand Russell

Thabo Mbeki was born into a political family. His father, Govan, one
of the Robben Islanders, was a member of the Communist Party
throughout his life and a colossus within the ANC. Their life was
about politics almost to the exclusion of emotional ties of family.
Thabo was a son of the ANC, groomed to lead the party from the age
of 16, when he left South Africa for London. His formal qualification
is a Master's in Economics from the University of Sussex, but the
breadth of his intellect extends far beyond the dismal science. People
who knew him in London say he was angered at being rejected by
Oxbridge, and that his tweed jacket and ubiquitous pipe were somewhat out of place at left-leaning Sussex. After his studies he served the
ANC in a number of roles: personal assistant and speech writer to
party President Oliver Tambo, Head of International Affairs based in
Lusaka, and then again London. When rapprochement began to
take place between the ANC in exile and white South Africa in the
1980s, Thabo's urbanity, charm and obvious intellect won over all
who had contact with him.

A diminutive man, amongst some ANC exiles he had a reputation
as a womaniser and a drinker. Within the ANC I often heard of his
amorous exploits, but only occasionally, at times of great stress, of
any excessive drinking. He is psychologically complex: a man who
struggles to show emotion and comes across as insecure and on edge.

He resents criticism and when angered becomes tight-lipped and curt, his small penetrating eyes moist. He is at once an Africanist and an Anglophile who quotes from the western classics while championing a New Partnership for Africa's Development (NEPAD).

The frequent literary quotations reflect someone who quite self-consciously enjoys displaying his learning and intellect. His need to be the brightest person in the room has led him to surround himself with advisors of varying quality. Essop Pahad, his closest ally for a long time, is an uncouth enforcer of limited principle. Mbeki's long-time Chief of Staff, Frank Chikane, is a man of far greater principle, courage and personal kindness. However, he has been competent rather than outstanding in the role, and is perceived as not standing up to the President. Mojanku Gumbi, the President's legal advisor, started badly with an ill-considered report exonerating Allan Boesak, who was later convicted and imprisoned. She is often described as prickly and difficult by ANC MPs and accused of being reluctant to listen to views emanating outside the Presidency. The one obvious exception is Joel Netshitenzhe, the head of government communications. A well-read but humble intellectual and a very good strategic thinker, Joel is also immensely likeable. The extent of his influence on the President is, however, moot.

On the whole, Mbeki's advisors are intellectually inferior to him and do not challenge his views vigorously. Like all national leaders, he lives in an artificial world, insulated from daily reality. But the quality of those he relies on means that this world is insufficiently perspicacious or honest.

*

NEPAD's first real test came as Robert Mugabe, desperate to retain power as he lost sanity and support, plunged Zimbabwe into autocratic, violent chaos.

At first, Mugabe was an impressive post-liberation leader – suave, urbane, combining competent economic management, reconciliation and productive efforts to address inherited inequities. I visited the newly independent Zimbabwe in the early 1980s and was swept up in the spirit of hope and progress captured in the stirring, popular song of the time, 'Zimbabwe, the new-found land'.

116

Mugabe had given some indication of a harder edge when he had ordered a crack North Korean-trained squad of special forces into Matabeleland in 1983 to quell dissident activity. Tens of thousands of atrocities, including murders, mass physical torture and arson occurred. Despite this he remained popular throughout most of the rest of the country, upholding a democratic system comprising an independent judiciary and a relatively free media. However, as his grip on power began to slip, so his initial pragmatism started to give way to a cruder populism. In the mid-1990s his support began to ebb as a consequence of economic difficulties and the emergence of a new opposition force with its roots in the trade union movement. Mugabe's initial response to this electoral threat was to style himself as a more traditional, populist African leader. Early on in this metamorphosis his urbanity started to give way to a crude homophobia. After years of apparent pride in the annual Zimbabwe International Book Fair, in 1995 Mugabe banned a gay and lesbian stall from the event. In his opening remarks to the Fair – on its theme of Human Rights and Justice – he defended his actions by describing gays and lesbians as 'worse than dogs and pigs'.[1]

His waning popularity became apparent in February 2000 when voters in a referendum, encouraged by the emerging Movement for Democratic Change (MDC) opposition, rejected a constitutional amendment designed to increase the already considerable powers of the presidency. Angered and insulted, Mugabe started seizing white-owned land and handing it over to his supporters and cronies. At the same time he set about destroying the MDC. He ignored Supreme Court rulings against his actions and restructured the judiciary, violently forcing out many independent jurists and replacing them with his supporters. He also clamped down viciously on the independent media.

The inevitable outcome of this descent into barbaric populism was economic collapse and starvation in a country that had been an exporter of its staple foodstuffs. Outrage from world leaders, and Tony Blair in particular, was dismissed as neo-colonial rantings by the 'gay Prime Minister and his gay gangster cabinet'.[2]

Eventually Thabo Mbeki and other southern African leaders flew to Victoria Falls in April 2000 to see the Zimbabwean President. They lavishly praised Mugabe in public (and, it is assumed, chided him to

117

some extent in private). This was described by South Africa's Department of Foreign Affairs as the 'quiet diplomacy' approach; indeed, initially it seemed to make sense for Mbeki to keep open a channel of communication while the world's larger powers shunned Mugabe. Mbeki left the Falls thinking he had negotiated a deal guaranteeing the withdrawal of the so-called war veterans who had occupied white farms, in return for an undertaking from Britain to restore promised funding for land reform. A few days later Mugabe publicly reneged on the deal.

In August 2000 Mugabe and Mbeki met again and announced together on television that the so-called war veterans who had led the expulsion of white farmers and occupied their land would be recalled. Before Mbeki had even landed back in Pretoria Mugabe recanted, saying this was just the start of land grabs.

Despite these humiliations, Mbeki stuck to his softly-softly approach. It would have had a devastating and possibly terminal impact on Mugabe if he had been isolated politically, diplomatically and financially by his southern African peers, and especially South Africa. As far as I can establish from people within the ANC, Mbeki never considered this option. His failure to act not only condemned hundreds of thousands, if not millions, of Zimbabweans to starvation and brutal repression; it had a deleterious impact on the South African economy, with the rand hitting record lows in the wake of the upheaval to our north.

South Africa's policy has never changed substantively. In rigged elections in March 2002 only the ANC observer mission regarded the process as free and fair, with the rest of the world united in condemning an act of political thievery. In the aftermath of the election Mbeki, as part of a three-person Heads of State Task Team, prevented Mugabe from being thrown out of the Commonwealth. In the ensuing years of economic chaos, repression and flagrant abuse of human rights the South African government refused to criticise Mugabe. In early 2007, as a divided opposition took to the streets, his thugs clamped down, arresting hundreds and savagely beating key opposition leaders, including the MDC's Morgan Tsvangirai. They also publicly molested senior members of the legal fraternity who attempted to protest against these activities. Despite international condemnation of Mugabe, South Africa remained silent for days before issuing

118

a weak statement. Eventually the SADC convened an emergency session to review the growing crisis and appointed Mbeki to mediate between the Zimbabwean government and the opposition. Mugabe returned home claiming support from his southern African colleagues and describing the summit as a victory for his tough approach. The next day Zanu-PF nominated Mugabe as its candidate for the presidential elections in 2008, despite his having agreed under pressure, months before, to stand down at these elections. The SADC session seemed to have bestowed a further lease of political life on him.

Only a few years earlier, Thabo Mbeki had eloquently declared that 'the one party state will not work'[3] and 'Africa [has no] need of the petty gangsters who would be our governors by theft of elective positions, as a result of holding fraudulent elections, or by purchasing positions of authority through bribery and corruption. The time has come to say enough and no more, and by acting to banish the shame, remake ourselves as the midwives of the African Renaissance.'[4]

What happened? Why did the one international leader who more than any other could have brought change in Zimbabwe, stand back and allow anarchy to flourish, allow his midwifery to result in stillbirth as NEPAD became consigned to the mountainous scrapheap of good intentions in Africa? Logical explanations include Mbeki's belief that his quiet approach would eventually resolve the situation. But even if the crisis were eventually to be ended by Mbeki it would be after over seven years of political brutality, economic destruction and untold suffering, whereas a more principled interventionist approach might have removed this tyrant far earlier with far less trauma. Mbeki may also have feared economic meltdown in Zimbabwe increasing the flow of refugees into South Africa and jeopardising South Africa's not insignificant economic relations with its neighbour. But these consequences were inevitable with the failure of quiet diplomacy anyway. Millions of Zimbabweans have managed to make their way into South Africa in search of food, work or respite. So why not up the ante, restore some sort of economic and social calm and win plaudits for Africa? Perhaps there were more subliminal reasons in play.

Mbeki has struggled to emerge from the gargantuan shade of

Mandela, as would any successor. Where Mandela and Mugabe's relationship was tense at best, Mbeki established a good rapport with the Zimbabwean leader. Mugabe felt that his status as the premier southern African liberation leader had been usurped by Mandela on his release. Mbeki, as the younger man willing to show respect to his elder, was able to build a warm personal relationship while Mandela had little time for Mugabe. I would not be surprised if Mbeki prized this relationship as an example of an area where he had succeeded and Mandela had failed. These contrasting attitudes to Mugabe reflect an important difference between Mandela and Mbeki's world views. Mandela, steeped in the ANC's Congress tradition, based on the values-driven, nationalist, non-racial Freedom Charter, despised the excesses of African dictators. Mbeki, an Africanist, refuses to criticise the 'liberation movements' and, on occasion, appears more interested in the rest of the continent than his own country.

There is also a more tangible political explanation for Mbeki's stance – namely his fear that success for the trade union-led opposition in Zimbabwe could embolden South Africa's union movement to consider abandoning the alliance with the ANC and become an opposition formation seeking power together with the SACP. In 2000 Mbeki's relationship with the union movement was dismal. They had been on opposite sides of the macroeconomic debate for years; the unions were public in their criticism of Mbeki's stance on HIV and AIDS and were hardly thrilled by his support for Mugabe against the MDC. Some in the ranks of Cosatu and the ANC spoke covertly of whether Thabo should even see out his two terms.

Mbeki exhibited a deep mistrust of the MDC, informing an ANC caucus soon after it was formed that we should have no contact with it. Rumours abounded that it had links to the CIA. Cosatu, on the other hand, has offered support to the opposition in Zimbabwe throughout the on-going crisis and has remained highly critical of the ANC government's refusal to adopt stronger measures. On two occasions Cosatu delegations have crossed Beit Bridge to deliver memoranda to the Zimbabwe government. On the first occasion they were arrested and briefly detained, with no support forthcoming from the South African government. On the second occasion they were turned back. This difference of approach was again apparent in early 2007 as Cosatu instantly and forthrightly condemned

Mugabe for the assault on the opposition while the South African government and the ANC remained silent for days. So it is quite likely that Mbeki's spineless approach to the tragedy in Zimbabwe is born partly of his fear of a trade-union-led opposition triumphing over a party of liberation.

*

In the early days of the Zimbabwean crisis Cosatu was not alone in taking on Mugabe. A few ANC parliamentarians joined the chorus of disapproval, most notably Pallo Jordan. Jordan is regarded within the ANC as a theorist and intellectual. He has often been on the margins of the organisation, at one point during the exile years even being held captive by the ANC in Quattro camp in Angola. He was appointed a Minister in Mandela's first government but lost his job when Thabo took over, regaining it again in a later Mbeki administration.

In May 2000 Pallo proposed a motion in Parliament condemning Mugabe's actions and questioning whether free and fair elections were possible in Zimbabwe. The leadership – that is, the President – was furious and a few days later he had to recant. I baulked at the sight of Pallo engaging in verbal contortions to repudiate his initial passionate opposition to the President's stance. This behaviour, in which acceptance of the leader's thinking is linked to a lack of meaningful debate within the organisation, was totally out of character for the ANC, but was the beginning of an insidious change ... what some in the party described at the time as its Zanu-isation. I recalled how I had felt during the meeting about inflation-targeting and how easily we had given way. But far more was at stake here.

*

As worrying a development was the use of state means to fight internal political battles. In April 2001 the languid Minister for Safety and Security and Mbeki ally, Steve Tshwete, shocked the nation by announcing at a specially convened press conference that a plot had been uncovered to undermine and possibly physically harm the President. The plotters were identified as Tokyo Sexwale, Cyril Ramaphosa and Mathews Phosa, former Premier of the Mpumalanga

121

province. The country as a whole, and particularly people within the ANC, were astonished by the accusations. Some saw in it the hand of Mbeki firing a warning shot across the bows of his opponents before the start of regional ANC conferences that were to elect representatives to the ANC National Congress later that year. The delegates to the Congress would then be responsible for electing or re-electing the President and office-bearers. It was common cause within the ANC that the three named people and others were organising slates of delegates to Congress who were unlikely to support Mbeki's candidates. It was also highly unlikely that Tshwete would have made such a statement publicly without clearing it with the President.

It had the desired effect politically. People were too frightened to lobby or promote anti-Mbeki nominees. But there were wider ramifications than intended. I was in London at the time on a road show promoting investment in South Africa. The day the story broke in the City of London's early morning paper of record, the *Financial Times*, I had a meeting scheduled with the head of an asset management company which had arguably the largest investment in South African equities of any foreign fund manager. As I walked into the office of this stern, opinionated man, he showed me the page of the *FT* with the article about the plot allegation, followed by an opinion piece on Mbeki's extreme levels of paranoia. These were carried alongside an item on a new threat from Robert Mugabe to expropriate the property of businesses in Zimbabwe and Mbeki's inaction on the matter. 'We have nothing to talk about,' he said.

CHAPTER 12
Dying of Politics

In the end, we will remember not the words of our enemies,
but the silence of our friends.

Martin Luther King, Jr

In a wonderful irony of history, the ANC parliamentary caucus meets in what was the debating chamber of the old apartheid Parliament. The leader of the ANC, of the country, occupies the seat of the former apartheid leaders, the seat in which Hendrik Verwoerd – the architect of apartheid – was stabbed to death by Dimitri Tsafendas. The Chamber itself draws its inspiration from the Mother of All Parliaments, with faded green leather benches, dark panelled wood tables and a web of thin, hanging microphones that pick up every word, sigh, jeer and cheer.

During the Mandela years the caucus room had resonated with sharp debate and discussion, passionate argument and profound polemic, the discourse that characterised the ANC and the internal resistance movement, a broad church all of whose congregants felt able to speak their mind and argue their view. On 28 September 2000, two years after Thabo Mbeki had assumed the leadership of the ANC, the caucus reflected a more disciplined, choreographed and constrained party, a party fearful of its leader, conscious of his power to make or break careers, conscious of his demand for loyalty, for conformity of thinking.

Two days before this caucus Mbeki had seemed to end two years of bitter controversy by announcing – under constant pressure from the international media on his foreign sojourns – that he was withdrawing from the public debate on the science of HIV and AIDS, a debate he had brazenly stepped into, fuelled by his views that HIV did not necessarily cause AIDS, contrary to the vast, vast majority of scientific and public health thinking.

This denialism had cast a fatal shadow over the provision of treatment to the ever-growing millions of HIV-positive South Africans and had prevented the clear, coherent public education that was needed to stem the inexorable spread of the virus. However, a number of us in caucus, ashamed and embarrassed by our failure to speak up, believed that at last the opportunity was upon us to have our say. Indications were that the President had seen the deadly impact his denialism was having and was about to lead us back to the moral high ground.

The chairperson of caucus, Thabang Makwetla, invited 'comrade President' to address us on this crucial issue. Mbeki stood up and shifted a little to the side of Verwoerd's execution chair. The caucus was silent, in anticipation. The following are the notes I took at the time on my Psion mini computer:

(He is looking terrible. Rheumy eyes. Quite nervous and fidgety.)
'We haven't spent enough time discussing issues of transformation.

'These issues are about changes that are a threat to the established order. Those who want to protect the old order will see SA as a problem and want to undermine us.'

On AIDS: the Uganda conference (attended by about 60 dissident scientists) agreed that nonsense was spoken about Uganda and its 'success'. He quoted from a conference document on HIV and AIDS. 'Vaccines give rise to other diseases.'

'The international panel has decided to carry out experiments for HIV isolation, because the question is unresolved. They also want to know what the HIV testing kits actually test. Montagnier[1] and his US counterpart didn't isolate the virus.

'There is a huge amount of literature on these issues that we must read so that when we are bombarded with huge propaganda we can respond.

'If we say HIV = AIDS then we must say = drugs. Pharmaceutical companies want to sell drugs which they can't do unless HIV causes AIDS, so they don't want this thesis to be attacked. That's one problem.

'The other one is the international political environment where the CIA has got involved. So, the US says we will give loans to Africa to pay for US drugs.

'As the conference in Uganda said, there are all sorts of other things that cause immune deficiency (starvation, poverty, etc.). The US denies this because their companies need it to be a virus.' He repeated figures on the main killers in Africa: respiratory, then malaria. 'Only 10% died of AIDS. Why focus on the 10% and not on the 90%. It's absurd.'

A few comrades cheered. It was clear that he was not recanting. He might have withdrawn from the public debate but, within the family of the ruling party, he was sticking to, further entrenching, his views in a web of conspiracy theory and fabrication that was an insult to his intellect.

I felt my stomach hollow, my cheeks redden, my mind was swirling. Surrounded by comrades of this organisation of which I was so proud, I realised that what was being said was nothing less than a continued death sentence for those babies born to HIV-positive women, for those South Africans who had contracted HIV but were too poor to afford the medicines to stay alive. I forced myself to refocus on what the President was saying, feeling that this was so much more important than all the other megabytes of notes I assiduously took in meetings. He continued:

'What do we do about orphans? We can't chase them away if they are not orphaned by AIDS. We have allowed ourselves to be led by the pharmaceutical companies. ...

'People are working on where this campaign is coming from. The British press describe the SA President as "deranged".

'The Treatment Action Campaign is leading the statements and vitriol against one [I was always struck by, and uncomfortable with, his pompous use of 'one' when referring to himself]. They are funded by pharmaceutical companies in the US. They also say they can't just dismiss Mbeki's views.

'The drug manufacturers must give scientific proof which will take 18 to 24 months.

'One of the major pharmaceutical companies told me that they've spent billions researching a vaccine but have given up because they can't find the virus. Meanwhile their website says by the end of 2000 they will have a vaccine, because if they didn't their shares would collapse.

'An article in the *Sunday Tribune* in late July made clear that health objectives won't be pursued if they clash with profits. So this is a revolutionary struggle for cures to TB, etc. As against people who make profit on the basis of ill-health.'

Comment by Martin Williams in *The Citizen*. He supports the President but 'where are the Ministers on this matter?'

'We have these challenges which comrades have now understood. The Treatment Action Group [sic] has a campaign to get doctors to write to papers, to identify unionists, etc. to speak out. Comrades must understand what these people are doing. We mustn't be scared to take on a lobby that is too strong (when this is only about 10% of the deaths in Africa).

'"One" met with a church leader who said they are discussing what area to focus on. It will be poverty, racism, crime, new morality and health. What are we doing as the ANC to ensure we are empowered to deal with these issues as the church is? These challenges on the movement are going to mount. We must be prepared to respond to these challenges and be aware of the links between the AIDS agenda and the IMF agenda.'

As the President took his seat cheers broke out, grew in volume, interspersed with cries of 'Viva Thabo Viva'. The psychosis of the crowd enveloped many of the 260 MPs crammed into the Chamber. I was sweating profusely, pretending to type on to avoid meeting anyone's eye. I looked up briefly at some of my ululating comrades and noticed a few seats in front of me the stunned, flushed face of Dr Essop Jassat, a medical doctor who was one of the few ANC members to voice his concern to close comrades of the devastating impact of the President's views on AIDS.

Makwetla suggested, to further cheering, that clearly no further discussion on the matter was required, and caucus was closed. Comrades jostled to leave through the narrow doors, chatting excitedly. As I gathered up my Psion and my papers I stood up; sat down again, feeling weak, nauseous. I noticed a few others straggling out, not a part of the buzzing surge … Pregs Govender, Barbara Hogan, Essop Jassat, Laloo Chiba … I couldn't bring myself to speak even to Barbara, my closest comrade and friend in the caucus. I walked down the grand passages of Parliament, the walls swaying, the carpet wave-like beneath my feet; feelings of self-loathing mixing with a visceral anger. I made my way up to my office, closing the door behind me with relief at being in my own insulated little world where Martin Luther King Jr and Mandela kept me company. I sat at my desk, shaking, unable to think clearly. Who did I hate more? Thabo for his deadly views, my colleagues who had cheered the empty, pathetic rhetoric, or myself and other colleagues who were unable to stand up and say what we knew to be so clear: 'No! Stop this fulminating nonsense. This is about the lives of our people, of many of us. These views are killing people every minute of every day.'

On auto-pilot, almost unthinking, I hooked up my Psion to the printer and watched, dazed, as the pages of deadly rhetoric emerged through the Epson and one by one, slowly, drifted to the floor. The printer silent, I picked up the papers, put them in a brown envelope and with that mixture of dread and determination that accompanies impulsive actions telephoned the Political Editor of the country's leading political weekly, Howard Barrell of the *Mail & Guardian*. Trying to sound matter-of-fact, but with strange anxiety and vulnerability in my voice, I greeted Howard: 'Can you meet me, now? There's something I need to talk to you about. No, not in the parliamentary precinct. Can you meet me in the Gardens in 15 minutes? Please.'

Up to this point in my political career I had had extensive contact with journalists but had never provided them with confidential information. Like many others, I had become adept at talking to journalists with great sincerity and limited substance. I regarded some as acquaintances, but had never broken confidences. I was aware that many politicians did so as an everyday part of their machinations, but I felt that to do so was to betray the ANC, to 'rat' on the organisation that had brought liberation to South Africa, which had embraced me and allowed me to play a small part in this extraordinary struggle.

I waited for ten minutes in my office, anxious but angry, scared but knowing that I was going to give these notes to Howard, that I was going to betray Thabo Mbeki, the man at whose inauguration I had so proudly carried my young son on my shoulders. I tried to rationalise in my own mind that many in the organisation would do the same … self-protection, self-justification?

I walked out of my office and out of the building, crossed the cobblestones of the precinct, exited the gates at the southern end of

Parliament Street, turned left, past a disapprovingly glowering Queen Victoria. I felt a little easier among ordinary Capetonians going about their lunchtime business. I hurried into the VOC Gardens, the clusters of dark green vegetation on the site of the vegetable gardens grown by the first white settlers at the Cape.

Howard was sitting on a bench – studious, academic; a long pale face, high forehead and bald dome with wisps of long hair softening a cerebral head troubled by his own traumas with the ANC in exile. I asked him if we could walk to another, less conspicuous seat and hurriedly told him what was in the envelope, pouring out my anger, trying to overcome my impotence. I asked him to protect my identity.

The next week's *Mail & Guardian* was headlined: 'Mbeki in AIDS Conspiracy Outburst'. The paper reprinted my notes almost verbatim.

My fear on reading the headline was not of exposure. Rather I thought: what if I've got it all wrong, misheard, misunderstood? Clearly I hadn't. For on the next working day the ANC ordered all the microphones in the caucus room ripped out and replaced, believing the room to be bugged. 'How else could someone have got, word for word, what the President said?'

At the next caucus meeting the Deputy President was seething. He bellowed from his podium that some members of the caucus must have spoken to the media to contextualise the remarks they had clearly recorded. I felt as if my whole body had turned a deep pink. The air-conditioned room was oppressively humid. I was convinced that all 259 pairs of eyes were focused on me, aware of the reason for my physical discomfort. I typed furiously.

*

South Africa has more people infected with HIV than any other country. A conservative estimate put the figure at 5.4 million in early 2005, with about 530 000 new infections between mid-2004 and mid-2005 and around 340 000 AIDS deaths in the same period. Over 930 people die every day from AIDS.[2] It is estimated that 1.5 million South Africans have died of AIDS since the start of the epidemic.

HIV and AIDS is in the process of destroying the extraordinary, hard-won gains of the struggle for liberation from apartheid. Projections are that by 2016, 6 million South Africans will have died from AIDS, the same as the number of Jews who perished at the hands of the Nazis in World War II. At the end of July 2005, 520 000 South Africans were sick with AIDS, untreated and in need of anti-retroviral therapy; 120 000 people were receiving anti-retrovirals (ARVs) through the private and public health systems.[3]

*

In 2001 I met Thabo Mbeki's nemesis, Zackie Achmat, one of the founders and leaders of the 'too strong lobby' against which the President had railed in that awful caucus meeting the previous year.

Charismatic but humble, strong yet vulnerable, Zackie joined the struggle during the 1976 student uprising. Detained and imprisoned on more than five occasions, he has a deep commitment and a brutal honesty. As an active ANC cadre he was not afraid to take on his own organisation, not questioning its legitimacy as the democratically elected government but critical of its economic policies and particularly its policy on AIDS. In the early 1990s he helped found the National Coalition for Gay and Lesbian Equality, a precursor of TAC. Zackie lives with HIV and refused treatment until it was generally available through the public health system, despite exhortations from Madiba to save himself.

Zackie and the other TAC leaders introduced me to a deeper understanding of the pandemic in South Africa, characterising it as a tale of missed opportunities, inadequate analysis, bureaucratic failure and political mismanagement.

The impact of AIDS in Africa is the most profound threat the continent has ever faced. From the mid-1970s to the end of the century the pandemic claimed 14 million lives. This is a holocaust in Africa equal to the slave trade. South Africa's pandemic is typically African in that it is characterised by heterosexual transmission and is exacerbated by poverty and extensive transport links between high-prevalence areas.[4]

AIDS is more deadly in Africa as a consequence of a number of factors. It might have to do with the type of HIV virus found here, the so-called HIV-1 (clade C). But it goes deeper than this, including the social and structural consequences of colonialism and slavery, poverty and malnutrition, sustained civil and military conflicts, geographical disadvantage, patterns of migration, poor governance and the effects of structural adjustment policies which denuded the public sector. Sexual culture and behaviour – and the 'sexual economy' in which women often feel their continued economic well-being is dependent on the provision of sex – is also an important driver of the pandemic. But it is the combination of socio-economic and biomedical factors, together with unsafe sexual practices, that produces the lethal basis for the spread of HIV. [5]

Poverty, lack of education opportunities and low skills levels heighten vulnerability to HIV infection, with HIV prevalence falling sharply as skill levels rise. Findings such as these highlight education and economic development as important components of an integrated approach to combating AIDS. Obviously there are other structural issues, such as addressing the migrant labour system. Ultimately an effective strategy against AIDS in Africa requires a combination of anti-AIDS interventions and pro-poor development strategies.

*

There is no doubt that weak policy responses by most African govern-ments contributed to the AIDS pandemic. This is especially the case for South Africa, which had more resources than other African coun-tries to combat the pandemic. In the early 1990s antenatal surveys indicated that less than 3 per cent of pregnant women attending government clinics were HIV-positive, but that there were some early warning signs of an impending AIDS pandemic. In 2005 that figure was 28 per cent.

The apartheid government's early response to HIV and AIDS was lukewarm because of a Calvinist prejudice against homosexuals and lim-ited motivation to promote condom use among the African population where in any case the state had minimal legitimacy or credibility.

Initially the ANC took the pandemic seriously, leading to the launch of the National AIDS Committee of South Africa to co-ordinate the response during the transition. This body developed a far-reaching and progressive plan which took the consensus view of the science of HIV and AIDS. The country's first two democratically elected Health Ministers, Nkosazana Dlamini-Zuma and Manto Tshabalala-Msimang, were centrally involved in the drafting of the document. The challenge of HIV and AIDS for the new democracy was included in the ANC's Reconstruction and Development Plan and the National Health Plan for South Africa, which included a National AIDS Plan. However, political and organisational imperatives then marginalised the AIDS issue.

When the ANC assumed power the dominant issues were reconciliation, the economy, the drafting of a final constitution, the deracialising of existing government and social institutions and the building of new state structures. I experienced this personally in Gauteng, where my immersion in creating a new department and effective committees in the Legislature caused me to all but ignore the pandemic. At the time, the disease hadn't touched me personally. I knew no one who was openly living with HIV or AIDS.

A National AIDS Programme Director was appointed, with the initiative veering away from the direction outlined in the AIDS Plan. Rather than place the Directorate in the Office of the President and provincial Premiers, AIDS was recast as a purely health issue, with Directorates restricted to health departments staffed by people from low levels within the civil service.

As the extent of the pandemic filtered through to government we looked for quick fix solutions with disastrous consequences. 'Sarafina II' was an expensive flop that did little for AIDS education and even less for the reputation of government. The so-called Virodene debacle in 1997 was to shred that reputation even further. A group of researchers from the University of Pretoria, who claimed to have developed a truly African cure for AIDS, gained access to Deputy President Thabo Mbeki. Such was his excitement at the prospect of an indigenous cure that when told by the researchers that the Medicines Control Council (MCC), the guardian of medical, scientific protocol, had been hindering their ability to develop the product, he invited them to address Cabinet. Immediately after the Cabinet meeting government announced the breakthrough, criticising the MCC for its obstructionism. The medical fraternity was flabbergasted, especially when tests on the product found it to be based on an industrial solvent with no medicinal benefits. In the aftermath of this unfortunate incident not only was the chairperson of the MCC replaced but rumours circulated of ANC involvement in the company set up to market and sell Virodene. (At the time I thought there was no way the ANC – or Thabo – would promote something prima-rily or even in part for financial gain.) Tensions with the scientific community were heightened and relations between the Health Department and civil society damaged.

Calls for a Mother to Child Treatment Plan (MTCTP) started to gain ground in the late 1990s, at the time that Thabo Mbeki assumed the Presidency of the ANC. In late 1998 the Health Minister announced that South Africa would not make AZT – the most suitable ARV at the time – available for MTCTP because of its cost and the inadequate health infrastructure. From the outset, affordability was touted as a central issue. This unleashed a storm of protest and precipitated the founding of the Treatment Action Campaign. At the funeral of his friend, the courageous activist Simon Nkoli, who was among the millions who could not afford ARVs to keep them alive, Zackie Achmat announced that he was launching a campaign to make treatment and care available to poor South Africans and to promote greater openness about and accep-tance of the pandemic.

TAC quickly gained momentum as a community-based re-sponse to HIV with a majority black membership. At its formation it had assumed that there would be resistance from pharmaceuti-cal companies whose profiteering it criticised, and from some NGOs that were not activist-based – but never that the most in-transigent opponent of a treatment campaign would be the lead-ership of the ANC. Surely, once the efficacy of ARVs was brought to the attention of government and prices reduced through pres-sure on the pharmaceutical companies and domestic production of generics, government policy would be enhanced to include the provision of treatment?

TAC's approach to activism drew on the experience of the libera-tion movement: organising at community level, using demonstrations, marches, civil disobedience and letter-writing campaigns, seeking national and global solidarity and unearthing impressive local leaders. As Achmat said: 'It is a cruel irony of history that at the very moment when all the people of our country removed the shackles of racial oppression and created a free political life for all, that HIV/AIDS establishes a new apartheid. The new apartheid exists between those who can buy health and life and those who die because they are poor.

The tools we used against the apartheid regime we now utilise to demand the right to life and social justice for people living with HIV/AIDS.'[6]

*

At the same historical moment, Thabo Mbeki was placing his own centralising, technocratic stamp on the movement, rowing back from the days of mass protest and community organisation. This stamp included the Presidency's active involvement in and often domination of every area of policy making, and the emergence of a small clique of trusted advisers which usurped the place of collective debate within the ANC. In October 1999, a few months after he was elected president of the country, he raised the problem of toxicity in relation to AZT in a speech to the National Council of Provinces. This was the first glimmer of his unorthodox views on HIV and AIDS. Within the ANC in Parliament there was talk of Thabo's late-night sessions surfing the Internet and becoming drawn to the work of a small group of AIDS dissidents who claimed that HIV was a harmless passenger virus and that the symptoms associated with AIDS were the result of poverty and lifestyle choices – and even the result of anti-retroviral medication.

The notion of dissidence is one that normally appeals to me. Not so in the case of AIDS dissidents who ignore the vast scientific evidence that has established a causal link between the HI virus and AIDS. Their denial of this causality is not just bad science – the problem with the dissident thesis is that if you don't believe AIDS is infectious but merely a deficiency disease you will not practise safe sex and the disease will spread exponentially. This is especially so if the belief is held by a country's leader in a culture in which the leader's view is enormously influential on public discourse and behaviour.

As Sparks suggests in *Beyond the Miracle*, there might be some validity in the view that Mbeki's engagement against the pharmaceutical companies – as elucidated below – would have been at its height as he became aware of the dissidents' work. The marrying of their criticism of the pharmaceutical companies, who undoubtedly profiteer, and their cranky views on the science of the disease might have been easy to conflate in the mind-set he occupied.

133

The President's intervention in the debate caused the Health Minister, a doctor, to alter the views she had held when engaged in the pre-1994 planning for the pandemic. She claimed that AZT weakened the immune system and could lead to mutations and birth defects.

I recall meeting Dr Manto Tshabalala-Msimang at the time of my swearing-in at Parliament. A short, neat woman with small spectacles and a precise bob of dark, thick hair, she came across as kind, concerned, a little insipid. Her history in the ANC was anything but: she had founded the movement's health department in exile and had been deeply involved in positioning the ANC to address the epidemic as a priority. Before joining government she had worked for a respected NGO, the National Progressive Primary Health Care Network.

Tshabala-Msimang had initially established good rapport with TAC. However, on becoming Health Minister after the 1999 election, amid the President's new-found aversion to ARVs, she had a choice: to take the President on and use her medical background to persuade him of the views she herself held, or to establish a new policy on HIV, very different to that which had gone before. Manto's statements on AZT's dangers made her choice clear. By these comments, the abandonment of scientific principles and protocols and by giving dissident voices equal status with the MCC, the South African government regressed AIDS policy-making into a scientific dark age that saw the purging of public scientific bodies of people critical of government's stance, and the creation of a National AIDS Council with no medical or civil society representation.

In addition the President announced the creation of an International Panel of Scientists of HIV in Africa comprising conventional scientists and dissidents in equal number. This created an air of unbelief among scientists, confusion among those at risk of HIV and consternation among AIDS workers. In April 2000 Mbeki wrote a letter to Bill Clinton, Tony Blair and other foreign leaders trying to justify the role of maverick scientists on the panel. In it he said: 'Not long ago in our country people were killed, tortured and imprisoned because the authorities believed that their views were dangerous. We are now being asked to do the same thing that the racist apartheid tyranny did, because there is a scientific view against which dissent is prohibited.' It appeared the President genuinely believed that poverty and its consequences actually caused AIDS rather than exacerbated it.

A month earlier Parks Mankahlana, the President's media spokesperson, wrote in an article that ARVs were expensive and toxic and were part of a corporate conspiracy to benefit from Africa's poor. Seven months later Parks died of AIDS (although neither his family nor the ANC would admit the cause of death).

Up to this point Nelson Mandela had remained relatively quiet on the issue, conscious of not treading on the toes of his successor. However, he became so deeply concerned by the tenor of the debate that at his concluding address to the 13th International AIDS conference in Durban in July 2000 he appealed for 'the dispute about the primacy of politics or science [to] be put on the back burner and that we proceed to address the needs and concerns of those suffering and dying'. In September he told the *Daily News* that HIV definitely causes AIDS.[7] It was well known in the ANC corridors of Parliament that Mbeki was incensed with Mandela's intervention.

At the same time, and in response to government's concerns about the cost of Nevirapine, its German manufacturer offered to provide it to the state for free. The Minister of Health rejected the offer, insisting that she first required the results of research from operational pilots in a handful of sites, despite the drug having been cleared by the US's Food and Drug Administration and the WHO, among others. She announced to widespread disbelief and anger that these trials would only be completed in December 2005. In fact, the Minister had asked the Cochrane Centre, the gold standard of medical research literature, to look into the efficacy and risks of Nevirapine as early as December 1999, and they had reported back to her later that month that it was less expensive than AZT, safe and effective. She had allowed the report to gather dust.[8]

While the Minister was prevaricating it was estimated that 70 000 babies born to HIV-positive women were affected every year. Public outrage grew. In September 2001, after his attempts to meet Mbeki to discuss the matter had been rebuffed, Nelson Mandela again publicly urged government to take action. TAC began an intensive campaign of mass action and took the government to the High Court, demanding that the state provide MTCTP as fulfilment of the right to life enshrined in the constitution. Government replied in court papers that MTCTP was unaffordable and would put too much strain on the health system.

In a momentous victory for the people of the country and the integrity and independence of its judiciary, on 14 December 2001 the court instructed government to provide MTCTP. It was a strange feeling, as a recent MP of the government, to be overjoyed at its legal defeat.

Government appealed the decision to the Constitutional Court, which upheld the High Court decision and reiterated that the government was to provide Nevirapine through the public health system. The Health Department reluctantly started rolling out MTCTP. However, by mid-2003 South Africa's MTCTP roll-out was still being described as 'a shambles'.[9] The lack of national government will to make it work led to sub-optimal implementation and unresolved operational problems. Conservative estimates suggest that these delays cost the lives of about 35 000 babies every year.[10]

*

This was not the first court case dealing with HIV and AIDS in post-apartheid South Africa.

The cost of ARVs and other drugs to treat opportunistic infections associated with AIDS was a severe obstacle preventing access to treatment for the poor. A key contributor to the high cost of essential drugs is the global system of patents, as the most effective way of reducing the cost is either through the generic production of the medicines or their parallel importation from a country in which they are available more cheaply. As Cameron[11] points out, 'poor people are denied access to life-saving medications because of patent rights every day across the world'. The reality is that the unjust application of patent laws in poorer countries which can't afford to pay high prices for patent medicines but are prohibited from manufacturing or accessing much cheaper alternatives, results in death from poverty.

In 1997 the government had introduced legislation to enable parallel importation and compulsory licensing of essential drugs. The pharmaceutical companies, through the Pharmaceutical Manufacturer's Association (PMA), instituted court proceedings against the government, claiming that the law was in violation of World Trade Organisation (WTO) agreements and, thus, South Africa's constitution. South Africa was placed on a US watch list of countries that were implementing unfair trade policies against US companies. At the time I assumed it was not coincidental that the pharmaceutical industry had been big contributors to the Clinton-Gore re-election campaign.

In 1998 Minister of Health Nkosazana Dlamini-Zuma had told TAC: 'If you want to fight for affordable treatment, then I will be with you all the way.' The case eventually came to court in 2001, with TAC admitted to the proceedings as 'friend of the court', increasing media interest in the proceedings and the four-year-old stand-off. This intervention and the accompanying publicity caused the PMA to settle. The Health Minister, now Tshabalala-Msimang, never acknowledged TAC's role in the case and denied that the court victory enabled government to introduce an ARV programme.

Interestingly, when quite legitimately attacking the pharmaceutical industry for pricing policies the President was never minded to negotiate for bulk discounts, nor did he consider ways of accessing generics. Instead a statement from the President's office likened antiretroviral therapy to the 'biological warfare of the apartheid era'. It said, 'Our people are being used as guinea pigs and conned into using dangerous and toxic drugs.'[12]

*

Civil society continued to criticise government's stance. Professor Malegapuru Makgoba, a leading scientist, president of the Medical Sciences Research Council and a fervent supporter of Mbeki's African Renaissance, told a meeting at Rhodes University in Grahamstown that South Africa could afford no more mixed messages and blunders in its fight against HIV and AIDS. Great care had to be taken with 'political and scientific choices' if the country was to avoid history recording that it collaborated in 'the greatest genocide of our time'.[13]

The President's views split the alliance, with the SACP and Cosatu speaking out publicly against the President and Health Minister's obfuscation. Within the ANC itself, those who supported the President were vociferous; those who opposed him generally quiet. The only example of anyone in the ANC raising the issue directly with the President was when Nkosazana Dlamini-Zuma, now the Minister for Foreign Affairs, privately warned Mbeki in mid-2000 (according to the ANC rumour mill in Parliament) that his international panel was creating confusion on the issue. The current Health Minister and the President's chief enforcer at the time, Essop Pahad, were dismissive of the concern.

In September that year Parliament's Health Committee bravely urged the Minister and President to state publicly that HIV causes AIDS. The ANC members of the committee went silent thereafter. In 2001 Parliament's Joint Monitoring Committee on the Improvement of the Quality of Life and Status of Women, led dynamically by ANC MP Pregs Govender, held hearings on the impact of HIV on women and girls. Their report, which called for ARVs to be distributed to the poor, was blocked by the ANC leadership and not discussed until March 2002. In March 2003, Barbara Hogan initiated hearings in the Finance Committee on the fiscal viability of treatment, debunking the propagated cost myths.

The opposition in Parliament vilified Mbeki for his stance but their electoral weakness and lack of credibility neutered the criticism.

In 2000 Mandela continued to try and meet with Mbeki to raise his concerns. The President refused to take his predecessor's calls as he was furious about Mandela's criticism. Then, under pressure from the ANC's allies, with a local election looming and intensifying criticism from the international media, Mbeki reluctantly announced that he was withdrawing from the scientific debate and would desist from making comments on the matter in public. This was followed by his tirade in the ANC caucus that I leaked to the *Mail & Guardian.*

Advised by Pahad that he had silenced dissent within the party, Mbeki proceeded to attack the media who had run the leaked story. He was particularly vituperative towards Sipho Seepe – who took over as political editor of the *Mail & Guardian* when Howard Barrell became its editor – and TAC, especially Zackie Achmat, attempting to label it a stooge of the pharmaceutical companies in spite of the fact that TAC has never received a cent from a pharmaceutical company, directly or indirectly. Essop Pahad weighed in as well, decrying local medical experts as pseudo-scientists.

With the ANC NEC reiterating their appreciation and full support for the President's initiatives on the issue, Mbeki refused to take an AIDS test in early 2001, suggesting that it would be interpreted as 'confirming a particular paradigm'.[14] Later that year he misused out-of-date WHO statistics to claim that only 2.2 per cent of deaths in South Africa were caused by AIDS and suggested therefore that health and social policy should be re-evaluated. Delivering the ZK Matthews Memorial lecture at the University of Fort Hare in October 2001, he implied that the conventional interpretation of the African AIDS pandemic was racist.[15]

Mandela again endeavoured to meet Mbeki and his wife, Zanele, to plead with them to lead the fight against HIV and AIDS publicly and prominently. Again he was rebuffed. The former President restated his concern about time being wasted on the scientific debate while people were dying.

Mbeki was now so outraged at 'the old man's meddling' that he eventually arranged a meeting with Mandela and the ANC National Working Committee (NWC). Mandela and the NWC turned up for the meeting but Mbeki never arrived. Madiba used the opportunity to urge the NWC to introduce ARVs immediately, for pregnant women at least, as had been demanded by the constitutional court. He voiced his concern that communities were beginning to see the ANC as uncaring. Former Archbishop Desmond Tutu also made public statements about the issue. The feud that this sparked between Tutu and Mbeki has still not been repaired. Even business weighed in to the debate, suggesting that the controversy was economically damaging. Faced with this intensifying pressure, at a Cabinet meeting in January 2002 the President finally agreed that the AIDS issue was undermining the country's interests. At the opening of Parliament the following month he spoke about government's intentions to intensify its comprehensive programme against AIDS.

A special meeting of the ANC's NEC to which Mandela was invited was called for March 2002 to discuss the issue further. In the build-up to the meeting Mandela was attacked in the media by Mbeki loyalists as 'meddling' and 'out of touch'. Peter Mokaba, my erstwhile guide in Hong Kong, co-ordinated the writing of a 114-page rant (claimed by some to have been written by Mbeki himself) against those who opposed the President on the issue. It was circulated within ANC ranks.

At the NEC meeting Mandela, dignified and restrained as ever, voiced his concerns. He was heckled and jeered by Mbeki's supporters. The loyalists urged the President to bulldoze ahead with his controversial AIDS policies. And after Peter Mokaba and others spoke in a carefully orchestrated onslaught the NEC agreed not to provide pregnant women, rape victims or health workers with ARVs because 'they remained unproven'. They also supported the appeal against the ruling by the Pretoria High Court that Nevirapine be given to pregnant women. The Health Minister had said earlier on television that government would not obey the order.

According to a former colleague of mine who is close to Mandela, this was among the lowest moments in his life's devotion to the movement. Madiba even said privately that he felt people were justified in seeing the ANC as a party that did not care about those dying of AIDS. With Mbeki's attacks on TAC and Zackie Achmat intensifying, Mandela made a symbolic visit to Achmat at his home. He lauded Zackie as a long-time ANC comrade of great integrity and pleaded with him to take ARVs.

Mbeki's 'dead hand of denialism'[16] continued to weigh heavily on AIDS policy making throughout 2002 and 2003, and besmirched the ANC during years that should have been among the new democratic South Africa's finest. In late 2002, after months of formal negotiations between the state, business, labour and community representatives in the National Education, Development and Labour Council (Nedlac), government was on the brink of signing an agreement that would have committed it to providing ARVs in public hospitals. At the last moment, government pulled out of the negotiations, citing the cost and complexity of implementing ARV treatment. In response, TAC leaked details of the costing plan that government had undertaken but not released, showing that treatment was affordable.

The arguments about the cost and efficacy of ARVs continued unabated. In early 2003, Trevor Manuel, socially progressive and a committed community activist prior to becoming involved in government, said in Parliament that '... I think there is a lot of voodoo being spoken by the likes of [IFP MP Peter] Smith ... This notion that it's ARVs or bust is bunkum. It's a position that can only be taken by pharmaceutical companies. It's not supported by fact ... We need to recognise that the term we use: "medically appropriate treatment" will cover a range of issues. But the bulk of our investment has to be in prevention, because you can put people on ARVs but they are not going to cure them.'[17] While Manuel's position was to prescribe a holistic approach on both prevention and treatment, it is not unknown for some economists and public health specialists to suggest a focus on prevention rather than using resources to provide treatment to those who are already sick. I have fundamental moral problems with this latter position. In practical terms, prevention efforts will be less effective unless treatment is offered as an incentive for testing.

Nicoli Nattrass at the University of Cape Town has illustrated that the cost of comprehensive treatment and prevention interventions is manageable within South Africa's existing budget constraints. She has also demonstrated in a rigorous economic analysis that the health costs of dealing with the pandemic without treatment would be far higher than the treatment option.[18]

The issue of toxicity of the drugs was best addressed by HIV-positive activist Nontsikelelo Zwedala, who said simply: 'I would rather live with the side effects [of medication] than die of AIDS.'[19] Any concerns around the implementation of treatment could be allayed not only by the successful experience of many developing countries, including Brazil and Haiti, but also closer to home in Khayelitsha and Lusikisiki.

The stark reality is that it was not the technicalities that delayed government action for so long, it was the lack of political will on the part of the President and the Minister of Health, and the acquiescence of their colleagues in the leadership of the ANC.

Eventually it was a combination of economics and politics that pushed the President and his Health Minister into changing government policy. Members of the President's International Investment Council (including global business luminaries Tony O'Reilly and Jurgen Schrempp) warned him that investors found the chaos around government's views on AIDS unsettling and frightening and that it was fuelling negative perceptions about South Africa as an investment opportunity. Trevor Manuel and Tito Mboweni also started to talk to him about the negative economic consequences, while Archbishop Ndungane – Tutu's successor – was moved to say at the South African AIDS Conference in Durban in early August 2003 that the government's inaction on HIV and AIDS was 'a world disgrace as serious as apartheid'.

These messages, together with the pressure of a civil disobedience campaign led by TAC and an impending election, eventually caused the South African government later that month to state that 'ARVs do help to improve the quality of life of those at a certain stage of the development of AIDS'. It was a highly qualified statement, citing the issues of toxicity, procuring and costing. But it was a massive step forward. The Cabinet then asked the Health Minister to develop a plan for a national roll-out of treatment including ARVs to start just before the April 2004 elections. This reversal of policy was met with great joy and relief.

In April 2004, just before the country's third democratic national election, Sankie Makhanyale-Mthembu, Deputy Secretary-General of the ANC, admitted that the party was wrong in respect of AIDS policy and must now take the correct route. Was this just a pre-election ploy, or had the Minister of Health and the President accepted the overwhelming scientific evidence and the compelling moral arguments in favour of ARVs?

*

By this time I was living in London. At the request of Zackie Achmat, a London-based South African writer, Rachel Holmes, myself and a few others founded the Friends of the Treatment Action Campaign (FoTAC). Our first meeting took place in a pub in central London. The group comprised expat South African lefties, for whom this was something of a reunion, and British activists with a fervent commitment to South Africa and the struggle against HIV and AIDS. In a move engineered by the visiting Zackie I was elected Chairperson and Rachel Secretary. A former UCT and Cambridge friend, Oliver Phillips, was made Treasurer. Shula Marks, a revered progressive academic, was among the trustees.

We dragooned a list of supportive celebrities into raising the profile of the South African AIDS issue in the UK. Annie Lennox, Archbishop Desmond Tutu, Sir Anthony Sher – who grew up in my former constituency of Sea Point – Gillian Anderson, Sharleen Spitteri, Jeanette Winterson, Gillian Slovo and Ann Grant (a former British High Commissioner to South Africa) are among our patrons. Having demonstrated outside South Africa House against apartheid it was a sad experience for me to lead a FoTAC delegation into the same building on World AIDS Day to deliver a statement calling for greater action on AIDS from the democratic government.

We were among many activists in South Africa and abroad who hoped that the President would illustrate the strength of his commitment to fighting the pandemic by appointing a more pragmatic, honest and committed Minister of Health. Annie Lennox and I appeared on the BBC to call for Tshabala-Msimang to be sacked and for Mbeki's government to show leadership on AIDS. But in early May 2004, after the ANC had increased its share of the vote to an astonishing 70 per cent, Manto Tshabalala-Msimang was reappointed. In the post-election euphoria government committed to the aim of having more than 50 000 people on treatment by March 2005. However, by June 2005 this figure had still not been achieved.[20]

The roll-out of a holistic prevention and treatment plan including ARVs remained slow and piecemeal for years, not helped by continuing confusing statements from the President and his Health Minister. Stock shortages, poor counselling, perpetuation of myths in communities and obfuscation by politicians all contributed to the slow pace.

TAC was again forced to seek a High Court injunction in November 2004 to compel the Minister to publish the Appendix to the roll-out plan, which was supposed to cover the details of the roll-out, including phasing and time scales. Eventually, in court she admitted that no such appendix existed.

The reality that in March 2005 over half a million South Africans desperately needed ARVs and that a similar number of people again were infected during the prior year is a shaming indictment of government's efforts. Why the torpor?

Taking its lead from the President, denialism has been widespread in the country. In 2004, on a visit to Johannesburg, I took a minibus taxi drive past the informal settlement of Elias Motsoaledi near the Chris Hani Baragwanath Hospital, Africa's largest. Three young Sowetans were sitting behind me. As we drove past the hospital a sign came into view with a picture of the President emblazoned across it with a message about safe sex. The three young men giggled. I asked them what was funny. The eldest pointed to the President and, with a smirk, remarked: 'He doesn't believe in AIDS, why should we?'

Speculation is rife that numerous prominent South Africans have died or are dying of AIDS: politicians, football stars, actors and musicians. But in the vast majority of cases the family, like the President, will not admit the cause of death. The ANC has never acknowledged the death of a member from AIDS. I remember vividly the case of a fellow MP who died just before I left Parliament. We all knew he had AIDS, but no one said a word. I asked a close comrade of his why no one said anything. He replied that we didn't want to shame our comrade in death.

Peter Mokaba, tourism deal maker, former President of the ANC Youth League and chief author of the vitriolic defence of the President's denialism and the fatal evils of ARVs, took the drugs for years, as did more than 20 other MPs through Parliament's medical aid scheme while the country's poor were unable to access the life-saving medication. Three months after writing his polemic, Peter died of AIDS. Did he come off the ARVs because he couldn't justify his outspoken views while keeping himself alive on the drugs? Or was he persuaded that the drugs, not AIDS, were killing him? A close friend of Peter's who spoke to me recently about his death claimed that Peter was caught in a battle between Winnie Mandela and Mbeki over his care; that he was confused and frightened and eventually 'ran away, didn't have medication and just wasted away'.

Even after Peter and Parks had died, when questioned in late 2003 at the Plaza Hotel in New York, where he was attending the opening of the UN General Assembly, President Mbeki said: 'Personally, I don't know anybody who has died of AIDS.' Asked whether he knew anyone with HIV, he added quietly, 'I really, honestly don't.'[21] This was in sharp contrast to the courageous public announcement in January 2005 by Nelson Mandela that one of his children had died of AIDS. Mangosuthu Buthelezi, to his credit, did likewise.

The ANC's deafening silence on the cause of death of countless of its own activists from AIDS is indicative of why there has been so little hope of a comprehensive and honest public education campaign while Mbeki is still in office. This is in stark contrast to his counterpart in Uganda, President Museveni, who has taken the lead in a highly successful awareness and education campaign that has contributed to the decline of infection rates. These denials also perpetuate stigma. The ANC as a progressive social formation should be leading the destigmatisation of AIDS. Mbeki should talk of AIDS as openly as the socially more conservative and less democratic Museveni. Instead he refuses even to say the virus is sexually transmitted.

Privately, the President remains an unrepentant AIDS denialist. I was told this as recently as late 2006 by someone who has extensive access to Mbeki and is sympathetic to him, if not to his views on AIDS. The same source further characterises the President's attitude towards the roll-out of ARVs as 'passive-aggressive'.

The Health Minister and the President have never once explicitly told people with AIDS to take ARVs. Instead the Minister posits garlic, the African potato, olive oil, lemon and vitamins as alternatives. It would be amusing if it wasn't so tragic.

The Minister also has form when it comes to supporting AIDS denialists. In March 2005 she appointed a leading dissident, Roberto Girraldo, as a consultant on nutrition, giving him and other dissidents the opportunity to address senior members of the Department of Health. She has also appeared supportively in a marketing video for another denialist, Tine van der Maas, whom she personally asked to cure Khabzela, a prominent South African DJ afflicted with AIDS, who would not take ARVs. Within a month of Van der Maas's intervention Khabzela was dead.[22]

Additionally, she has refused to criticise or take action against a dangerous charlatan who encourages people to come off ARVs and take up his alternative regimen of vitamins, from which unsurprisingly he profits. German pharmaceutical proprietor Matthias Rath, who calls himself a doctor although he is not registered with any of the relevant professional bodies in the country, has conducted experiments on humans without the approval of the MCC, and his vitamins are not registered for the treatment of AIDS.[23] Since November 2004 he has openly undertaken these activities in South Africa with the knowledge of the Minister.

Rath's activities directly contradict government policy and often flout SA Medical Association guidelines and requirements. However, no state authority will take any action against him despite TAC and other organisations' repeated requests. He has been condemned by a range of local and international organisations, and has court judgements against him in Germany and Holland. But government does nothing; rather the Minister's actions have emboldened him. When asked to condemn him at a community meeting in Khayelitsha, she refused to do so. She admitted in Parliament to having a meeting with him to discuss his concern for people infected with HIV and AIDS, and invited his agents, fellow dissidents David Rasnick and Sam Mhlongo, to present their claims to the National Health Council in September 2005. The Minister has never distanced herself from any of the statements Rath has published in which her support for him is outlined. And when a consignment of his vitamins was seized by customs officials, the Director-General of Health personally secured their release.

In October 2005 it was reported that two women whom Rath had presented to the media in June as examples of how his vitamins reverse AIDS had admitted they were on ARVs all along. A third woman, a high-profile Rath Foundation agent who had been promoting vitamins in Gugulethu, died a few months after rejecting ARVs.[24]

President Mbeki's 2006 State of the Nation address made only a fleeting reference to AIDS, noting that 100 000 people were receiving ARVs. This was succour to some, who were elated that at least the President regarded the provision of ARVs as an achievement. But they were soon disappointed again. In early 2006 Willy Madisha, leader of the South African Democratic Teachers' Union, expressed his concern about the impact of teachers dying of AIDS. He quoted HSRC figures that in 2005, 12.7 per cent of teachers had HIV (about 40 000), while a minimum of 10 000 teachers living with AIDS urgently needed to be put on ARVs. The President responded that there was no AIDS crisis in the public service, despite his own government having reported in 1994 that 100 000 public servants were HIV-positive, presenting a real threat to governance.[25]

Wole Soyinka, the Nigerian Nobel laureate and one of the continent's greatest poets and writers, suggested that democracy alone is not any guarantee of sound governance. As an example he likened Mbeki to imams who fought a WHO campaign to eradicate polio, saying: 'I find his position virtually as illiterate as the position of Muslim fundamentalists here in Nigeria who say they read somewhere in the Koran that polio immunization is anti-Islamic.'[26]

*

But why this denialism? How does a highly intelligent, progressive, committed and sensible man close his mind to the reality unfolding around him?

There are three broad views on this. The 'psychotic denialist' account suggests that Mbeki himself might be HIV-positive and is in an extreme form of denial, or is in denial as a consequence of the number of people around him who are HIV-positive. The 'rationalist-economic' position holds that Mbeki believes that to acknowledge the extent of the pandemic will bankrupt the state and undermine hard-won economic stability at just the point when economic take-off seems likely. The 'defensive Africanist' explanation posits that Mbeki sees HIV and AIDS as another weapon in the hands of those who demonise black Africa and see the sexually rapacious African male – evocative of colonial and apartheid horror stories – as the cause of untold evil.

The first view can only be conjecture. The psychodynamic under-standing of denial suggests that something that is too unpalatable for the rational, conscious mind to cope with remains repressed, uncon-scious in the face of even compelling rational information to the contrary. Mbeki has always refused to take an AIDS test – supposedly because he believes doing so would be a tacit acknowledgement of the evidence-based link between HIV and AIDS. His health certainly appears good. It is also possible that he is in denial not because of his own health status but due to the devastation wreaked around him. Not only Mokaba and Mankahlana have perished from AIDS. While I was in Parliament at least two other MPs died of AIDS and over 20 were on ARVs.

In the face of the overwhelming evidence that prevention com-bined with treatment actually costs the fiscus less, the economic rationale for the President's denialism could only hold for the eco-nomically illiterate. Mbeki is certainly not that. His degree in Eco-nomics from Sussex and his detailed involvement with economic policy formulation testify to his strong grasp of the discipline. To suggest that the cost of providing ARVs would undermine the fiscal stability engendered by GEAR might make some sense if the South African government had not agreed to spend what will eventually be between R45 and R100 billion on defence equipment in 1999.

Mbeki's Africanism is complex. Some see it as a heartfelt belief

147

that the only way forward for any country on the continent is the development of Africa as a whole. Others believe his very self-conscious invoking of this pan-Africanism actually conceals a (possibly unconscious) antipathy, even embarrassment towards the continent. They would add that he is far more an Anglophile than an Afrophile, that he is more comfortable at the G8 than the African Union. Again, this can only remain in the realms of conjecture.

Assuming as I do that his Africanism is genuine, Sparks suggests[27] that somehow in this complex man there seems to be a deep-seated anger that the disease and those who point to its catastrophic scale in Africa are maligning black people, that the whole thing amounts to a calumny against African culture and sexual behaviour; that the disease is being used as a means to smear black people the way homosexuals were demonised when AIDS first appeared in the US. There is considerable evidence to support this view. Referring to a declaration signed by 5000 doctors at the international AIDS Conference in Durban, Mbeki wrote in a letter to the Leader of the Opposition, Tony Leon, in July 2000: 'To me as an African it is both interesting and disturbing that the signatories of the so-called Durban Declaration return to the thesis about the alleged original transmission of HIV from (African) animals to humans, given what science has said about AIDS during the past two decades. I accept that it may be that you do not understand the significance of this and the message it communicates to Africans …'[28]

During an outburst in the speech at Fort Hare University in October 2001 Mbeki implied that AIDS scientists were denigrating black people as vice-ridden germ carriers. He said: 'And thus does it happen that others who consider themselves to be our leaders take to the streets carrying their placards … convinced that we are but natural born, promiscuous carriers of germs, unique in the world, they proclaim that our continent is doomed to an inevitable mortal end because of our unconquerable devotion to the sin of lust.'[29]

In autumn 2002 Mbeki sent an e-mail of the 114-page diatribe written by Peter Mokaba to members of his Cabinet. Heavy with sarcasm, it read: 'Yes, we are sex crazy! Yes, we are diseased! Yes, we spread the deadly HIV through uncontrolled heterosexual sex! In this regard, yes, we are different from the US and Western Europe! Yes, we the men, abuse women and the girl-child with gay abandon! Yes, among

148

us rape is endemic because of our culture! Yes, we do believe that sleeping with young virgins will cure us of AIDS! Yes, as a result of all of this, we are threatened with destruction by the HIV/AIDS pandemic! Yes, what we need, and cannot afford because we are poor, are condoms and anti-retroviral drugs! Help!'

Mbeki's vituperative attacks on a white female journalist, Charlene Smith, offer further evidence. Smith, herself a victim of rape and an erstwhile supporter of the ANC, suggested that society had to address the sexual mistreatment of women as part of the response to the pandemic, stating that the AIDS epidemic in South Africa was being spurred by men's attitudes towards women. She wrote: 'We won't end this epidemic until we understand the role of tradition and religion – and of a culture in which rape is endemic and has become a prime means of transmitting the disease to young women as well as children. There is no doubt in my mind: attitude is the father of rape and the incubator of AIDS.'[30] This is not an unreasonable statement in a country in which over 130 people are raped every day. But Mbeki responded belligerently, describing it as a nakedly racist declaration.

All of these theses may play a role to some extent in the President's profoundly irrational outlook. It is extraordinary that someone who embraces notions of historical and political renaissance rejects scientific enlightenment on this issue, especially as he has accepted global economic orthodoxy which is driven by a group of technicians on the basis of claimed empirical evidence. This makes his rejection of scientific orthodoxy on HIV and AIDS, and his extreme defence of the AIDS dissidents, all the more difficult to fathom.

*

Why was the rump of the ANC silent for so long?

The ANC has, since its early years, been home to a wide range of perspectives and ideologies, an eclectic grouping with a tradition of robust internal debate. Thabo Mbeki's personality and politics do not sit comfortably with this tradition. He is deeply paranoid. His mindset is not too different from that of Margaret Thatcher, captured so brilliantly by Hugo Young in his biography, *One of Us*.[31] In it he evokes a dogmatic, driven woman who believes that everyone is either with her or against her.

Mbeki is the same. He takes criticism of government very personally and believes that those disagreeing with him either hate him or want to topple him. The manner in which he dealt with the 'threat' of Tokyo Sexwale by resorting to the spreading of rumours, and the plot allegations against his political rivals, were the most obvious manifestations of this. His own insecurity leads him to personalise criticism and demonise those who disagree with him, seen most obviously in his virulent reaction to Mandela and Tutu's polite and reasoned opposition to his views on AIDS. He refuses to countenance that he might be wrong, as if admitting error would collapse the frail carapace that guards his sense of self.

He seems to trust no one, wanting to be involved in every area of policy making, centralising power in his Office, even writing his own important speeches into the early hours of the morning. The small clique he allows around him is unthreatening, intellectually and politically. They are his eyes and ears on the world, creating a bubble of mediocrity and partial knowledge in which he exists. This is sad at a personal and political level for a man of such immense talent and intellect. It is disastrous for the country he leads.

The ANC and SACP's vanguardist and paranoid style of organisation in exile – in which Mbeki was steeped – and which was required in the face of efforts by the apartheid government to fatally undermine the liberation movement, inhibits the questioning, pluralist tradition of the organisation that flourished inside the country and even, as far as was possible, on Robben Island. South Africa's party-led proportional representation system lends itself to centralisation and control. Add to this the patronage benefits of being the party in power – not necessarily bribery or corruption, but appointment, retention and opportunity within government and possibly business – and one has the ingredients of a dangerous political brew.

The consequence of these institutional and personal factors, as Pregs Govender suggested in her Ruth First Memorial Lecture in April 2004, has led to the ANC's tradition of collective and open debate being reduced to group think, with its naïve and unquestioning acceptance of the leader as infallible. The most shameful example of this is Manto Tshabalala-Msimang: a doctor who altered her orthodox views on HIV and AIDS to accommodate the President and secure her political position. So disturbing had the closing-down of debate within the ANC become that Nelson Mandela was motivated to write in 2004: 'More than ever we need debate in South Africa today – debate for, against and among.'[32]

I was viscerally angry that no senior member of the ANC spoke out publicly on HIV and AIDS, making clear that there were internal differences with the President. I am ashamed that I said nothing, besides my 'ratting', until I was safely ensconced in London.

I cannot explain my own silence while I was in Parliament. My involvement in other issues and battles is hardly justification, especially given my commitment, expressed in the debate on the Holocaust, to seek out and name perpetrators of injustice. I initiated that debate to make clear the dangers of remaining silent and then inexplicably couldn't find my own voice on the greatest shame of the post-apartheid era.

*

Hope rose in late 2006. While the Health Minister was ill in hospital the Deputy President, Phumzile Mlambo-Ngcuka, stepped in to chair the SA National AIDS Council and together with the Deputy Minister of Health, Nozizwe Madlala-Routledge, began to interact with those most affected by the pandemic. Nozizwe, a Quaker whom Mbeki had previously appointed Deputy Minister of Defence, had been uncompromising since assuming her role in the Health Ministry in 2004. She admitted the government had handled the pandemic poorly, spoke out against her bosses' denialism and obfuscation and called on the President and other senior politicians to take public AIDS tests.

Nozizwe and Phumzile embraced organs of civil society, including TAC, and agreed to work with them to draw up a new strategy to deal with AIDS. They engaged in an inclusive consultation process that by March 2007 had produced a new strategic plan involving all relevant players that sets targets for treatment, education, research and monitoring. For the first time since Thabo Mbeki's accession to the Presidency it appeared as though South Africa was poised to tackle the pandemic in a coherent and united manner.

The Minister attempted to row back this progress in a diatribe posted on the ANC website. However, her Deputy and the Deputy

President held firm, leading Zackie Achmat to say to me in March 2007: 'The civil war seems to be over.' At the time, someone close to the President suggested to me that while the President's personal views hadn't necessarily changed he realised he had to accept a shift in approach and strategy on HIV and AIDS if he was to achieve his stated objective of a third term as ANC President.

However, on the night of 7 August 2007 the President announced that he had fired the Deputy Minister of Health at a meeting attended by the Deputy President. The ostensible reason for the firing was a contested trip the Deputy Minister had made to an AIDS conference in Spain. ANC insiders sympathetic to Nozizwe claimed that it was a calculated set-up, with the hand of the recovered Health Minister prominent. The supposed misdemeanour – confusion over whether the trip had been authorised by the Presidency – paled into insignificance against the abuse of public funds allegedly perpetrated by the Deputy Minister of Home Affairs and the Deputy President herself and the failure by the Minister of Defence to declare his interests in a range of companies as required by Parliament's Code of Conduct. No action has been taken against any of them and they still serve in Cabinet. The difference, of course, is that they are all political allies of the President, whereas Nozizwe was a source of significant anger and political embarrassment to him.

Her boss, the Minister of Health, has proved not just incompetent but highly damaging to the nation's health and its reputation around the world. Recently the *Sunday Times* went so far as to accuse her of drunkenness, theft and obtaining a liver transplant against accepted guidelines.[33]

As this book went to print it was too early to say whether Nozizwe's firing marked the reassertion of the denialist agenda. But the Health Minister's reversal of instructions given by her former Deputy to address the needs of HIV-positive prisoners in Westville prison, to proceed with action against Matthias Rath and to finalise a new policy for the prevention of mother-to-child-transmission do not bode well. This led former UN envoy on AIDS to Africa, Stephen Lewis, to remark: 'Every time there is evidence of progress, the president and the health minister combine to crush the glimmers of hope.'[34]

In a statement made after her sacking Nozizwe captured the real challenges facing the country:

We have made progress recently, and I would be saddened and disappointed if we were to be taken back to a time when people were confused about AIDS treatment.

I am certain now, that if our Health Minister goes back to talking about garlic and beetroot, she will face only ridicule. ... But we are dealing with a modern disease and ... we have to subject whatever we propose as a cure to rigorous scientific testing.

I don't regret saying that our political leaders should show the way and undergo HIV testing, in public. ... When you are in charge of the country, you have to offer leadership.

It is also important for us to hear Mr Mbeki's voice, encouraging people, leading, and showing that HIV and AIDS, with treatment, can be managed.[35]

Indeed it is crucial for Thabo Mbeki to emerge from the morass he has created and lead the country out of the moral void of AIDS denialism that has already lasted far too long.

CHAPTER 13
A Story That Had To Be Told

Certain people told me that this story was too disgraceful, too shameful, that it should
be concealed …There were others who claimed that it was a matter for tears and sor-
row, that it should be suppressed so that we should not shed tears a second time.
I asked them: How can we cover up pits in our courtyard with leaves or
grass, saying to ourselves that because our eyes cannot now see the holes,
our children can prance about the yard as they like?
Happy is the man who is able to discern the pitfalls in his path,
for he can avoid them.

Devil on the Cross
Ngugi Wa Thiong'o

At first glance Joe Modise was a roly-poly, grandfatherly figure, a
short, stout man with a wide girth and a chubby face of multiple
chins. You could well imagine him playing Father Christmas to a
horde of excited grandchildren. Up close, however, his skin was pock-
marked and arid, a strange 1970s wallpaper brown.

Modise was both a hero and a villain of the struggle against
apartheid. As commander-in-chief of Umkhonto we Sizwe (MK), the
armed wing of the ANC, he was revered by some of his guerrillas and
by militant youths in the townships of apartheid South Africa. He was
reviled, however, by those who were aware that he sometimes sent
guerrillas into South Africa and into great danger to shop for the
luxury goods he so coveted.

Modise was the democratic South Africa's first Defence Minister.
In this role, together with then Deputy President Mbeki, he spearheaded the largest procurement in South Africa's history, about R50
billion worth of arms.[1] At the time hundreds of thousands of South
Africans living with AIDS and desperate for anti-retrovirals that might
prolong their lives were told by the ANC government that the drugs
were unaffordable.

154

In the early years of the democratic government Parliament had conducted a Defence Review proposing modernisation of the country's defence force, emphasising a non-offensive defence posture and pledging to contain military spending in favour of socio-economic development.[2] So why did the country spend this obscene amount of money on arms at a time when it faced no internal or external military threat, but when the social needs of its people were vast? Was it to placate the apartheid-era military leaders, whose buy-in was important to the nascent democracy? Or was there a less strategic imperative?

During 1998, as competition for the lucrative arms contracts intensified, British Aerospace, now known as BAe Systems, made a generous donation of R5 million to the MK Veterans Association, whose Life President was Joe Modise. One of the bidders allegedly bought Modise millions of shares in defence company Conlog, which was likely to benefit from sub-contracts if successful in its bid. [3] It was, and Modise became chair of Conlog weeks after leaving office.

It is alleged that Modise also received between R10 million and R35 million in cash from a variety of the bidders. Other key government players in the deal are alleged to have received millions in bribes. In addition, speculation has refused to go away that the ANC received millions of rands from the successful bidders, money that was probably used in our 1999 election campaign.

*

Cape Town's De Waal Drive on a mid-September morning, the first winter of the new millennium. The thick clouds veil Table Bay and Robben Island on my right. To my left Table Mountain and Signal Hill are similarly obscured. I have always loved the gently curving drive from the southern suburbs into the city centre. As I wound my way along the contours of the mountain's foot the radio news mentioned an imminent report to Parliament by the Auditor-General (AG), the country's key financial watchdog. It concerned corruption allegations surrounding a massive arms deal. Patricia de Lille, a fiery Pan-Africanist Congress (PAC) MP, had first raised these allegations a few months previously based on a memo she had received from a couple of ANC MPs on Parliament's Defence Committee.

I had been caught up in a flurry of activity on the Finance Committee and the Public Accounts Committee, on which I was the ranking ANC member. In this capacity I chaired the majority ANC component of the committee, which involved interacting with the leadership of the party on behalf of the ANC members, acting as the party's spokesperson on Public Accounts issues, and working closely with the non-ANC chair of the Standing Committee on Public Accounts (Scopa) in determining the committee's *modus operandi* and approach to each issue brought before us. This frenetic work, a busy constituency and a young family meant I had barely registered the arms deal allegations when Patricia first raised them. I also knew nothing about the arms industry.

Each time I entered the Parliamentary precinct, with the colourful flag of our new democracy flapping in the ever-present Cape wind, I was struck by a feeling of pride and disbelief, both engendered by my role as a Member of Parliament. I parked my car in the underground garage, whistling contentedly as I made my way towards the ANC pigeon-holes. Almost as an afterthought, I popped into the Chief Whip's office to mention what I had heard on the radio. Tony Yengeni, the proud political ringmaster, nodded as I told him of the imminent report.

Later that day I returned to my pigeon-hole. Amidst the multi-coloured papers that determined the day's parliamentary proceedings lay the familiar cover of a report from the AG's Office. These reports, stiff and formal in their embossed, lacquered, off-white covers, provide the information on the basis of which Scopa examines the government's financial management. The Committee did so in a non-partisan manner, steering clear of debate on underlying policy issues and focusing instead on whether the money had been spent in accordance with the regulations and procedures laid down.

Under the searching leadership of the IFP's Gavin Woods, the committee had developed a cross-party camaraderie, taking pride in this most important of oversight functions. We were doing great work, as the media regularly acknowledged. We had formed an effective team when questioning officials of the old order and the new on subjects as varied as the failure to spend more than 70 per cent of the welfare budget in the early post-apartheid years, and Winnie

Mandela's unauthorised travel and crashing of government cars. Our investigations included the surreal in the form of getting to the bottom of the apartheid state's inexplicable rebuilding of a privately owned hotel in the Seychelles (which had initially been constructed with South African government funding) after it had been destroyed by South African mercenaries. And in a particularly noteworthy endeavour the Committee undertook an investigation into the Correctional Services Department after a report from the AG was deemed inadequate. We recommended to the President that the Commissioner of Correctional Services be dismissed. The President followed our advice. In July 2000 we conducted a hearing with the National Police Commissioner, George Fivaz, who was less than candid in his evidence. We tore into him. The Commissioner's Minister, Steve Tshwete, was none too pleased about our interaction. However, ANC members encouraged Gavin not to back down in the face of Executive pressure. He held fast.

Gavin is an intense, smallish man with a weathered face lined by a straggly beard and moustache. He always reminded me of a slightly thinner, less manic Joe Cocker. Gavin grew up in a large, poor family and was weakened by polio at a young age, leaving him with a withered leg, but wore his disability lightly despite requiring a crutch to walk. He had interacted with the IFP from the 1980s and joined the party in the 1990s, rising to head its research wing, the Inkatha Institute. ANC members from KwaZulu-Natal were suspicious of him, assuming that he must have been aware of IFP involvement in township hit squads during the 1980s and 90s. I certainly had little time for the ethnic, moderate politics of the IFP, but found Gavin open to criticism of his own party and its leader. In fact, I often wondered why he had not joined the ANC. With the combination of an impartial, forensic mind and a punishing work schedule, he led the committee superbly.

The Office of the Auditor-General was crucial to the success of the committee. Constitutionally independent, thorough and meticulous, the body under the leadership of Henri Kleuver was seen, somewhat unfairly, as a relic of the past. That perception had started to shift from 1999 when Barbara Hogan, Gavin, myself and others had overseen the appointment of Shauket Fakie, a quietly determined accountant, as the country's first black Auditor-General. Younger,

157

more dynamic investigators were recruited. The racial demographics of the Office began to slowly change. Its industry and impartiality were unquestioned.

*

Sitting in my office overlooking the presidential gardens I began to read the Auditor-General's initial report into the arms deal.[4] It found that there had been a litany of irregularities in the procurement of the armaments and weapons. These included conflicts of interest among key decision makers, the contentious awarding of a contract to provide fighter and trainer jets to BAe and SAAB, the controversial decision to grant the German Frigate Consortium the right to build four ships, the allocation of a naval sub-contract to a French company at a substantial increase in cost over a local company tender, inadequate offset guarantees and a disregard for the staff requirements to operate the systems purchased.

The report identified 'material deviations' from generally accepted procurement practices and stated that it would be necessary to also investigate the allegations of irregularities in contracts awarded to sub-contractors. Its most remarkable findings were to do with the inadequacy of efforts to address conflicts of interest of key role players, and the practice followed in awarding the largest contract. The former allegation referred to the Director of Procurement in the Defence Force at the time, 'Chippy' Shaik, and Defence Minister Joe Modise. On further enquiry the Committee was told by the Auditor-General that it was alleged that Shaik had favoured his brother, Schabir, while Modise may have benefited materially from the deal.

In language about as incredulous as an accountant can venture, the report revealed that in by far the most expensive of the contracts, the decision was taken to exclude cost as a criterion. In the costed option, an Italian jet produced by Aeromacchi won out over one produced by BAe/SAAB. The two were pretty much neck-and-neck even in the non-costed technical evaluations. Despite this, the contract was awarded to BAe/SAAB, whose tender was almost twice as expensive as that of the Italians. The report raised concerns about the cost of the overall deal, suggesting that the final cost to the country might be significantly more than revealed by government.

Finally, the AG recommended that a further investigation was required on highlighted aspects of the deal as well as the awarding of sub-contracts by the winning contractors.

Once I had read the report I realised that this was a huge political issue. But I didn't realise quite how it would change my life.

*

The ANC Study Group or component of Scopa that I led comprised a formidable mix of old ANC stalwarts and newer politicians. Robben Island veterans Laloo Chiba and Billy Nair remained part of the group. Among the younger members, Bruce Kannemeyer, a rotund, smiling Western Cape MP, had a sharp financial mind, while Serake Leeuw, a Free Stater, took his role on the committee extremely seriously, reflected in an assiduous approach to the work. Nomvula Hlongwane shared this work ethic but was a little quieter in meetings. Her thoughtfulness and good humour, especially in Study Group meetings, counted for as much as her diligence. Don Gumede, the son of a prominent UDF activist, was slightly aloof, worked hard but occasionally struggled to get to the core of an issue. However, when he had formed an opinion on a matter it was virtually impossible to change his mind. Another Free Stater, Beatrice Marshoff, was a little less engaged in the committee but forthright and to the point whenever she was with us. Rhoda Joemat, a long-time Western Cape activist, was steadfast in her commitment to accountability.

The Study Group met on two occasions to discuss the import of the AG's explosive report. We agreed that we should deal with the matter in the usual non-partisan manner that characterised the committee and decided that the next step would be a public hearing on the report. The only dissension came from Vincent Smith, a little-known Gauteng MP whose abrasive manner had sat uneasily in the committee since his recent arrival. To accommodate his desire to ask the leadership for direction I agreed to talk to the government and party hierarchy, not to seek a steer but to ensure the leadership was informed.

The Leader of Government Business in Parliament at the time was the country's Deputy President, Jacob Zuma. I arranged to see JZ during the next sitting of Parliament.

Zuma is a barrel-chested man with a large, open face which regularly breaks into a wide, brilliant white smile. Down the right side of his ebullient face is a long scar which attests to a life of struggle and hardship. Arriving illiterate on Robben Island in his early twenties, Zuma revealed not only a great capacity for learning quickly but also a political shrewdness and a tough, unbreakable spirit that saw him rise to become the head of ANC Intelligence after his release. I had encountered JZ in his capacity as Minister for Economic Affairs in KwaZulu-Natal while I was working in the Gauteng ministry. He had always been friendly and warm.

It was a relaxed, amiable Deputy President I encountered in a room behind the ANC benches in Parliament. I briefed him on the report and our proposed way forward. He thanked me for informing him and insisted that we continue with our constitutional role along the lines I had suggested. Later that afternoon I bumped into Zuma's Parliamentary Advisor, John Jeffrey, at a urinal behind the Chamber. I repeated JZ's instruction. John asked whether I had heard anything from the Auditor-General's office about JZ's relationship with Schabir Shaik. I hadn't – mainly because, embarrassingly, I had never heard the name before.

Laloo Chiba and I were designated by the ANC Study Group to lead the questioning at the forthcoming public hearing. Laloo prepared with an intensity and rigour that was awe-inspiring.

The day before the hearing, the Speaker of Parliament, Frene Ginwala, called Gavin Woods and me to see her. She informed us that before mentioning any implicated MPs we would need to provide those names to her together with any documentation pertaining to their behaviour. We agreed. She then encouraged us to pursue our enquiries 'fully and comprehensively', and offered material support for additional research capacity if required. Both Laloo and I gave separate, short and informal briefings to the Minister of Defence, Mosiuoa 'Terror' Lekota, who said that we must pursue the matter and that we had 'nothing to be inhibited by'.

On the morning of 11 October Laloo and I met in his office to go through our questions one last time before the hearing. We were both nervous but determined, knowing that this was likely to be the most important oversight meeting in the democratic Parliament's history. Smoke swirled towards the gabled roof of his small office as we worked. The phone rang. Laloo answered, paling as he did. 'The Chief Whip wants to see us,' he said.

'Look, comrades,' Yengeni began in his clipped, sharp tone once we were seated in his palatial office, 'this is a big matter. How do you propose handling it?' I explained what we were planning to do, mentioning that I had briefed the Deputy President. He asked us what a 'forensic investigation' involved and looked pained as Laloo explained that investigators would scour bank accounts, minutes of meetings and even telephone transcripts.

'I don't think a public hearing is a good idea,' he continued. 'This matter should be dealt with internally, like the Maduna matter.'

As mentioned earlier, the Maduna matter referred to unconstitutional remarks about the AG made by Penuell Maduna, then Minister of Mineral and Energy Affairs. Misunderstanding a fairly standard accounting entry, he had accused the AG of hiding a significant loss in oil reserves for nefarious, apartheid-era reasons. Even after the error had been pointed out to him by Barbara Hogan, the Minister refused to retract, creating a minor constitutional crisis. Rather than allow a full investigation, the ANC decided to exonerate the Minister through the creation of an ANC-dominated *ad hoc* committee of Parliament chaired by an ultra-loyal ANC whip, Andries Nel.[5] Despite hearing damning evidence against the Minister, the Committee found in his favour. This was the precedent our Chief Whip wanted us to follow.

'Unfortunately, the hearing starts in five minutes, Comrade Tony. We can't cancel it now.' With those departing words Laloo and I fled the angry Chief Whip. Laloo was furious. 'How dare he try and pressure us in that way,' he said. 'Let's go and do this before he tries to stop us.' I was more nervous than I had been, realising that this was likely to be the start of significant political pressure. As we approached the room where the hearing was scheduled to take place, a throng of witnesses and other interested parties had gathered. Yengeni joined the crowd a few minutes after we did. I saw him in conspiratorial conversation with Ron Haywood, then the Chairman of Armscor, the state arms company. I ambled closer to where they were standing, ensuring that Yengeni couldn't see me, and overheard him say: 'I've called the two main chaps in and I've laid down the line.' I rushed off to inform Laloo that what had just happened in the

Chief Whip's office was the laying down of the line on behalf of Armscor and God knows who else. We chortled, but both of us felt even more determined than before.

*

E249 is a modern, characterless and functional parliamentary committee room. Pale wooden desks for the members run down either side of the narrow room. In the front stands a larger ceremonial bench from where the meeting is chaired. A small gallery for observers and the media abuts the other three walls. Usually only two or three journalists would occupy these benches. But on the morning of 11 October 2000 the room was crowded with media, embassy, NGO and corporate representatives. The tense anticipation was palpable. I sat in my usual position: the front row to the right of a clearly nervous Gavin Woods in the chair. Laloo was in the back row behind me, his desk overflowing with papers and documents.

A thickset man with cropped hair, hunched shoulders and darting eyes took his seat at the head of the rows of uniformed witnesses.

'Who's that?' I whispered to Serake Leeuw, sitting nearest to me.

'That's Chippy Shaik.'

After Gavin's measured introduction, Laloo posed a series of characteristically blunt questions about the rising costs of the deal. Pointing out that no one seemed to know the likely scale of the escalations, he asked: 'What will be the total package – R50 billion or R70 billion? Have you made a calculation? If you have not made a calculation, how would you motivate agreement on figures that you do not know?'[6]

After a mealy-mouthed response from Shaik, Laloo demanded that he furnish us with the complete costs of the package within seven days. We finally managed to ascertain from one of the other defence department officials that, at that point, the cost of the deal was already R 43.8 billion, excluding financing costs, rather than government's claimed R29.8 billion. Nobody was able to say what the final costs might amount to.

Moving on to the 'industrial offsets' that had been used to justify the deal to the South African public, Gavin first explained the term. Common practice in arms deals, they are ostensibly industrial investments and trade opportunities that bidding contractors agree to undertake if they win the contract. So, for instance, a winning contractor might agree that it will build a factory in South Africa to produce widgets which it will import to the UK. The cost of its investment plus what it generates in export sales are counted as offset credits in fulfilment of its obligation.

Penalties for failing to meet offset obligations are usually set at about 5 per cent of the contract price. They have been pilloried in academic literature as so much sophistry. Most arms companies have little intention of fulfilling these obligations and tend to build the penalty costs into the price they charge.[7]

Laloo was nevertheless dissatisfied with the low level of offset guarantees, which had been set at 10 per cent of the contract price, arguing that if the officials were sure the defence firms would deliver on their undertakings, why not insist on much higher guarantees?

I then posed the obvious question around industrial offsets and received a surprising answer:

[Mr A Feinstein] (If we) spend R43.8 billion and receive R104 billion worth of new economic activity creating 65 000 jobs [as claimed by the contractors], why do most countries not spend the vast majority of their budget on arms? It does not make sense. ... If one looks at the literature on the matter what comes through is that while industrialized countries often benefit from the economic multiplier effects, developing countries very seldom do. What often happens is that the offsets can be significantly diluted ... or the bidders simply factor the penalties into the purchase price. I have not heard anything that convinces me why South Africa is going to be different.

[Mr S 'Chippy' Shaik] I think too much emphasis is being put on the fact that the Department of Defence acquires equipment because of counter trade.[8]

In response to my stating that we wanted surety that these promised economic benefits would be forthcoming, Jayendra Naidoo, a charming, handsome activist who had been retained by government to negotiate the offsets, said: 'It is a highly questionable proposition that offsets will generate economic development ... the exercise was to maintain a neutral economic impact,'[9] thus destroying one of government's two primary justifications for the deal. Cabinet had argued – and would continue to do so – that the offsets were a major motivation for the deal.[10] Laloo was outraged, asking whether Cabinet had been misled and if they had had appropriate information on which to base their decisions. Gavin noted that the figures were malleable and conditional and that the agreements were fudged.

We turned our attention to conflicts of interest. Chippy outlined a complicated four-tier decision-making hierarchy and points system that made the process as secure as possible. However, under further questioning he admitted that no declarations of conflicts of interest had been signed as this wasn't standard Armscor practice – which is what was being used for this deal. He also acknowledged that deals could have been struck between the main contractors and sub-contractors before any main contracts had been awarded.

Without stating his name explicitly, we focused on Chippy himself and his perceived conflict of interest due to his brother, Schabir, being a director of African Defence Systems (ADS), a company bidding for sub-contracts. Under repeated questioning from me he claimed that he had recused himself from the chair and physically from the room when any discussion involving his brother's interests arose. I was sceptical and requested the minutes of meetings that would confirm his assertion. He did acknowledge that a person with such a conflict might have had informal communication on the matter with those who remained in the meeting(s) and with the sub-contractors involved as well.

Gavin asked what role ADS had played in the deal. He was told that 50 per cent of ADS was owned by Thomsons, the company that had been chosen by the German Frigate Consortium to provide the combat suites for the ships. Gavin repeated the question about conflicts of interest and Chippy reiterated that he had recused himself from 'any decision relating to the combat suite'.[11]

During a break in the hearing I was chatting to Jayendra Naidoo, whom I knew from ANC circles and in his capacity as Coordinator of Nedlac, where Simone had worked. His cell phone rang. A loud voice boomed out of the earpiece: 'Jay, it's Mo, what's happening there?' Jayendra hurriedly ended the call and smiled at me. It was Mo Shaik, brother of Chippy and Schabir, who was at the time South Africa's ambassador to Algeria. Clearly there was a family interest in the hearing and its consequences.

When the meeting resumed we enquired about other failings in the process. Gavin asked Chippy to confirm what would happen if bribery/corruption was discovered, and was told that the contaminated contract would become null and void.

There was intense discussion, led by Nomvula, on the combat suite for the ships, which the Navy had appeared to want to award to a long-time technology partner, C^2I^2. However, it was ultimately awarded to Thomsons/ADS. The MD of C^2I^2, who was observing the hearing, sent a note to Gavin that he was being quoted out of context on a number of matters. Chippy waded in, in defence of Thomsons/ ADS. He showed remarkable mastery of the detail of an aspect of the deal he had supposedly recused himself from. Gavin then questioned the Navy's representative, who conceded that the Navy had in fact preferred the technical potential of C^2I^2. Our questioning failed to lift the murk shrouding this aspect of the deal, so we asked for additional information and moved on.

Chippy then attempted to explain why it had been decided to exclude cost from the most expensive component of the procurement, the fighter and trainer jets. It was clear that the Minister's Committee, chaired by then Deputy President Thabo Mbeki, had taken the final decision to go with BAe/SAAB rather than Aeromacchi, the Italian equivalent which was the preferred technical choice of the South African Air Force and half the price of the BAe/SAAB equivalent. Under intense questioning from Serake Leeuw and Bruce Kannemeyer, Chippy stated that it was impossible to compare competing bids when the price differential was so large. We eventually established that for 17 per cent greater technical value (which was not required by the Air Force) the Ministers had decided on 72 per cent greater cost!

We were further concerned that the price charged was higher than on either of the equivalent deals done by BAe with India and Australia. We assumed that a significant miscellaneous amount built into the pricing was to cover offsets and commissions.

Having exhausted what we could ask without additional information Gavin suggested I make some concluding remarks:

[Mr A Feinstein] I am sure all members on all sides of the House will agree that this is the most difficult, the most material and possibly the most important issue to come before the Committee. ... The issue has been characterized by an enormous amount of rumour and conjecture. I think it is critically important that we, as elected representatives, know everything there is to know about this deal. That we consider this information in a non-partial, non-party political and fair manner, so that we can once and for all either deal with any irregularities, regardless of what those irregularities might be or who is involved in them, or clear the air once and for all.

As a committee I would like to suggest that our integrity in dealing with this issue must be unequivocal. Public Accounts is about public accountability and public accountability is about strengthening and deepening our nation's democracy and the institutions of this democracy. ...

The Committee needs to ... pursue these issues ... as in all of our work, with the understanding that we at all times work in the interests of the people of South Africa, whose money we are, after all, talking about today.[12]

The media and civil society organisations immediately praised the hearings. The respected Institute for Democracy in South Africa (Idasa) described the process as 'demonstrating the central role that parliament can play in ensuring there is meaningful oversight of executive power'. It further noted: 'it is really a litmus test for the various institutions of democratic accountability.'[13] The international media were similarly fulsome: 'The arms deal is a test case for anti-corruption efforts and for this new democracy. Parliament is turning out to be not just a rubber stamp,' said the *Christian Science Monitor*.[14]

After a frenzied round of media interviews I eventually made my way out of Parliament and back up towards the foot of Table Mountain. I was both elated and wary. This was what our new democracy was about: elected representatives ensuring that citizens received value for money from their government. This could never have happened under apartheid. At the same time I feared Tony Yengeni's response and wondered whether the ANC was going to allow us to continue this search for the truth. At the back of my mind I knew that this could lead to trouble for Laloo, myself and the other ANC members of Scopa. We needed to move quickly but carefully.

*

The natural next step in the accountability process was for the committee to submit a resolution to Parliament on the way forward. Reflecting on the hearing, we felt that the Defence Department had been evasive, especially Chippy. As Parliament was due to break for two weeks we formed a small sub-group comprising Laloo, Bruce, Gavin and me. We agreed to submit a request for a wide range of documents. A navy official, Rear Admiral Johnny Kamerman, arrived with box loads of paper. As the others were campaigning for local elections or on holiday, Gavin and I went through the key documents. We soon realised that there was far more going on in the deal than anyone had grasped. In fact we felt that the AG's Office had been superficial in its initial report and decided to use this new information to draft our resolution.

In the days following the Scopa hearing Gavin's and my phones rang incessantly. Now that the investigation had gone public, people who had information, or an axe to grind, knew who to contact. Among the callers was a former diplomat who had acted for one of the tendering companies. He asked if we could meet as soon as possible. A few days later, over a coffee, this measured, unassuming man told me that he had worked as a consultant for a well-known international entity which had considered tendering for certain of the contracts. He had attended a meeting that one of the company's Vice Presidents had with Chippy Shaik. What he said made me worry.

He suggested that it became apparent early on in the process that putting together an excellent programme of investment together with a superior product would not be the deciding factor in determining which companies would win the bids. He went on: 'The first warning signals came with our first meeting with Chippy Shaik. We met him in his office at Armscor. No one else was present. In my experience as a diplomat (and a military man) in any sort of discussions involving military purchases or agreements there would always be more than one person present from each side. It was clear that Mr Shaik, by the tenor of his remarks, wanted no such constraints. Thereafter he only wanted to meet in informal venues, so we met him at the Northgate shopping centre and at a coffee shop in Pretoria on another occasion. While Mr Shaik never gave us anything in writing or said outright that a special consideration of some sort (a bribe) would help our cause, he made it clear that the procurement process was not going to be nearly as transparent as government claimed it to be. He recommended that to stand a chance of winning the contract we get in touch with one Tsepo Molai. When I tried to contact him it appeared that Mr Molai's business consisted of a cell phone. We didn't know that Molai was linked to Joe Modise.[15] When we met with Molai he proposed that the bidding company hire him as a consultant, suggesting a $250 000 start-up fee and $25 000 a month retainer. We declined the offer. Clearly this was the death knell for our bid.'

I asked my contact whether the Vice President of the company would be prepared to give evidence. He said that he would.

Was this a one-off, or part of a broader trend that characterised the deal?

A few weeks later I received another call, this time from someone I had worked with in Gauteng. This source had information from an Italian company that was bidding for both the frigate and submarine contracts. Fincantiere had had an almost identical experience with Chippy. They were asked to meet at an informal venue, not at his office. At the meeting Chippy suggested his brother Schabir as an appropriate empowerment partner, implying that failure to follow his advice would hinder their efforts to secure a contract. Someone acting for the company was so shocked by this that they approached senior ANC leader Steve Tshwete. He listened attentively, but did nothing.

Fincantiere were told that they had won the submarine contract, and their President flew to South Africa to conclude the deal. However, despite them scoring the highest number of points, they were then told that the decision had changed. The contract had gone instead to a German consortium. The Italians were approached by someone allegedly sent by Chippy, who suggested that for a payment of $15 million they could still 'better the Germans'. A second source, this time within the Navy, confirmed the gist of this story, and the battles that had gone on around the decision and its reversal.

After we had started the investigation, people associated with Fincantiere were told not to co-operate with the investigators as the Italians 'didn't want to upset the South Africans'. I had no reason to doubt the sources and felt that a second account very similar to the first was sufficient grounds for pursuing a more extensive investigation into the deal.

Between these two meetings I was encouraged by Gavin to go and see a man by the name of Bheki Jacobs, at the Africa Institute in Pretoria. I was told he was an ANC intelligence operative who had been a source of information for Patricia De Lille.

A small man with an animated, bird-like face greeted me in the Institute's spacious and largely empty offices. He introduced me to the Institute's Director, Eddie Maloka, before secreting me into a small office that comprised a bare table and three hard rudimentary chairs, one occupied by a colleague.

'So – tell me a bit about your background,' I said.

He laughed: 'Call me Bheki or Hassan or Solomon or Uranin.' He then proceeded to show me three different passports. 'I have about six at the moment,' he said with child-like pride. He told me how he had been an ANC agent, trained and based in Moscow for many of the exile years. He professed to know more about the ANC leader-ship than anyone. He further claimed to have fallen out with some of them and to be working for others. There was a sinister undertone to his bragging. I had never knowingly met a spy, let alone one who was so compulsively verbose.

Over the next three hours Bheki/Hassan/Solomon/Uranin spoke almost without pause. He claimed the arms deal had been plotted during the World Trade Centre negotiations in the early nineties by Tony Georgiadis, a shadowy Greek/South African businessman, and the then Foreign Minister, Pik Botha. They had allegedly persuaded Joe Modise and Thabo Mbeki that the ANC could access millions of dollars from arms companies if there was sufficient contractual reward for the companies once the ANC was in government. He then went on, crazily, to allege that the ANC was full of murderers, drug dealers and common criminals. When I eventually emerged, punch-drunk and exhausted by this verbal onslaught, it gradually occurred to me that over the past few hours almost the only people in the ANC Bheki hadn't maligned were Barbara Hogan and myself.

Were there any elements of truth in what Bheki had said about the arms deal, or was it part of a vast, sprawling fantasy that he had woven in his head? This was, after all, a man who, uniquely, had been both jailed briefly for plotting to kill the President and, at virtually the same time, accused of being Mbeki's master spy! My instinct was that there were kernels of truth embedded amidst flamboyant hyperbole and some outright fabrication.

169

Less surreal and of greater import were a number of briefings Gavin and I received from a variety of investigators. Two of them intimated that there were very real concerns that Joe Modise, among others, had benefited personally from the deal, and that the ANC might also have benefited. They undertook to provide us with further information.

At Gavin's insistence I accompanied him to meet another player in the drama. Richard Young ran C^2I^2, the technology company specialising in the design and manufacture of combat suites, the 'brains' of military hardware.

At Richard's drab offices off Rosmead Avenue in Claremont, a lower middle class suburb of Cape Town, all the windows were blocked with vector blinds, the doors reinforced with metal grilles. Richard met us at reception accompanied by two attractive blonde women, neither of whom was introduced to us. We were taken through to a nondescript boardroom. The two women settled in opposite Gavin and me. Richard had prepared a comprehensive dossier of overheads and a mound of documentation. Throughout his presentation the two women stared intently and silently at Gavin and me. We couldn't figure out whether they were there to distract our attention or merely flashy adornments like Bialystock & Blum's buxom receptionist in Mel Brook's *The Producers*.

Richard's basic contention was that the C^2I^2 system, which is South African, had been selected by the South African Navy. However, late in the process the contract was granted to French company Detexis. The significance of this was that Detexis was owned by the defence company Thomson-CSF. Thomson also owned the South African company African Defence Systems (ADS), which was appointed to drive South African participation in the 'fighting' components of the naval programme. A main South African director of ADS was Schabir Shaik. In addition, the wife of Chippy worked for the marketing department of ADS at the time. Other directors included Lt Gen (Rtd) Lambert Moloi – Joe Modise's brother-in-law and former MK chief-of-staff – and Tshepo Maloi (Moloi's son-in-law).

Richard suggested that Chippy's claimed recusal from meetings where his brother's interests were discussed was bogus. He produced minutes of a meeting that suggested that far from leaving the session when ADS was discussed, Chippy continued to chair the meeting and intervened in the discussion in support of his brother. In other words, Chippy lied to Parliament. This was damning evidence, later confirmed by a source in the Defence Force. I felt a little uneasy, not only because of the two disarming women but also because Richard had worked with the South African Defence Force during the apartheid years and he was a failed bidder with an obvious axe to grind. However, a review of his extensive documentation showed compelling support for his thesis.[16]

A fellow MP came to see me at my constituency office in Sea Point. Sitting in a café on Sea Point's Main Road, my colleague, who had a reputation for integrity within the ANC, told me that, as a one-time member of Parliament's Defence Committee, he was aware that both Tony Yengeni and his then deputy on the committee, Ntsiki Mashimbye, had received money and/or gifts for 'various roles played in assisting international defence companies'. He mentioned that a Defence Committee visit overseas generally meant that Ntsiki (now chair) would be whisked off by representatives of one or other arms company to return laden with suits and other gifts. Two other ANC colleagues of his on the Defence Committee confirmed this allegation with me over the following months.

*

After each of these meetings I reported the salient features to the ANC Study Group, minus the details of who I had heard them from and the names of the ANC people involved. All the members, bar one, were committed to a large-scale investigation to get to the bottom of those aspects of the deal that, if anything, concerned us more after the public hearing. These included the spiralling cost of the deal, significant departures from accepted procurement practices, and the limited enforceability of the industrial offsets. The puny penalties for not delivering on offset obligations and the inflated contract prices that probably factored in these penalties only exacerbated our suspicion of offsets, the impact of which would be economically neutral at best.

We were worried about the role played by a range of 'influential parties' in the selection of sub-contractors. Of especial concern was Chippy's conflict of interests, his undue and inappropriate influence over the process and the discovery that he hadn't recused himself from meetings as claimed.

We again pondered the most extraordinary of the decisions taken: the Lead In Fighter Trainer (LIFT) contract, involving BAe/SAAB and Aeromacchi.

Minutes of the Cabinet sub-committee at the time, which we had been given among the documents requested, showed Joe Modise questioning why the Hawk had been eliminated. He was told it was because of cost. 'We need a visionary approach. Let's rerun this without costs,' came the reply. The Armaments Acquisition Council, the body tasked with overseeing the bids – on which Chippy and Modise's advisor, Fana Hlongwane, were the main movers and shakers, and which in addition was sometimes chaired by the minister – then formally requested a non-costed option on the basis that the price differentials were so big and because the Hawk exceeded the technical requirements. So, on this, the biggest single contract negotiated by the post-apartheid government, cost was excluded as a criterion.

At the next meeting, even with cost removed, the Hawk was not number one. The Aeromacchi still came out top of the technical evaluation even when price was removed as a consideration. However, on an evaluation that included the dubious industrial offsets and excluded costs, the Hawk just pipped the Aeromacchi. BAe/SAAB were awarded the contract. Casting a pall over the whole deal were the allegations of corruption that we had heard from the investigators and others and which I outlined to the Study Group in broad terms.

With these concerns in mind, the committee set about refining the resolution that Gavin and I had drafted during the parliamentary break and that we would put before Parliament. We felt that what was required was an extensive forensic investigation involving all available expertise and resources. We proposed an exploratory meeting with the main investigating agencies in the country. In addition to the Auditor-General, this would include the Public Protector (a constitutional body established to investigate public complaints of government lapses), the Directorate of Serious Economic Offences, the Heath Special Investigative Unit (SIU) (an anti-corruption body headed by Judge Willem Heath, which not only investigated corruption but, where it was proved, was empowered to recoup public money from beneficiaries of corruption) and 'any other appropriate investigative bodies'.

We met with key members of the ANC Study Group in a deserted Parliament one late Sunday afternoon. Gavin was invited to present the proposed resolution. As my colleagues intently read the draft I was anxious that they might not agree with key aspects of it. We discussed the resolution at some length and made a few changes before unanimously approving it. We were of one mind about the issues and the way forward.

The full committee deliberated formally over the draft during a meeting the next day. Throughout the deliberations I would regularly take comfort breaks. Once in the toilet I would call John Jeffrey and keep him updated with information on the direction the resolution was taking. It was understood that he was transmitting this to Jacob Zuma, thus ensuring the ANC leadership was informed of developments. Surprisingly, none of the other parties questioned my suddenly weakened bladder. I felt a bit stupid huddling in a toilet cubicle every couple of hours making furtive phone calls, but it relieved the tedium of a painstaking process.

Before finalising the resolution Gavin and I met with Bulelani Ngcuka, a former ANC MP and at that time the Director of Public Prosecutions. Bulelani was enthusiastic about the investigation and the message it would send. He claimed this was going to be the biggest investigation in South Africa's history and detailed the foreign resources he had already lined up to assist with the international dimensions of the probe. He was comfortable with the composition of the investigating team. So was the Public Protector, Selby Baqwa. We also separately briefed the Minister of Defence, Mosiuoa Lekota.

Finally Gavin and I met with Frene Ginwala to brief her on the resolution. Frene, who had championed Parliament's independence from the executive since 1994, was enthusiastic about the investigation and the Committee's role in briefing the relevant bodies and receiving regular reports from the investigating team. She again offered us any additional resources we required for the investigation, suggesting we talk to her legal advisor, Fink Haysom, about the nature and extent of our involvement with the investigating team. At

173

a subsequent meeting with her on my own I mentioned the Chief Whip's concerns about the public hearing and the process. In rousing style, she said that if anyone attempted to subvert our investigation she would publicly resign in protest.

After another conversation with Jacob Zuma in which I told him I felt Tony Yengeni was intimidating the ANC component of Scopa, the Deputy President instructed Yengeni to have no contact with the committee or its members.

With this ringing endorsement from the presiding officer of Parliament and Jacob Zuma's bold intervention, Gavin and I believed we were about to set the stage for the most comprehensive and important investigation since the Infogate furore of the mid-1970s.[17] The difference was that the Infogate exposé was undertaken by journalists in the face of intense opposition from the government of the day. In our case the investigation was about to be sanctioned by the country's democratically elected representatives.

Our resolution was to be tabled in the National Assembly on 2 November. The ANC duty whip on the day was a garrulous old sports administrator and veteran of the National Party, the Democratic Party and finally the ANC, Jannie Momberg. I informed Jannie that the report was being submitted and that both the Deputy President and the Speaker were aware of its content. In his usual inimitable manner Jannie responded: 'What *kak* are you causing now, Feinstein?'

Gavin, Laloo, Serake, Bruce, Nomvula and I sat anxiously on our different benches in the Chamber, wondering whether Tony Yengeni might have a trick up his sleeve to scupper the adoption of the report. Vanette van Huysteen, our committee secretary, had fortunately placed our resolution in the middle of a pile of end-of-session committee reports. It was rushed through along with all the others without even a murmur. As the parliamentary official announced that the 14th Report of the Standing Committee on Public Accounts had been approved unanimously we grinned in triumph and relief. Now the real work could begin.

Later that afternoon I began to hear whispers about Yengeni's volcanic response when he realised what had been passed. Clearly neither the Speaker, the Deputy President or Jannie Momberg had informed him. Jannie came scuttling after me later that day: 'Fuck, what was in that report, man? The Chief has gone ballistic.' He wasn't the only one. We soon started to receive reports of the President's apoplexy.

*

A few days later, on 8 November, the Study Group was called before a meeting of the ANC's Governance Committee, a body recently established to provide 'political leadership' to the ANC in Parliament. It comprised the Chief Whip, the Speakers of both the National Assembly and the National Council of Provinces, the Leader of Government Business (JZ), the Minister in the Office of the President (Essop Pahad), the President's Parliamentary advisor (Charles Nqakula), the chair of the ANC caucus (Thabang Makwetla) and a range of other trusted loyalists. In addition, for this meeting, Sue Rabkin, advisor to the Defence Minister, was also present. Sue, the partner of Pallo Jordan, had made sure we were able to brief her boss and had privately been very supportive of our efforts. Essop Pahad objected to her presence but was overruled.

Pahad is a tall, wiry man with a mane of greying hair and small lizard-like eyes. Bluff, uncompromising and often rude, he has been close to Thabo Mbeki since they went into exile in their late teens and has been described as the only person he trusts, the President's rottweiler. As the Scopa Study Group sloped into the tense committee meeting room Pahad was sitting with his arm around Ntsiki Mashimbye, the youthful chair of Parliament's Defence Committee. Ntsiki's predecessor, Tony Yengeni, was on his other side. We were surprised to see Yengeni there, as we thought he had been told to keep out of this issue. JZ instructed us to sit on the opposite side of the table to them. We did so, quaking.

Mashimbye started a tirade against the Study Group, alleging that we didn't understand the deal and that it was a matter his committee should be dealing with. Throughout Ntsiki's harangue Pahad was clapping him on the back as if geeing on a promising colt. We were bemused and frightened.

Johnny de Lange, the avuncular chair of the Parliamentary Justice Committee, with whom I regularly played cricket for the aptly named Spin Doctors, weighed in that there was no evidence of impropriety and we were engaged in an unjustified fishing expedition. In addition, he said, the investigation should not under any circumstances involve the Special Investigative Unit of Judge Heath.

I was given a brief opportunity to try and explain the *prima facie* evidence that we had and the process we were following. Within a few minutes Pahad had launched into a ferocious diatribe, spluttering: 'Who the fuck do you think you are, questioning the integrity of the government, the Ministers and the President?' Pointing aggressively at me, he shouted that we should simply withdraw the resolution. Johnny de Lange quietly pointed out that we couldn't do that, but that we should use our majority on the committee to water down the effect of the resolution and ensure that the Heath Unit was excluded from the investigating team.

Pahad then announced that he had to leave the meeting to catch a plane. With his departure the atmosphere in the room changed. Quiet descended, a strange hush, as if a typhoon had moved on. Everyone was too stunned to react. After a few moments, for the first time in the meeting, JZ spoke. He stated calmly that he felt the Study Group was fulfilling its constitutional responsibility, that the organisation hadn't provided us with any leadership and that now they would. The key point, he said, was to ensure that Judge Heath was not part of the investigating team. He proposed convening another meeting at which we would be given the opportunity to put our concerns to the relevant Ministers.

The Study Group, with the exception of Vincent Smith, who had sat apart from us during the gruelling session with a patronising smile creasing his face, made our way to Laloo's flat next to the Parliamentary precinct. We collapsed in his lounge, shattered but defiant. One of the older comrades sat down next to me on the floor. 'You know, comrade,' he said softly, 'many years on the Island couldn't break me, but I think Thabo's ANC might.'

*

The next day details of the meeting were all over the newspapers. Someone had leaked the explosive deliberations. Pahad described reports that he had tried to derail the investigation as 'a litany of lies'.[18]

Around this time, Trevor Manuel asked me to have lunch with

him. I had greatly admired his robust intellect and his courage during the struggle, and was encouraged by rumours that he had never supported the arms deal in Cabinet, primarily concerned with its impact on fiscal stability.

We sat down at the appropriately named Speaker's Corner, a favoured haunt of parliamentarians. Trevor was friendly, warm, almost intimate. He summarised the extensive work the Treasury had undertaken before agreeing to the financing package, and suggested I talk directly to those officials. Towards the end of the meal came his real point: 'We all know JM [as Joe Modise was known]. It's possible that there was some shit in the deal. But if there was, no one will ever uncover it. They're not that stupid. Just let it lie. Focus on the technical stuff, which was sound.' I responded that there were even problems with the technical aspects, and warned that if we didn't get to the bottom of the deal now, it would come back to haunt us – a view I expressed over and over again within the ANC.

Another senior member of the ANC's NEC invited me to his house one Sunday. Sitting outside in the sunshine, he explained to me that I was never going to 'win this thing'.

'Why not?' I demanded.

'Because we received money from some of the winning companies. How do you think we funded the 1999 election?'

I didn't know what to say. I tried to think of a reason why this comrade might want to mislead me, but couldn't.

A few days later, with Pahad's harangue still ringing in our ears, members of the committee made our way to Pretoria for a meeting with the agencies we had recommended for the investigation. The Chief Whip initially refused to authorise our travel expenses, but we went anyway. Before the meeting got under way one of the investigators asked to speak to Gavin and me. He led us down through labyrinthine corridors, past rows of desks, into a basement and up to the gate of what looked like a prison cell. This was the secure storage area. He unlocked the gates and asked us to take a seat. Opening a safe he withdrew a sheaf of different-sized pages. We looked at the series of bank statements, signed letters, deposit and withdrawal slips. 'This,' said the investigator, 'is a substantial part of the paper trail linking money from a number of the successful bidders to Joe Modise.'

'How much of the trail is outstanding?' Gavin asked.

'Not much. With the resources and legal powers of the investigating team upstairs, we will complete it in a couple of weeks.'

Gavin and I were astonished.

The meeting of the investigators involved all of the agencies recommended in our resolution. It was clear that they were all required, including the SIU, which was in a position to consider the legal validity of the contracts and to seek civil remedy if any of them were found to be unsound. The mechanics of a joint investigation were then easily agreed, with the agencies comfortable to provide Scopa with regular updates of their progress before submitting a final report to us.

Any satisfaction we felt at the successful conclusion of the session with the agencies soon dissipated when we returned to Cape Town for the next round with the party leadership. The ANC component of the Committee was called to the President's office in Tuynhuys. Besides JZ, who was chairing the meeting, a number of participants from the Governance Committee were joined by the Minister for Trade and Industry, Alec Erwin, and the deputy ministers of defence and finance.

Alec had been a militant trade unionist in the 1970s, aligned with the anti-SACP 'workerist' traditions of the union movement. By the time we achieved power in 1994 he had transformed himself into a Deputy Minister of Finance committed to orthodox macroeconomic policy. He then took over at Trade and Industry, where he was responsible for opening up the South African economy to global forces while campaigning tirelessly for developing countries to be treated at least equally in international trade negotiations. I had always admired his sharp intellect and found him engaging and warm.

On this occasion there was no warmth as we sat around a huge oval boardroom table in Tuynhuys. JZ asked me to run through our major concerns. Alec responded frostily. He added nothing new and actually seemed confused on some of the detail. For instance, when we pointed out to him that the contracts were shoddy as in one or two cases they equated Dollars and Euros in value as credits, he answered that our point was irrelevant, as the two currencies were equal at the time. They had never been at parity, however: a very basic error from one of the country's leading economic thinkers. He also launched a most unconvincing defence of the industrial offsets. He suggested, focusing withering looks on me, that Cabinet was stung by our resolution, which criticised them and accused them 'of buying Ferraris with the peoples' money'. His ears reddened. Later in the meeting, he said that there was no way we would find anything if there had been corruption as it would have been too well hidden.

A couple of days after the meeting Alec was quoted in the *Cape Times* as saying that there would never have been an investigation by Scopa if Chippy had not been Asian. Implicitly accusing Gavin and me of racism was a little disingenuous.

The ever-kowtowing Ntsiki Mashimbye then read off a list of unacceptable contentions made in Scopa's resolution. Not only were the members of the committee able to respond cogently to each and every point, but the fuzzy nature of the accusations led me to feel that many of those accusing us of betraying the Cabinet and the ANC hadn't actually read the resolution, let alone any of the related documentation.

Charles Nqakula had had enough of our measured and persuasive responses. He stood up and glared at me across the table. 'Comrade Chair,' he intoned in his deep baritone, 'our last meeting was leaked to the media and today again there is somebody here who uses complicated technology that sends information straight to journalists. We have to stop this betrayal now.' He fairly spat the words out, the volume rising with his anger. His eyes were focused on me and my Psion mini computer, on which I was as usual taking notes. The meeting degenerated into chaos, with others joining the chorus of condemnation. No one mentioned my name, but it was clear that I was the focus of their ire. JZ ended the meeting. I went up to him afterwards and said I needed to speak to him. He said he would call me later.

I emerged shocked into the piercing brightness of the Cape Town sunlight. Bruce Kannemeyer asked: 'Why didn't they have the balls to say it was you they were talking about? Fucking cowards.' As we walked towards the Parliamentary buildings, Gavin shuffled across the piazza. Seeing us emerging from Tuynhuys, he assumed we had been brow-beaten, and possibly directed, by the Presidency and the Cabinet. He was furious. Laloo rushed over to explain what had just happened.

I spent the evening at home waiting for the Deputy President to call. The knowledge that I was seen as betraying the organisation hurt, although I saw the irony in this false accusation, given that I had leaked Thabo's AIDS remarks to the *Mail & Guardian* a few months before. Eventually, just after 10 pm, my cell phone rang. I answered it before the second ring. 'I'm sorry it's so late. I've been in meetings. Can you come down to my office now?' I was so relieved that JZ had phoned, I ran all the way down the hill to Parliament and arrived at Tuynhuys breathless, sweat coursing down my bald head.

The normally busy Presidency was virtually deserted. A few bored bodyguards slouched around the ornate stairwell. I was shown into the Deputy President's office. My anxiety was relieved as he greeted me warmly and asked me to sit close to him. I immediately and a little manically started explaining that I had not leaked information from the Governance Committee meeting. He stopped me: 'I know it wasn't you.' It was clear he knew who it was. Thinking about it later, I assumed that JZ's office had fed the media in an attempt to embarrass the President.

JZ encouraged me to press on with the investigation, reiterating that he believed we were fulfilling our constitutional responsibility. His only caveat: we ensure that Heath was not part of the investigating team.

I walked back up towards Table Mountain, calm and satisfied but a little perplexed. Why was Zuma supporting us in the face of such hostility from the President? With the limited knowledge I then had, I assumed that JZ saw an opportunity to further destabilise a teetering President. At the time Mbeki was at his most isolated since his election: his orthodox economic strategy, the HIV and AIDS debacle which was at its height, his weak approach to Zimbabwe and his generally autocratic leadership style were all contributing to his alienation from the ANC's allies and many in the organisation itself. Perhaps JZ felt that if Mbeki was intimately involved in the less salubrious aspects of the arms deal, exposure might turn the ANC whispers of preventing a second Mbeki term into a crescendo. Zuma would have seen himself as the most likely beneficiary of such a scenario. Bizarrely, this naive thesis gave me succour. I thought it was possible that within these political shenanigans Scopa might be given the latitude to continue a meaningful investigation.

Comforted, I then pondered why everyone in the ANC was so

keen to exclude Judge Heath and his highly successful investigating unit from the probe. Willem Heath came across as a rather grey accountant. However, contrary to this 'bean-counter' image he enjoys the limelight. A man of the old National Party, he had been a judge in the former homeland of Ciskei. Post-1994 he had become one of the country's leading crusaders against corruption. The unit he had built up was tenacious, illustrating its competence to Scopa by its recovery of almost half of the money wasted on the 'Sarafina II' AIDS fiasco. However, he was perceived by some as liable to jump in and out of issues, depending on their profile. The unit claimed to already have significant evidence of wrongdoing in the arms deal, and importantly was the only entity in the proposed investigating team that would have the power to annul the contracts if any corruption was proven. In addition, Heath was the only actor in the drama who had little connection to or sympathy with the ANC.

The party developed a coordinated and aggressive campaign to enable the President to refuse Heath the proclamation he required to participate in the investigation. Johnny de Lange wrote a 17-page article to explain why the judge should be excluded on legal grounds. The Speaker entered the fray. Within the ANC Study Group there was debate on the issue. Some wanted him excluded either because that was the wish of the leadership or because they just didn't trust him. Laloo, myself and a few others felt it was important to have Heath involved, but that he needed to be kept within the parameters of the investigation and work cooperatively with the other bodies. To this end, we insisted that the Joint Investigating Team (JIT) report to Scopa at regular intervals, a prospect the JIT was comfortable with. However, the Speaker informed Gavin and me that it would be inappropriate for us to instruct the JIT, or have regular interaction with them. We were surprised, given her earlier support for our proposal, and approached her legal advisor, Fink Haysom, who had fulfilled the same role with distinction for President Mandela. Fink made clear that there was no problem with the JIT keeping Scopa informed of its progress or our interacting with them as long as we were not seen to instruct them. The Speaker was unmoved and took the extraordinary step of editing Gavin's letter to the JIT, imposing her view on the correspondence.

Prior to this onslaught the JIT had written to Gavin asking him to request the President to include the Heath Unit. The media too clamoured for his inclusion. Gavin duly wrote to the President, requesting him to provide the Heath Unit with the required proclamation. He and I also released a joint statement containing the advice we had received from Fink. However, after meeting the President, Selby Baqwa and Bulelani Ngcuka changed their minds about the need to involve the Judge. Even the Auditor-General equivocated. Just before changing his mind, Selby Baqwa was accused, in the media, of sexual harassment. Remarkably, once he had recanted on Heath the allegations were dropped. His accuser spoke to the media and said she had been compensated for withdrawing charges.[19]

Soon afterwards the ANC hierarchy received a massive fillip when, in another matter, the Constitutional Court ruled it was inappropriate for a judge to lead the unit (even though the application of the ruling was delayed for a year and didn't affect the day-to-day activities of the SIU). The Speaker issued a statement claiming Scopa's report did not call for Heath's inclusion in the JIT and alleging that Gavin was in conflict with Parliament for writing to the President. I was outraged. The media claimed she was trying to stymie the investigation.[20] She hated bad publicity, especially when her ethics were questioned.

Frene started calling me frantically. As this was now in Parliament's end of year recess I was holed up at my sister's house on the beach at Kommetjie. Initially I avoided her calls. When we eventually spoke she complained that Gavin had overstepped the mark as he claimed to be acting on behalf of the committee when the committee hadn't met for weeks. I pointed out that he was acting with my support and in accordance with Parliamentary rules, which stipulate that the chairperson acts on the committee's behalf during the recess. She asked me to come and see her at her official residence.

I did so on 2 January 2001. Passing through the security barriers into Groote Schuur, the official compound of the Cabinet and parliamentary office-bearers, I was a little cowed by the display of importance and power. Frene's official house was dark behind drawn curtains. Inside the dull furniture and lingering damp added to the soullessness of this temporary home. She explained to me that the JIT could not report to us and that she would come to the Study Group to explain her reasoning. She also made clear that Parliament would decide that our resolution did not include Heath, and that she would inform the President accordingly. I asked her what had happened to her initial enthusiastic support for the investigation, and she mumbled a response about Gavin exceeding his powers. She hinted that my close working relationship with him was untenable and left the room to take a call.

As I sat on my own in Frene's inhospitable lounge I began to piece together what had been going on. Later my suspicions were confirmed by a variety of journalists and senior comrades who remained sympathetic to me. Key political functionaries in the ANC, the President's office and Parliament had been communicating either in a variety of sessions or in one large meeting that could have included the Speaker of both houses of Parliament, Yengeni, Pahad, Ngcuka, Peter Mokaba and others. At this meeting or series of deliberations in mid-December it had been decided that the ANC Study Group would begin to row back the resolution, Heath would not be given a proclamation and the remaining investigators would be directed as to the parameters of their enquiries. At the same time, senior ANC leaders had started to brief individual members of the ANC Study Group against me, claiming that I had an anti-ANC agenda. The harsh reality and inappropriateness of this scenario were only fully brought home to me when I was told by someone involved in the JIT about a meeting with the President at which they were castigated for publishing their initial report and effectively told who they could and could not investigate.

I left Frene's residence appalled that someone who a few weeks earlier had fervently supported Parliament's independence and threatened to resign if I was intimidated or stopped from pursuing the truth, was now a key player in neutering the investigation.

I drove back to Kommetjie through the fynbos-strewn mountains of Silvermine. A fog settled over the winding road. I realised that it was going to be increasingly difficult to have an unfettered investigation. In the early stages of the Scopa process I had been warned by my friend and closest political confidant, Barbara Hogan, that pursuing the truth of the arms deal might bring a premature end to my political career. That moment seemed closer now.

With Frene's support evaporated it was imperative that I spoke again to Jacob Zuma and attempted to persuade him why the Heath

Unit was essential to the investigation. I left urgent messages for him and John Jeffrey. I never heard from either of them again. The future was bleak. I made my way down to Long Beach. Unfashionable, a little wild and often windswept, the area is buffeted by the cold waters of the Atlantic. I gingerly entered the sea. My body stiffened at the cold as if a long blue shaft of stainless steel was being inserted first into my toes up through my legs and into my back. My testicles shrivelled in fright. In those ice-cold moments I asked myself repeatedly why I was putting myself through this agony. And then, as a massive grey-blue wave crashed in front of me, I dived into its frothing head. The tumultuous micro-currents seemed to hit me from every conceivable angle. For a few freezing seconds I lost all bearings. My body was pushed, pulled and pummelled in countless directions. I had no control.

*

Gavin and I met to strategise. We had a day-long Scopa workshop scheduled for 22 January. I advised him to get legal backing for the view that he had every right to act on behalf of the Committee during the recess. I told him I might not have the support of the full ANC Study Group any more; that the ANC would reject what he had done and insist that we agree to exclude Heath.

On 8 January the Parliamentary Legal Advisors produced an opinion that Scopa's resolution did not insist on the inclusion of the Heath Unit. The ANC National Working Committee discussed the matter and decided to campaign against Heath's inclusion. A five-member task team was set up to deal with the Heath issue. The following week the decision was endorsed by the ANC's National Executive Committee.

In a *pas de deux* of political choreography Frene issued a statement suggesting that Scopa had acted inappropriately with regard to the JIT, thereby contradicting the view of her own legal advisor and a sympathetic senior ANC-aligned judge we had consulted. The judge reiterated that, in legal terms, our intention for all four agencies to be included was clear. He also stated that he thought it was inappropriate and wrong for the Speaker of Parliament to intervene in the way she had.

A few days later Alec Erwin, Trevor Manuel, Jeff Radebe and Mosiuoa Lekota held a press conference to criticise Scopa and argued that there was no need for an investigation as it was 'the firm view of Cabinet that this process was undertaken with the utmost integrity. Accordingly, the government rejects with contempt any insinuation of corrupt practice on its part.' [21] They further suggested that the Office of the Auditor-General and Scopa had failed to understand this very complex deal. In a remarkable display of political doublespeak, they took particular issue with the cost we had reported even though this was the figure their officials had presented to us. 'The cost price which was calculated in 1990 rand is R30.3 billion. In keeping with standard government accounting practice it is the actual payment to suppliers that represents expenditure to the State. Interest costs are part of deficit financing and not the cost of the equipment.' [22] No mention was made of the cost of currency fluctuation or that deficit financing is paid for by the taxpayer, the point we made explicitly in our resolution. Alec Erwin then attempted an explanation of the controversial Hawk contract. Judging by their bemused expressions, his Cabinet colleagues were as confused as the baffled journalists.

I started to ring round the ANC Study Group members to try and arrange a meeting. Pierre Gerber, who only a couple of years previously had joined the ANC from the National Party, responded that now was the time to take a stand: 'We must bite the bullet. Honesty must take preference. The goings-on make me suspicious.' Bruce Kannemeyer questioned why the ANC and the Speaker were making a statement on Heath without consulting me. But the party was in full assault mode. The NEC member who had previously warned me about the consequences of continuing the investigation contacted me on 17 January to say that the NEC was 'monumentally pissed off. They believe they can just tough it out.' He repeated his view that I was on a hiding to nothing, because the party had received money from some of the bidding companies.

This was the context in which the decision on Heath, a determination that would be a touchstone of our new democracy, was to be made. The progressive *Mail & Guardian*, in an editorial headlined 'A test of integrity looms', opined:

185

Let there be no mistaking the moment. The ruling ANC, the government and particularly President Thabo Mbeki face a decisive test of their integrity and will to combat corruption in the attitude they adopt to the investigation into the R43.8 billion arms deal.

Either they give the investigation presided over by Scopa, their patent and unqualified support and co-operation or they risk grave consequences for themselves and the country. ... The government needs to dispel all doubt that it is committed to a full and unfettered investigation by Scopa. Its members need to demonstrate unambiguous support for one of the organising principles of our constitution: That Parliament, in this case represented by Scopa, exercises as primary representative of the people, oversight over the executive arm of government.

Our greatest expectation lies with Mbeki. ... if he acts decisively in support of Scopa's investigation – whatever the discomfort this may cause old comrades – he will be seen to have favoured the public interest over the comfort of elements in his party; he will have ensured Parliament's and the people's oversight of the executive; he will have laid down a marker that he will not tolerate corruption of any kind, no matter how high it might go.[23]

The *Sunday Independent* editorialised that:

For the Executive to be seen to be contradicting the recommendations of this Parliamentary watchdog body in any way is, at best, unseemly, and, at worst, a sign that powerful people do not want it to dig too deep. The old adage that it is not the scandal but the cover-up that is more damaging is once more being proved true. Had the executive allowed the legislature to get on with its work, its claims that it has nothing to hide would have more credence. Instead the executive has decided to shuffle about, saying it has not yet made a decision about whether Heath should investigate the matter. In the end, the damage done by corruption – real or imagined – is being compounded by the taint of a cover-up.[24]

A few days before the President was to announce his decision, Penuell Maduna – rewarded for his unconstitutional attack on the Auditor-General a few years earlier by being made Justice Minister –

186

advised the President that it would not be appropriate or necessary to include the Heath Unit in the investigation. On hearing of the Justice Minister's advice to the President, Idasa stated that 'it deeply regrets this decision because it undermines the constructive role that parliament through Scopa had defined for itself in giving life to the constitutional obligation to hold the executive to account'.[25] Even Transparency International wrote to the President that 'the perception locally and internationally is that the integrity of the government is in question'.[26] Ironically, Frene Ginwala, one of Transparency International's South African patrons, castigated the body for commenting on the matter. The Archbishop of Cape Town appealed to Mbeki to put the country first and argued that a failure to do so 'would pose a very serious threat to the country's democracy. Were the executive to override Parliament and set up its own terms of reference for this investigation as the apartheid government used to do, South Africa would enter into the downward slippery road to becoming a banana republic.'[27]

On 19 January Thabo Mbeki appeared on television to address the nation. He announced that he would be following his Justice Minister's advice in refusing Heath a proclamation. In support of his decision he cited additional legal opinion that he had sought from the Director of Public Prosecutions in the Western Cape, Frank Khan, and Advocate Jan Lubbe. However, when the full text of the so-called Khan-Lubbe report was inadvertently presented to the media it was clear that they had advised exactly the opposite. They stated quite unequivocally 'In addition there are sufficient grounds in terms of the Special Investigating Units and Special Tribunals Act No 74 of 1996 for a Special Investigating Unit to conduct an investigation and, in our opinion, such an investigation is warranted. We agree with the conclusions of the Special Committee on Public Accounts (sic) ... that all the agencies referred to above be involved at the earliest possible stage.'[28] They went on to say that Judge Heath should be replaced as head of the unit as soon as possible to give effect to the recent decision of the Constitutional Court.

Mbeki's selective use of the opinion was a shameful distortion of information by a Head of State. The *Sunday Independent* editorialised that his action 'constitutes at best a cynical distortion of the report and at worst a wilful misrepresentation of its key findings'.[29]

President Mbeki ended his address to the nation with the following extraordinary statement:

Our country and all our people have been subjected to a sustained campaign that has sought to discredit our government and the country itself by making unfounded and unsubstantiated allegations of corruption. Among other things this campaign has sought to force us to do illegal things, to break important contractual obligations, to accuse major international companies of corrupt practice and to damage our image globally ... We know that various entities have been hired to sustain this campaign ... I would like to assure you that the campaign will not succeed.[30]

The level of paranoia bound up in these conspiracy theories is quite remarkable. In fact the only conspiracy about at the time was that being manufactured by the President, who held a highly inappropriate meeting with the Auditor-General, the Public Protector and the Director of Public Prosecutions three days before coming to his decision. Given that the President had acted as chair of the Cabinet sub-committee that made the key decisions in relation to the arms deal, it was improper for him to be setting the terms of the investigation into his own conduct.

Responses to the President's exclusion of the Heath Unit were fevered. Political analyst Xolela Mangcu commented that 'what is at stake is the integrity of Parliament [and] the Presidency'.[31] The *Sunday Independent* editorialised:

Any suggestion that criticism of the Executive is subversive, is a subversion of democracy. We would argue that Mbeki's decision to exclude the unit and publicly accuse the AG and Scopa of wrongdoing subverts the separation of powers between the legislature and the executive and undermines the instruments of accountability in so fragile a democracy. Clearly Mbeki has the political power to bludgeon into submission those ANC members who supported the decision to include the unit, but his action could do the cause of democracy irrevocable harm.[32]

During these tumultuous days I had tried incessantly to contact Jacob Zuma. Neither he nor John Jeffrey would return my calls. Soon I understood why. On the same day the President announced he was excluding the Heath Unit, a letter arrived for Gavin, purportedly from the Deputy President. It was a thirteen page excoriation of the committee for the same offences highlighted by the President. Using Johnny de Lange's words from the governance committee meeting, it stated that 'the investigation is tantamount to a fishing expedition'. Describing the arms companies as 'well-known and prestigious international companies', the letter fulminate against our rather measured statement that the arms industry was prone to corruption. It continued: 'Natural justice demands that you both substantiate the allegation that the persons, governments and corporations ... are prone to corruption and dishonesty ... it is a most serious matter indeed for our parliament or any section of it to level charges of corruption against foreign governments and corporations without producing evidence to back up such allegations.' After further attacking Scopa for unfounded allegations and our *ultra vires* support for the Heath Unit the letter concluded with the familiar, paranoid refrain: 'The government will also act vigorously to defend itself and the country against any malicious misinformation campaign intended to discredit the government and destabilise the country.'[33]

This laughable defence of the innate purity of governments and arms companies seems particularly absurd in light not only of the extensive documented history of global arms deal corruption[34] and the accepted investigative process of compiling *prime facie* evidence and then launching a full investigation, but also what has subsequently emerged (and continues to emerge) about the South African deal. Laloo, Barbara, Gavin and I were convinced that this diatribe could not have come from the Deputy President, who was out of the country at the time. It has since come to light in the lead up to the recent corruption trial of Jacob Zuma, that it was written by President Mbeki.[35] What was clear to us even at the time was that the Deputy President was either no longer driving the agenda on the ANC's response to the arms deal crisis or had changed his tune quite dramatically.

The ANC members of Scopa were shocked. Having been informed of the support we were getting from the Deputy President, they couldn't understand this letter in his name. In addition, they were being briefed against me and the investigation by Vincent Smith, the Chief Whip and the Presidency. They were now faced with a choice: continue to support the investigation and alienate the party, or support the party and become part of the leadership's effort to stymie any meaningful investigation. This was a manifestly unfair choice as, within South Africa's pure proportional representation system, rebellion against the party inevitably results in exclusion from Parliament, either immediately or most certainly at the next election.

On 21 January the Study Group met. It was a chastened group of people. Bruce Kannemeyer and Serake Leeuw looked devastated, defeated, which was how I felt. Laloo was regrettably in Gauteng attending to party business. Vincent Smith was leering with delight. Don, Beatrice and Billy, who had been determined in their support of the route we were taking, had clearly had their minds changed. The three of them turned on me, accusing me of not keeping them informed, of failing to keep the executive up-to-date, and of pursuing an anti-ANC agenda. Serake and Bruce fought my corner, reiterating that we had briefed the Deputy President, the Defence Minister and the Speaker on a number of occasions. They also insisted that information had regularly been shared with the Study Group. Don stated brutally and crudely: 'The President has spoken. What more can we be expected to say?'

Even Bruce and Serake were feeling the heat of the Executive; as they realised the tide was turning against us they moderated their positions. Beatrice alleged I was providing Gavin with confidential ANC information.[36] When Vincent started to accuse me of wanting to damage the ANC and especially the Executive, my resistance broke. The situation was out of control. I was being bullied into accepting the leadership's line, and if I didn't it would be clear that I was a traitor with an agenda of my own. I felt tears well up. I excused myself and fled the meeting room as I began to cry. Not quite the hard-nosed politician, I made for the nearest bathroom, closed the cubicle door and sat on the toilet seat holding my head, trying to stop the tears and to think clearly. My composure eventually regained, at least superficially, I returned to the meeting. It was suggested that we reconvene the following day with the Whippery present.

I was confused and fearful. That evening I went down to our local corner café to use the pay phone. Too nervous to use my cell or home phone, I felt comfortably anonymous amidst the homeless 'bergies' and night-time revellers in need of cigarettes or something to absorb the alcohol. I called Barbara and asked her advice. As we started talking an effusive member of the opposition DA greeted me loudly and came over to talk. The last person I wanted to see was a fellow MP. Eventually I phoned Gavin to let him know that things were unravelling. He asked me whether I thought the Scopa workshop scheduled for the next day was likely to proceed. I told him I didn't know.

The following day the Study Group reconvened. Geoff Doidge, the Deputy Chief Whip, had joined us at Vincent's invitation. A pleasant apparatchik, he told us that the Speaker and the chairperson of the NCOP wished to join us as well. Given the sensitivity of their positions, he suggested we invite them to the meeting. Frene swept in wearing a dour grey sari. Naledi Pandor, a business-like, officious politician, was dressed in a dark blue trouser suit. They were ready for action.

Frene led the charge: 'We think you should issue a press statement stating that you support the exclusion of Heath, that the investigation should not report to Scopa, and that you apologise for the inference of wrongdoing by the Executive.' The Speaker left as we started drafting, but Naledi remained and took an active part in the crafting of the statement. I argued that we had to recommit ourselves to Scopa's 14th Report. They accepted that, in return for my agreeing to state that we had not specifically identified the Heath Unit as an essential part of the investigating team. Extremely edgy and unsure what to do, I felt torn between loyalty to the party and my convictions. Encouraged by my comrades, I agreed. With the backtracking statement complete, the group insisted that I be the person to read it to the media. I could see no way out.

As we filed into the meeting room where the press conference was being held I felt the journalists were focusing on me in an attempt to establish whether I had been turned. I read the statement sheepishly. A barrage of questions followed, all aimed at whether we were still committed to the investigation. I attempted the contortionist's trick of suggesting nothing fundamental had changed. Geoff Doidge brought the briefing to a close. I felt miserable. Weak, pathetic and ashamed.

I now had to travel to the venue where Scopa was scheduled to meet, knowing I had to confront Gavin Woods. The Conference Centre was set among the undulating fields and aged oak trees of Constantia. As I drove, fast, through Cape Town's premier southern suburb the justifications were running through my head: This is the only way to keep the investigation afloat. A strategic retreat in a much bigger battle, etc, etc.

On arrival at the quaint venue I avoided the growing number of journalists and camera people outside. I asked the committee clerk where Gavin was. She pointed to the back garden. Across the grass, next to a gentle brook, Gavin was sitting on a chair, paler than I had ever seen him. He saw me and looked away. As I came closer he looked up, devastation etched on his face: 'So, that's it, then?'

Time seemed to stop. The birds and brook fell silent. The top of my head was freezing cold but pricked with sweat. My heart was pounding, my arms and hands numb. I took a deep breath, put aside my well-prepared rationalisations and responded as I instinctively felt: 'I'm sorry, I should never have agreed to be a part of the press briefing. Nothing will change. Let's go and tell the media that we will still pursue this thing even if Heath isn't involved.'

I could see the relief course through Gavin's body. He warned me as a friend of the consequences of what I was about to do. We talked animatedly for a few minutes, wondered what we would do about the Scopa workshop, and then walked round to speak to the media. We told the journalists that we were united. On Heath I said there were different interpretations but that I had understood when we drafted the resolution that we did want him in. Gavin and I promised to continue to fight for an unfettered investigation. Both of us realised that we had to compromise to see this thing through. But we also understood, perhaps more than ever before, that we needed each other.

We cancelled the workshop, as the ANC members had no desire to participate, and I headed back to Parliament with a sense of relief and trepidation – relief that I had separated myself from the contortions of the press statement, that I had made the right decision, the only decision I could live with. I also knew that this stand would be my last; that my political career in the ANC was over.

*

The following day, the ANC issued an endorsement of the Executive's view. In a section entitled 'the REAL Arms Scandal', the statement suggested it was extraordinary that 'so few people have been able to make so much noise on the basis of so few facts'.[37] They identified four 'myths' propagated by the troublemakers:

- The involvement of the Heath Unit is a test of government's commitment to fight corruption
- The President does not respect the oversight role of Parliament.
- The ANC is trying to prevent a thorough investigation.
- The arms procurement process is riddled with corruption.

The statement ended with Leninist flourish:

'Forward to Democracy and the Liberation of the People of SA
Down with Corruption
Down with the destabilization of our democracy'

These 'myths' were actually a fair encapsulation of what was happening. However, the statement served to further isolate me and to suggest that Gavin and I were part of a massive conspiracy to bring down the democratically elected South African government.

Scopa met again on 24 January. A sombre Gavin, still shocked by the previous few days' events, started the meeting by calling for the committee to rise above our political differences and continue the proud, non-partisan and consensual tradition of Scopa. I spoke strongly in support, as did Raenette Taljaard of the opposition Democratic Alliance. Some of the ANC members trumpeted the new line developed by the leadership. Gavin called for objectivity all round. I was out of kilter with the other ANC members of the committee, arguing that our resolution could be read both as insisting on including Heath and leaving it open for the subsequent meeting of the investigators to decide. I found myself contradicting many of my ANC colleagues who insisted we hadn't agreed to Heath's participation. I was torn between trying to keep the committee on an even keel, and my anger with some of my own comrades. The meeting ended with the formation of a small sub-group to resolve this and other issues.

193

Monday 29 January was another bright summer's day. I had spent the weekend back at Kommetjie trying not to think about the predicament I was in. The Study Group had been called to see the Chief Whip at 8 am. His meeting room, though grand, seemed tiny and suffocating to me. I felt like the proverbial dead man walking. Expressionless and talking in a flat tone, Yengeni said: 'Comrades, we have decided to strengthen the Public Accounts Committee. Feinstein will no longer chair the Study Group. Geoff Doidge will be the chair. He will be joined by comrade Andries Nel [the loyalist who had 'dealt with' the problem of Penuell Maduna's attack on the Auditor-General], Chair of ANC Caucus Thabang Makwetla and comrade Neo Masithela.' He continued: 'The ANC, from the President downwards, will now exercise political control over Scopa.' From that moment the role of the Public Accounts Committee as a non-partisan arbiter on matters of financial management was over.

I stared at Yengeni. This was the same man I had watched weeping during the TRC hearings as his torture was re-enacted. Even though I knew that some sort of reprimand or sacking was coming, when it actually happened I was still shocked. I went numb. My head throbbed. I couldn't think clearly. I couldn't think at all. I felt winded, as though a battering ram had been driven into the pit of my stomach.

And then: 'Questions? Comments?'

Silence.

I gathered up my Psion and left. The manner in which my fellow Study Group members shifted awkwardly out of my way, avoiding eye contact, made me feel like the political leper I had instantly become. It was a feeling I would have to get used to over the coming months.

I followed the worn pattern of the green, fraying carpet up to my usual refuge, my office. I phoned Barbara. She was outraged that no one had spoken up on my behalf. I was only too conscious of the extreme pressure they were under and understood the silence. My phone rang incessantly. I ignored it. My heart was pounding. Amidst the turmoil I tried to focus on a key question: do I resign or do I stay on and fight?

While I ruminated in my office the new Public Accounts Committee was being addressed by the Speaker. Claiming to be dispassionate on the matter, she said the Committee could not sub-contract its work to the JIT or give it instructions. She claimed that Gavin had exceeded his authority as chair. He disagreed with her vehemently on all counts. He later recounted to me how the ANC members, bar Laloo, were in jovial, relieved mood. They had been released from a horrendous bind. On the same day, Frene Ginwala wrote an obsequious letter to the Deputy President confirming that Scopa's allegations 'are not substantiated' and that the Committee could not instruct the JIT.

After the meeting Tony Yengeni held a press conference at which he stated that the ANC had decided to 'strengthen the ANC membership of Scopa', that I had 'drifted away', and that there was 'no committee in respect of the ANC which is above party political discipline'.[38]

The following few days were awful. I spent most of my time questioning whether I had done the right thing or not. Every time I felt an iota of pride in the stand I'd taken it was accompanied by a feeling of regret that I was doing the ANC harm. Had I just been caught up in some elaborate conspiracy to besmirch the ANC? Why had I relied on Zuma as the link to the party? What was his agenda? And why was the ANC going to such lengths to neuter the investigation? Surely if there was nothing to hide there should have been no objection to what we were doing?

I was instructed to attend a workshop of the ANC Study Group under its new leadership. As I arrived at the pseudo-Safari Lodge in central Cape Town, Geoff Doidge masqueraded at how pleased he was to see me and how we could now move on. The members who had been on the committee for a while were uncomfortable with my presence. The new members were openly hostile. After half an hour of discomfort I decided to leave.

After a few days' reflection and conversations with a small group of people either in or close to the ANC for whom I had enormous respect, I decided to issue a statement:

I have been saddened by the ANC's lack of confidence in my leadership of the Study Group on Public Accounts at such a crucial time in the Committee's life.

However, the issues are far bigger than my own position. They run to the heart of our democracy, specifically issues of good

195

governance and the accountability of the Executive to the Legislature.

In relation to the arms deal, it is critical that a comprehensive and thorough investigation take place that will determine once and for all the veracity or otherwise of the myriad allegations made. It is also essential that the investigators and MP's involved in the probe are free of any influence or pressure. The integrity of this process will be a touchstone of our new democracy.

It was hard not to let the personal hurt and emotion I was feeling stand in the way of the public good. For someone who takes any form of rejection to heart and who enjoys the theatre of politics it was difficult but crucial not to become self-indulgent. With the emotional support of my family and close friends and a surprising degree of praise in the media, it was possible, with the guidance of that small group of informal advisors, to keep focused on the national issues at stake rather than on myself.

The following evening I spoke in a debate at Rabbi Steinhorn's synagogue in Sea Point. I was overwhelmed by the response I received but restated my commitment to the ANC, much to the bemusement of most of the audience. A few days later I was given the opportunity to set out my credo on the issues at stake by my friend Richard Calland at an Idasa seminar on parliamentary oversight. I called on the members of Scopa to rise above party politics, suggesting that there was a need for the parliamentary rules to insulate the committee from party political influence.

*

Gavin and I started to meet in more secluded places. Meetings late at night on a deserted stretch of Mouille Point beachfront or during the day at Tokai forest were our favoured rendezvous. We had been told earlier by one of the investigators that our home phones and even cars were probably bugged, and had started to use pay phones to call each other. The thought of some unfortunate intelligence operative having to listen to endless repeats of Misha's favourite nursery rhyme, 'The Grand Old Duke of York', caused Simone and me no end of mirth at what was a very stressful time. We developed code names for each other and our key sources. One of the investigators who spoke to us regularly but clandestinely was referred to as Wallace while Gavin became Gromit.

Gavin was having a tough time in the committee since its 'thugging up', to use his words. Shauket Fakie, the Auditor-General, had disappeared from view. The Deputy AG, Terrence Nombembe, appeared before Scopa and undertook to report back to the committee on behalf of the JIT in July 2001. This never happened. Soon thereafter, staff in the AG's Office were instructed that they could not have contact with either Gavin or myself. This was a culmination of strange behaviour by Fakie since the beginning of the new year. Every time he saw Gavin and me he would become extremely agitated and nervous. He would sweat profusely while talking to us and obfuscate the state of play in the investigation. It soon became clear why.

The two senior members of his Office who had been directing the enquiries into the deal for over a year were removed from the investigation, with no reason given. A source in the Office suggested that they stood down because of the manner in which the process was being manipulated. I was later told by another source that the Auditor-General had been summoned to a couple of meetings with the President. In the first, Mbeki supposedly attacked Fakie and admonished him for writing the initial report. He also made it clear in no uncertain terms which aspects of the deal the AG's Office could and could not investigate. This pressure was intensified when they met again just before the President's announcement on Judge Heath. The AG was reportedly 'freaked out' by the meetings and very nervous. Exhibiting paranoia reminiscent of the President, the AG took the extraordinary step of administering lie-detector tests to his staff. Many were insulted and angry.

Gavin and I attempted to raise the issue of the AG's supine submission to the will of the Executive at the Audit Commission. This was a body appointed by the President to oversee the work of the AG's Office. I was Deputy Chair of the Commission. Pallo Jordan, the incumbent Chair and usually an independent-minded ANC MP, closed the door on any meaningful discussion of the AG's behaviour.

Meanwhile, the behaviour of the ANC members of Scopa had become ever more politically partisan and aggressive. Gavin felt that this inevitably spilled over to other areas of the committee's work unconnected with the arms deal. Whenever any matter arose that might cause embarrassment to the ANC leadership, Vincent Smith would begin filibustering, ensuring that the meetings lost direction and resolved nothing. The ANC component objected to anything that could be construed as critical of the governing party. At each and every meeting, the newly arrived Neo Masithela challenged Gavin's competence to chair the committee.

After a few more meetings the ANC contingent, responding to an instruction from the Chief Whip to move the committee away from the arms deal, decided that the committee should take no further action to follow up the 14th Report undertakings and should have no further communication with the Joint Investigating Team. The committee had been rendered toothless. Now its only remaining function was to play the compliant audience to a performance by the Cabinet Ministers involved in defending the deal. And for this performance nothing was left to chance. I sat astonished and angry in a Study Group meeting where the Cabinet Ministers who were to appear before the committee instructed us in exactly what questions to ask. Oversight indeed!

The hearing with the Ministers took place on 26 February in a dark, oppressive room in Parliament's Marks building. It was in this very room during the late apartheid years that the National Party held its caucus meetings, where its Parliamentary puppets would receive instructions from the leadership. While the ANC members asked their scripted questions and agreed with every answer supplied by the Ministers, Gavin, Raenette and I asked about the substantive issues pertaining to the deal. Trevor Manuel, Alec Erwin and Mosiuoa Lekota were belligerent and arrogant in their responses.

Alec was particularly aggressive and enthusiastic in defence of Chippy Shaik. In response to a question I had asked about the lack of declarations of conflicts of interest he responded:

> [Minister A Erwin]... when it was known to us, and it was known at an early stage, that a person in a relatively critical position, the Chief of Procurement [i.e. Chippy], and that there were now negotiations taking place between a company that his brother was involved in, we took specific steps to ensure that the person recused himself ... we were satisfied that we had taken sufficient precautions to deal with that.[39]

They fudged the issue of what influence Chippy had in the Cabinet sub-committee and were joined in their obscurantism by Geoff Doidge and Don Gumede. Gavin was polite and firm in the chair, successfully concealing his growing exasperation with the ANC members.

The Ministers continued their self-defence with the view that they had nothing to do with the sub-contracts and were responsible only for the main contracts, which were all above board. Gavin, Raenette and I wearily explained that if, as Chippy had made clear at our hearing, deals were done between the main contractors and the sub-contractors prior to the main contracts being awarded, it was the relationship between the two levels of contractors that was most open to abuse and about which we had received extremely worrying information of state involvement. Revealingly, after claiming initially that Government had nothing to do with sub-contractors, Erwin eventually stated that '... at various times ... each of us as Ministers probably met in one or other way subcontractors.'[40]

On the controversial LIFT deal with BAe/SAAB, Erwin made it

clear that the Ministers and not the Arms Acquisition Council made the final decision, and did so 'for the correct reasons and within the correct procedures'.[41] Creating even more confusion on the issue, he also said that the offsets were not a primary reason for the deal.

The Ministers endlessly repeated their mantra that the cost of the deal was R30 billion, even when shown that the Treasury's own Budget Review released the previous week referred to R43 billion. The Defence Minister attempted to enlighten the committee:

> [Minister M Lekota] ... let us say that South Africa committed itself to give 30.3 billion giraffes. Those giraffes are living animals and they will remain like that. Now paper money or a coin, which is a symbol of something concrete, its quantities change in relation to the commodity. The commodity does not change. And what we are saying here is that the amount of money South Africa signed that it is going to pay, in real terms, will remain the same, but because the nominal forms change, the quantities change.[42]

A little befuddled by this bizarre analogy, I attempted to infuse a bit of humour in to the proceedings while making a serious point:

> [Mr AJ Feinstein] ... what would happen if we gave the giraffes in twelve years time. We would have to hand over the offspring that they had in those twelve years as well. The key issue is the cost on the day of signing and the overall cost to the taxpayer. So, there was something that was omitted from the original statement from government on the cost.[43]

My levity was not shared by the Ministers, who, despite all indications that they had misled the public, remained angry that Scopa had raised this issue at all. They continued to defend their position, tying themselves in knots in the process, and proceeded to castigate the Committee for our prejudgement of the arms industry as corrupt, Minister Lekota stating 'that particular position is unacceptable'.[44]

Gavin was confronted with an almost impossible balancing act between being polite and courteous to the Ministers while exasperated by their constant obfuscation. He told me afterwards: 'I was a millimetre from going over the line at which all hell would break out and I would be totally rubbished. I had to literally bite my lip not to become personal, show anger or be rude to a Minister.'

The committee made no headway after the hearing. At the ANC's insistence it decided not to follow up the outrageous letter signed by the Deputy President. Its second report on the arms deal was highly contested. Unsurprisingly, the ANC's report, which had been drafted with the involvement of the Ministers concerned (which I had witnessed in a series of Study Group meetings and exchanges of drafts), reiterated that the committee had never called for the inclusion of the Heath Unit and expressed their confidence in the ongoing investigation. Equally unsurprising was the ANC's complete exoneration of the Executive. The document apologised for the 14th Report's unintended offence and accepted the Executive's take on the real cost of the deal. It criticised Gavin for the position he took on the involvement of the Heath Unit. It was a capitulation of Roberto Duran proportions, with which the other parties refused to be associated. But to the ANC it was a political job well done.[45]

Gavin tried to persuade the committee that they had an obligation to Parliament and thus to the country to continue to investigate aspects of the deal themselves. This was rejected by the ANC. Gavin claimed that 'the committee has been sidelined. We had interventions by the Speaker which by design created uncertainty about accountability. That uncertainty has been exploited to the point where we are in the dark.'[46]

The ANC members demanded a special meeting to discuss Gavin's remarks, at which Vincent Smith, rude and aggressive, warned Gavin not to speak on behalf of the committee without consulting its members first. Gavin pointed out that he was quite entitled to speak in his personal capacity. I was mortified by the ANC's conduct. It was not just the pathetic attempt to silence Gavin in his quite legitimate attack on the Speaker, but also the boorish, arrogant manner in which it was done. I stormed out of the meeting, shaking my head in disgust. As a consequence I was called to a disciplinary meeting with two senior whips. Reggie Oliphant and Mbulelo Goniwe[47] seemed slightly embarrassed by their task. 'The Chief Whip has asked us to speak to you to get more information about your behaviour in recent meetings of the Public Accounts Committee.'

On hearing that their brief was to communicate my side of the story to the Chief Whip, who would then decide what action to take, I responded: 'Unfortunately, I can't participate in this process, as I believe the Chief Whip is compromised and unable to rule fairly on the matter.'

The two were dumbstruck, so I explained: a few weeks before, an investigative journalist called Mzilikazi wa Afrika had broken a story in the *Sunday Times* that the Chief Whip and former Chair of Parliament's Defence Committee, Tony Yengeni, had received a 47 per cent discount on a luxury motor vehicle from EADS, a company which was a bidder in the arms deal. This was one of 30 luxury cars given at massive discount to key stakeholders in the deal. The very man who had ensured Scopa's investigation was stillborn appeared to have benefited from the deal himself.

The whips said they would 'consult and get back to me'.

The Speaker called on Gavin to apologise for his remarks about her. He refused. The following day the leader of the small United Democratic Movement, Bantu Holomisa, echoed Gavin's comments, suggesting the Speaker's conduct in relation to the arms deal was in dereliction of her duty to prioritise the integrity of Parliament. He said she was intentionally obstructing parliamentary processes on behalf of the Executive and was improperly interfering in the committee's functioning.

Sadly, I had seen at first hand how she had done this, changing her tune from a crusading defender of Parliament to a calculating accomplice of the Executive. This proud, intelligent woman who had served the struggle so courageously for decades and who had guided the democratic Parliament through its first difficult years, had capitulated in the face of pressure from the Presidency. In the final reckoning, she had chosen the party over the nation, the President over Parliament.

She defended herself robustly, pointing out how she had refused Executive demands for the return of documents. This was disingenuous, as in one of the more laughable moments of the saga, the Speaker had asked Gavin and me to speak to her 'intelligence advisor', Russell Christophers. He told us that he was concerned about our safety and asked us to practise a few cautionary exercises such as always looking underneath our cars before starting them. Gavin and I thought this was a little paranoid and melodramatic, but soon his real intention became clear. 'The Speaker suggests, and I agree with her, that it would be safer for you if I kept all your documentation under lock and key. You could obviously have access to it at any time. I'm worried that it might be stolen or fall into the wrong hands. It must also be very heavy to lug around.'

It took real effort for Gavin and me not to laugh out loud. The Executive were desperate to know exactly what information we had. Using Frene's none-too-smart intelligence advisor to scare us into giving up this information was hardly inspired sleuthing. In fact we had demanded documents from departments after our public hearing in terms of Section 56 of the constitution. As soon as we had received the documents the Minister of Defence wanted them returned, arguing that we had no right to them. Gavin and I decided we would not give them back, but the Speaker eventually demanded them, arranging as a sop to us that we could examine certain of the documents under supervision in the AG's office.

As *Business Day* noted with reference to the Speaker's behaviour: '[Her] interpretation of the 14th Report was seen by some commentators as the razor's edge which has sliced Scopa into party factions and been systematically used by ANC members to undermine Woods' standing ... The question could be asked "How easy is it to sit on the inner counsel of the party, to hear and take part in its most sensitive strategy debates and remain impartial in Parliament?"'[48]

The ANC's response was to call a debate in Parliament on a resolution showing support for and appreciation of the Speaker. On 7 June 2001, in the minutes leading up to the debate, I sat with Barbara Hogan in a locked meeting room on the fifth floor of the parliamentary building to discuss my options: I could absent myself from the debate, I could attend the debate but leave the House before the vote was called, or I could attend the debate and register my lack of support for the Speaker. Barbara left the room and made her way to the Chamber. I anxiously paced the impersonal, green-tinged room. This was the moment in which I had to decide whether to take my actions to their logical conclusion.

I made my way downstairs into the Chamber. Where a few months previously almost every MP I passed would have greeted me as I walked to my seat, now only one or two did. The rest avoided looking at me. Melanie Verwoerd gave me a supportive smile. Essop Jassat looked at me intently, worry creased across his forehead. I sat down next to James Ngculu, one of the original members of the Defence committee who had been caught up in the issue.

Opposition parties spoke of the importance of the Speaker's impartiality. Douglas Gibson of the DA alleged that the reason the matter had been so poorly handled by the Executive and so contro-versially by the Speaker was because '...substantial donations were made to the ANC election fund by many of those who have benefited from the arms deal.' [49]

The ANC rolled out the heavyweights to defend the Speaker, in the process illustrating how beholden to the ruling party she actually was. They cleverly used Pallo Jordan and Jeremy Cronin, the two long-time struggle heroes who were known for their sometime independence of thought. I was shocked. Jeremy launched a misin-formed attack on Scopa and Gavin. He endorsed the deal and de-bunked criticism of it from a variety of quarters. He suggested that the uproar about the deal was just the opposition parties trying to steal a march on each other. [50]

Here was a man I had spoken to about the investigation, who had encouraged me to continue the search for answers, doing the politi-cal equivalent of a belly flop. As Jeremy spoke and my anger rose I realised that I could not abrogate responsibility. I could not cop out by leaving the chamber, thus avoiding the vote. As the electronic vote was called I listened as the ayes were asked to press the green button, the no's the red button and the abstentions the orange button. I usually enjoyed the elongated ANC shout of 'Greeeen' as the appro-priate button was called. It symbolised solidarity, togetherness. Today it was a cry that marked my isolation, my loneliness. For the first time in my seven and a half years as an ANC representative, I didn't vote with my comrades.

I trudged out of the Chamber and made my way home. I had voted with my conscience, but all I felt was sadness. Sadness that it had come to this; that the ANC had behaved so despicably over the arms deal; that Parliament was being subjugated to the interests of the party. Sadness too that my political career was over.

As I walked up towards Table Mountain my cell phone rang. It was a parliamentary official.

'Mr Feinstein, it's Caspir Handink from Parliament.'

Handink was a deathly pale man, tall and thin. I had often thought he looked like an undertaker in a Norman Rockwell painting when he sat just below the Speaker's chair in his black and white robes.

'We have recorded your vote in today's debate as an abstention,' he continued. 'I just wanted to check that that was in fact how you voted and that there was no error. If it was a mistake we can correct it.'

A small chink of light. I still had a final opportunity to change my mind.

'No, there was no error,' I replied.

*

The next morning I received a call from one of the whips again.

'We need to talk to you.'

'I will not participate in a process that involves the Chief Whip. He has a conflict of interests.'

The phone went dead. An announcement was made by the Chief Whip's Office later that day that the matter of my disciplining had been handed over to Luthuli House, ANC National Head Office.

I arranged to go up to Johannesburg to see the organisation's Secretary-General, Kgalema Motlanthe. I didn't know Kgalema well. What I knew of him – his long history in the trade union movement, his dignified demeanour and his supposed disagreement with the President's AIDS denialism and autocratic leadership style – led me to respect him. His small white goatee and round spectacles suggested a thoughtful revolutionary, while his soft face exuded compassion.

He was understanding as I explained why I had taken the positions I had, how I was initially supported by the Deputy President and why I refused to cooperate with any enquiry involving the Chief Whip. He spoke about the complexities of the organisation's 'present conjuncture' and asked me to put the key issues I'd mentioned in writing, which I subsequently did. We agreed my position was untenable and that the best solution was for me to resign before the start of the next parliamentary session. As I left he hugged me and thanked me for coming to see him.

I walked through the ramshackle reception of Luthuli House, conscious that I would probably never return. Outside, the frenetic, chaotic bustle of downtown Johannesburg mirrored my emotions.

I was immensely proud to have been a part of the ANC during a crucial phase in the building of democracy in South Africa. I was devastated that my role had come to an end.

*

The following weeks before my formal resignation were spent trying to map out another life without the issues and organisation that had consumed me so totally since my late teens.

During this time I had an obligation to undertake an investment promotion trip for a couple of investment banks in the UK, something I had done regularly during my time as an MP. While in the UK I started exploring job opportunities. On my return, as I was walking through the arrivals area at Cape Town International airport, a large, ebullient man whom I didn't recognise took my hand and started shaking it vigorously: 'Comrade Feinstein, thank you for what you have done. Please don't desert us. We need more people like you in the movement, not less. Please don't go.' I felt tears welling in my eyes, thanked him and walked quickly through the concourse, riven with guilt and regret.

Over the following weeks I thought about how I could have been politically shrewder, built more of a support base within the ANC. Realistically, I had neither the necessary political skills nor the standing within the organisation to do so. Also I lacked the courage. A braver person would have endured the cold shouldering by many colleagues, would have embraced the conflict with the powers that dominate the party. I was emotionally exhausted and unused to being disliked and vilified by people I respected. Having initially enjoyed the media focus on the arms deal issue, I now longed for anonymity and a quieter life.

As agreed with the ANC Secretary-General, I began to prepare a statement of resignation which would take effect from the end of August. Towards the end of the month Vincent Smith began to leak my resignation and his imminent rise to head the ANC component of the committee. It was time to bring my political career to a formal end.

On 23 August I faxed a brief statement to the media. It read, in part:

It is with sadness that I intend to resign from Parliament with effect from the end of August 2001. I have realised over the past few months that I can no longer play a meaningful role in

Parliament under the present political strictures. I have been saddened by the manner in which government and the ANC in Parliament have handled the controversial armaments deal and the subsequent investigation thereof.

The manner in which this issue has been handled has, and will continue to, detract from many of the excellent things the ANC government has undertaken: from national reconciliation to sound economic management to delivery on key social needs.

In leaving I would like to thank my colleagues who, with a few exceptions, have provided comradeship and friendship over the past seven and a half years. An especial thanks to those, both inside and outside the ANC, who have been supportive during the past difficult year.

On 30 August, my last day as an MP, I faxed a final official letter to the one person I felt it most important to thank:

Dear Comrade Mandela
It is with sadness that I have decided to resign as a Member of Parliament.

The main reason for my resignation is the manner in which government has handled the arms deal and the investigation into it. It has become impossible for me to engage in Parliament on the matter without either raising the ire of the leadership or compromising my own integrity. I further believe that the way Parliament has been marginalised on this and other issues has potentially harmful consequences for our democracy.

I will, however, remain a member of the ANC. I will continue to be loyal to the principles of the organisation but will not hesitate to criticise when appropriate.

I write to thank you for the extraordinary opportunity that I have had of playing a very small role in the first seven and a half years of our democracy. It has been a privilege and an honour to serve you, the organisation and, thus, the people of South Africa. For this I will be eternally grateful.
Yours sincerely
Andrew Feinstein MP

CHAPTER 14

Hard-wired for Corruption

Simple maths tells us that arms is indeed the most corrupt of all legal trades. [It] is hard-wired for corruption.

Joe Roeber, Transparency International

On the evening of 21 October 2001 the SABC evening news announced that Tony Yengeni would be charged in relation to the inappropriate receipt of a luxury 4x4 Mercedes from one of the bidders in the arms deal at a massive discount. Immediately after this explosive item the news broke for adverts. The first ad showed the self-same luxury Mercedes disappearing gradually into a muddy swamp, accompanied by the 'glug, glug, glug' of the occupant as it descended. The car was soon to be known as a 'Yengeni'. This was either the most extraordinary piece of media buying in the history of advertising or one of those mischievous coincidences that seem to occur in this beguiling land.

When the allegations were first published, Yengeni took a full-page ad in a Sunday paper accusing his detractors of engaging in a 'racist witch hunt'.[1] However, his numerous appeals against his conviction only served to reinforce his guilt. Ultimately he was found guilty of making a fraudulent submission to Parliament in respect of this gift. Thinking he had done a deal with the prosecutors, he was shocked when given a custodial sentence, though it was only in late 2006 that he actually went to prison.

Before serving what was only four months of a four-year term Yengeni was delivered to prison by a cavalcade of cheering ANC luminaries, including the Speaker of the Parliament he had lied to. A similar reception greeted him on his release. The Chief Whip who had gone to great lengths to stop the arms deal investigation was a convicted fraudster and a feted hero.

When the matter had come before Parliament's Ethics Committee the ANC had opposed the Registrar of Members Interests' recommendation to investigate a breach of the Code of Conduct. Instead they argued that Parliament should wait until the JIT reported and that if anything was proven against Yengeni, only then should the Legislature consider action. They used the ANC majority to vote this unpopular approach through. With the investigation neutered, this was clever politics but displayed a shameful morality on the part of the members concerned. Like much else, the broader Yengeni allegations – including that he received a million rand from one of the bidders – were never meaningfully addressed by the investigators.

By preventing Parliament investigating whether one of its most senior officials had breached its Code of Conduct, the ANC was in effect stating that the interests of the powerful in the party came before the integrity of the legislative arm of government. This meant that another parliamentary committee was reduced to being a party political battleground of the ANC vs the rest, even though the Ethics Committee's founder chairperson, Prof Kader Asmal, felt strongly that its members should not sit primarily as party representatives but as representatives of the whole Parliament,

Yengeni has been the most ironic 'victim' of the arms deal, but certainly not the only one. In relation only to the gift of luxury cars, on 2 July 2001 *The Star* newspaper published a list of 33 prominent South Africans, a number of them linked to the arms deal, who had received special deals on such cars from EADS, a subsidiary of Daimler Chrysler which had an interest in the deal. They included the Chief of the Defence Force, senior personnel in the state-owned arms company Denel and a member of Jayendra Naidoo's negotiating team, Vanan Pillay.[2] The senior manager involved in the discounted sale of the cars was eventually forced to admit embezzlement in Germany and pay a fine of DM 15000. To add further fuel to the arms deal fire, the *Mail & Guardian* reported later in the same month that Denel had partly funded the construction of Joe Modise's six-bedroom luxury mansion.[3]

After he left Parliament in June 1999, Modise became chairman of Conlog Holdings, a company which had benefited from the arms deal. His multi-million rands worth of shares in the company had allegedly been purchased on his behalf by one of the successful contractors.[4] A subsidiary of BKS, another company of which Modise became chairman, was contracted to work on the Coega industrial development zone, which was strongly tied to the R4.5 billion submarine purchase. This led Colm Allen, Executive Director of the Eastern Cape-based Public Service Accountability Monitor, to comment: 'For Modise to benefit financially as a businessman from decisions that he made whilst he was a Cabinet minister is an astounding conflict of interests. You don't need a degree in ethics to recognise that.'[5]

On 15 June 2001, while my life was being turned upside down by our efforts to ensure an open and unfettered investigation into allegations of high-level corruption, the Deputy President (JZ) was, without a hint of irony, launching a National Anti-corruption Forum in Cape Town. The arms deal wasn't mentioned.

*

After my departure from Parliament Gavin tried courageously to salvage what he could of the investigation. The odds were stacked against him. The ANC component of the Committee had prevented any further consideration of the arms deal. The Auditor-General advised Gavin that his report would be ready in mid-September, but nothing was forthcoming for a further two months. The AG denied that the report was delayed because the Executive were making changes to it.

Parliament eventually received the report from the JIT on 15 November. Gavin and I were hardly surprised that it was a major disappointment. It was contradictory and avoided the key issues but nevertheless exonerated the Executive of any wrongdoing despite stating that most of the key allegations around corruption were still under investigation. The report 'regretted Joe Modise's behaviour' but exonerated him of the allegation that he 'paid for shares in Conlog with a bribe received from a successful prime contractor.'[6] No mention was made of any broader allegations against him.

The report revealed, as we had stated repeatedly, that Chippy Shaik had a massive conflict of interest and didn't recuse himself from relevant meetings. So he had lied to Parliament. At the Scopa public hearing he had been asked specifically whether he had physically left the meeting rooms whenever issues relating to his brother's company were discussed. He replied emphatically that he had. So much for Alec Erwin's contention that Cabinet took measures to ensure this conflict was addressed.

Still in South Africa at the time, I wrote an open letter to Speaker Ginwala suggesting that to protect Parliament's integrity Shaik's misleading of the Committee should be investigated. I never received a reply. No action was ever taken.

With respect to the procurement process, the report found around 50 instances of non-compliance, suggesting that 'proper evaluation procedures were not consistently and diligently applied and a proper audit trail was not established throughout the procurement process.'[7] In addition, 'the time allocated for each evaluation and execution was insufficient to ensure that it was done properly and efficiently,' and 'various key documents had not been finalised and/ or duly approved before the final contracts were concluded.'[8]

In auditing terms these are very serious failures. In fact, in numerous Auditor-General's reports such findings would lead to the AG expressing an adverse opinion or refusing to express an opinion at all. This would then lead Parliament to refuse to authorise the expenditure and require government to recover the monies spent. This was what occurred in relation to 'Sarafina II', with senior public servants losing their jobs. So why was this, the largest single procurement undertaken since the advent of democracy, and with arguably the highest incidence of non-compliance with accepted practices, treated differently by the AG?

The report, while containing a very weak section on costing and financing, avoided the key questions posed by Scopa of whether Cabinet was upfront with the South African public about the actual costs to the taxpayer of the deal – in other words, the real cost over 12 years, including inflationary and currency-related risks as well as the obvious cost of financing. In addition, the investigators stated that they had not looked at the sub-contracts in any detail. It was in the complex interaction between the main and sub-contracts that Scopa was concerned corruption might have taken place, especially given that Chippy had been involved at every stage of these processes.

Alec Erwin had repeatedly claimed that the government had had nothing to do with these sub-contracts but we saw letters in which the

Department of Defence and Armscor instructed prime contractors which sub-contractors to use. The AG decided this didn't warrant meaningful scrutiny, even though in his initial report he had high-lighted it as an area requiring further investigation.

The report was primarily the work of the AG's Office, with a few pages from the Public Protector and Bulelani Ngcuka's office. I was told by a reliable source that the investigators' contribution to the report included a far stronger section on Modise's involvement and recommended that the role of the ANC in corruption related to the deal be investigated. Unsurprisingly this draft never saw the light of day, and was replaced in total by a section written by someone only peripherally involved in the investigation.

In essence, the report asked as many questions as it answered. It was going to be up to Parliament now to ask the hard questions and demand answers. However, when Gavin attempted to arrange for the JIT to discuss its report with Scopa, the ANC and the Speaker rejected his request. Instead the Executive engineered a PR event in Par-liament where it stressed the report had exonerated any wrongdoing by government or ministers.

A two-day hearing was set up between the JIT and six of Parliament's committees. Four of these committees knew little about the investigation or the deal but served to ensure that tough ques-tions by Gavin and others were kept to a minimum and marginalised. Soon after the session began, Gavin decided to end his participation in what he described as a 'shameful charade'. Any tough questions about the report were simply avoided by the JIT.

When Scopa next met, the ANC produced and voted through a pre-written report as Scopa's final arms deal report, expressing total satisfaction with the quality of the JIT investigation and report and explicitly ruling out any further investigation. All other parties voted against the ANC report.

All the committees reported back to Parliament in December 2001, reiterating that the ANC's Scopa report was representative of the findings and reports of the other committees as well. As far as the ANC and government were concerned, the matter was at an end. There was no further report by the JIT, despite its having stat-ed that many of the corruption allegations had not been fully investigated.

Observing this from a distance, I felt sickened by the whole charade. For over a year now I had witnessed an offensive and deceitful, albeit well-executed, instance of 'power repeating untruths until they have the force of truth,' in the words of Edward Said.[9]

My biliousness was intensified when the *Mail & Guardian*, through the efforts of Richard Young, revealed that the President and the Ministers of Defence, Finance and Trade and Industry had received the report prior to its submission to Parliament. The AG had not mentioned this to Parliament.[10] The same newspaper had already revealed that the AG had shown a copy of his final draft report to Chippy Shaik before submitting it to Parliament, and that Shaik had meaningfully changed a part of the report that referred directly to his brother's interests.[11] Gavin had sight of a letter from Chippy to the AG insisting on the removal of a paragraph on conflicts of interest that referred to him. This was yet another indication of the power and authority that Chippy wielded over the process and its cover-up. While it was accepted practice for the Auditor-General to show a copy of his departmental reports to the relevant Minister just before submitting them to Parliament, it was highly unusual for the Auditor-General to change the content of a report substantively at the Minister's request, let alone at the request of significant players in the matter under investigation.

The extent to which the Auditor-General and the other investigators had kowtowed to the Executive became apparent through Fakie's behaviour. He was found by the High Court to be in contempt of court and threatened with a jail term before he would make the original draft reports available. It was soon clear why: the original draft report contained handwritten instructions indicating what was to be removed, amended or added. It was widely alleged that the instructions were written by the AG himself in meetings with the Executive. Without fail these instructions were followed in the final report, starting with the new first sentence, which completely exonerated the Executive from any wrongdoing. The most significant change concerned Joe Modise, where the entire meaning of a section of the report was fundamentally changed after the 'intervention' of the Executive.

These changes were so blatant they deserve quoting at length:

Original wording:

5.13 CONCLUSION

According to documentation the Minister could have influenced decisions made by certain role-players during the process to select BAe/SAAB as the preferred bidder for the Gripen and Hawk aircraft. Furthermore, during the investigation it became apparent that preference was given to BAe/SAAB by making changes to value systems midway through the process. This caused the Hawk aircraft to be ranked first, followed by the MB339FD (the Aeromacchi jet). The MB339FD could have been acquired much cheaper whilst also meeting the SAAF LIFT requirements adequately.

1.8 OVERALL CONCLUSION

1.8.1 The findings of the joint investigation support the majority of the key findings by the AG as contained in his Special Review dated 15 September 2000.

1.8.2 There were fundamental flaws in the selection of BAe/SAAB as the preferred bidder for the LIFT & ALFA programme.'

Adjusted wording after Executive intervention and as presented to Parliament:

14.1 KEY FINDINGS

14.1.1 No evidence was found of any improper or unlawful conduct by the Government. The irregularities and improprieties referred to in the findings as contained in this report, point to the conduct of certain officials of the government departments involved and cannot, in our view, be ascribed to the President or the Ministers involved in their capacity as members of the Ministers' Committee or Cabinet. There are therefore no grounds to suggest that the Government's contracting position is flawed.

14.1.6 The decision that the evaluation criteria in respect of the LIFT had to be expanded to include a non-costed option and which eventually resulted in a different bidder being selected, was taken by the Ministers' Committee, a subcommittee of Cabinet. Although unusual in terms of normal procurement practice, this decision was neither unlawful, nor irregular in terms of the procurement process as it evolved during the SDP acquisition. As the ultimate decision-maker, Cabinet was entitled to select the preferred bidder, taking into account the recommendations of the evaluating bodies as well as other factors, such as strategic considerations.

14.1.7 The decision to recommend the Hawk/Gripen combination to Cabinet as the preferred selection for the LIFT/ALFA was taken by the Ministers' Committee for strategic reasons, including the total benefit to the country in terms of counter trade investment and the operational capabilities of the SANDF.[12]

The unexpurgated version of the report thus revealed the full extent of the manipulation undertaken in order to award BAe the contract. The Hawk had been left off an initial shortlist in 1997 because of its cost and its failure to meet the operational requirements of the South African Air Force (SAAF). However, after the UK's Defence Export Services Organisation (Deso) met with Modise, a small team of officials was created to interact with Deso. One of the team's members, DW Esterhuyse, Armscor's general manager for acquisitions, was 'concerned about the actions of Deso and British companies regarding South African politicians and Parliamentarians'.[13]

So strong was the SAAF's opposition to the Hawk that the Chief of the force wrote that they would only accept it if 'politically obliged' to do so.[14] The Secretary of Defence, Pierre Steyn, in his evidence to the investigators, had stated that the selection of the Hawk/Gripen had been 'turned arse about face' – the SAAF's requirements had to be tailored to suit the decision-maker's choice. Steyn said that: 'the choice for the Hawk was clear from the start'.[15] Despite Steyn's objections, Modise insisted that the Armaments Acquisition Council send both the costed and non-costed options to the Cabinet sub-committee stating: 'We must not prejudge – let the politicians decide'.[16]

The politicians decided in favour of the Hawk/Gripen at an informal meeting attended by Mbeki, Chippy, Modise, Erwin and a few others in Durban. Steyn and Esterhuyse, who were also in attendance, were furious, as the relative merits of the Hawk and Aeromacchi were not even discussed at the meeting. Later the Hawk/Gripen was presented to Cabinet as the sole recommendation. Steyn resigned over the matter. Esterhuyse wanted to launch a full-scale enquiry, but left Armscor shortly afterwards.[17] No wonder the Executive wanted the AG's report edited.

The Auditor-General, for his part, issued a rejoinder in June 2003. It served only to repeat the President's laughable contention that elements who had criticised the report were the same people trying to use the arms deal to overthrow the government. So Shauket Fakie too had become a conspiracy theorist in order to cover up his capitulation to those in power, whom he was constitutionally bound to hold to account.

After Parliament's pitiful handling of the report Gavin wrote a conciliatory letter to all members of Scopa suggesting a new beginning for the committee. Vincent Smith rejected it out of hand. It was clear that the ANC wanted his head. In February 2002 Gavin completed his critique of the JIT report and resigned as chair of Scopa. The year and a half of intense pressure and vilification by the ANC had taken its toll on his health and his personal life. When I saw him just after his resignation he seemed a broken man.

Despite the fact that our political paths and philosophies differed, Gavin Woods is undoubtedly one of the heroes of the democratic South Africa: he fought with every bone in his weakening body to get to the truth. Not to destroy the democratically elected government but to ensure the state served its people by spending their money prudently and honestly.

It was with great relief that I saw Gavin again a few years later, after he had left the IFP, having been described by Chief Buthelezi, in recrimination for authoring a document critical of his leadership, as a 'token' member of the party because of his disability. Gavin's health had improved and his personal life was much happier. He was made Professor of Public Finance at the University of Stellenbosch, deserved recognition for the quality of his mind and the courage with which he pursued his laudable convictions.

By comparison the weak-kneed response of Frene Ginwala, Jeremy Cronin, Pallo Jordan and others to the arms deal imbroglio was a source of great consternation to me, not least because I admired and respected each one of them for the courage and commitment they had shown during the struggle and the fortitude with which they had, on occasion, defended Parliament against the Executive. However, when push came to shove they were found wanting and Parliament and South Africa's democracy has been the poorer for it.

*

In late 2001 Simone, Misha and I left South Africa for London. I felt it would be easier to find work outside politics in the UK, and both of us needed distance from the place and events that had made the past year of our lives so stressful. It had not been unusual for me to return home from Parliament towards midnight and find a journalist waiting at our gate – if not invited in for a cup of tea by Simone. Fearing the house was bugged, we had both tired of having to leave our home to have a conversation about what was going on in the investigation or anything of a personal nature that we didn't particularly want others to hear. A burglary in which the only things taken were four boxes containing arms deal documents hardly helped.

But while I had fled the arms deal, the arms deal and its ramifications hadn't released me from its grasping clutches.

In October 2001 the Scorpions, as part of their investigation into Chippy's brother, Schabir Shaik, carried out simultaneous raids on companies in France, Mauritius and Durban. During the raids they discovered, among other documents, Cabinet minutes relating to the arms deal. On 16 November 2001, Schabir was arrested. A few months later I received a phone call from Billy Downer of the National Prosecuting Authority, asking if he could meet with me on an upcoming trip to London.

I had never been inside the imposing South Africa House on Trafalgar Square. Like many, I knew only its grand façade, observed from the outside while demonstrating against apartheid. Pictures of Mandela and Mbeki peer down as you enter the reception area. Madiba's gaze enveloped me with a feeling of warmth, of having stepped inside my 'home'. The other left me cold, excluded, as though I didn't belong here.

Billy came to meet me. An energetic man, bespectacled and wearing a greying 1970s moustache, he exuded the camaraderie of an old friend. He showed me into a small meeting room where I was introduced to his two colleagues, Isak du Plooy and Advocate Johan van Rooyen. Billy informed me that they had all been involved in the arms deal investigation. I then gave them a run-down of my involvement and particularly my interaction with Jacob Zuma. They transcribed the conversation and gave it to me to edit and sign. They planned to use it in Schabir Shaik's forthcoming trial.

My admiration for Billy and his team grew over the following months as I observed the Shaik trial from a distance. They were thorough in setting out how Shaik had used his relationship with and financial support for Jacob Zuma to benefit himself and his companies. Shaik's legendary ego was to prove fatal as he insisted on answering questions at excessive length with himself at the centre of every story, slowly embroiling himself deeper and deeper into the mire. The image of that luxury 4x4 disappearing into a swamp recurred regularly as I read through the court transcripts.

A key aspect of the case was the relationship between Shaik, Zuma and Thomson-CSF, who were bidding to provide the communications suite for the ships. The chronology of events accepted by the court was that Shaik had met with Thomsons on 3 March 2000 to confirm a deal that involved an annual payment of R500 000 to Jacob Zuma. In return, Zuma would assist their efforts in relation to the deal and, crucially from my perspective, protect them from any investigation into the transaction. For many months after this meeting nothing further had been heard from Thomsons, despite a number of pleas from Shaik to honour the deal. During these months construction had started on a new home for Zuma in KwaZulu-Natal. Between 31 October and 4 December the builder became more and more demanding on the need for payment. On 8 December (the day Gavin Woods called for a proclamation for Judge Heath to be included in the investigation), a signed service agreement was sent by Shaik to Thomsons. The company signed the agreement and returned it to Shaik on 1 January 2001. The first instalment was paid on 9 February 2001.

While initially I had thought that Zuma supported Scopa and me either out of a commitment to clean governance or in a bid to further undermine a weak Thabo Mbeki, after seeing this chronology I couldn't but wonder whether his motives were more nefarious. Was it pure coincidence that Zuma abandoned Scopa and me just a few days after the service agreement was sent to Thomsons? Did he agree to sign the vituperative letter written by the President to Gavin Woods on 19 January because it showed Thomsons that he was acting on their recently signed agreement?

In my more conspiratorial moments I even thought that perhaps Zuma and Schabir Shaik had used Scopa and me to up the ante on Thomsons, on the assumption that they could put a lid on the investigation once their French friends had paid up.

*

In sentencing Shaik to 15 years in jail for fraud and corruption, the presiding judge described the relationship between Shaik and Deputy President Jacob Zuma as one of 'mutually beneficial symbiosis' and involving 'inappropriate behaviour.'[18] The next day *The Times* reported the stunning verdict thus:

> Judge Hillary Squires said that the businessman had facilitated a 500,000 rands (£41,000) annual bribe from Thomson-CSF, the French arms company, for the Vice-President [sic]. The bribe related to securing for Thomson-CSF a slice of a controversial £5.2 billion [arms] deal ...
>
> Mr. Zuma's part of the deal was, in his role as leader of Parliamentary business, to block any enquiry into the arms deal and to promote the French company's interests in Cabinet. ... Judge Squires said that the Vice-President had blocked a special investigation into the arms deal requested by Gavin Woods, the chairman of the powerful Parliamentary Public Accounts Committee.

219

Andrew Feinstein, an ANC MP, had publicly accused Mr. Zuma and three ANC Cabinet ministers of being corrupt beneficiaries of the arms deal. Mr. Zuma responded by sacking Mr. Feinstein from the Committee. Mr. Feinstein resigned from the committee and went into exile [sic].

Billy was back in London a few days after the court victory. He was understandably euphoric, and told me that the National Prosecuting Authority was about to charge Zuma. He asked whether I would be prepared to give evidence against the Deputy President. After saying goodbye to Billy I wandered from my City office, surprised that I felt a little confused. Did I have a moral obligation to testify? I questioned whether giving evidence against Zuma would be a betrayal of the ANC, the party I had served for almost eight years – and still, in spite of everything, revered? Would it serve President Mbeki's own political agenda of derailing a Zuma succession, thus paving the way for the President to be succeeded by his own appointee, whom he could continue to manipulate from behind the scenes? Did I want to get involved in what was fast becoming a battle between the centre (Mbeki) and left (Zuma) of the party? By not giving evidence, would I be condoning corruption? Could I face reliving a painful time in my life and surrendering the anonymity that London provided? How would it affect my wife and young family? Would I be in any physical danger if I returned to South Africa for the trial?

I walked past St Paul's Cathedral, beyond the bankers' minimalist gates, and stepped on to the Millennium Bridge, excited, apprehensive and confused. I thought of Jacob Zuma, in many ways a brave and courageous man. A pleasant and often friendly man; the man who had initially supported our attempt to investigate the arms deal, but then abandoned us to our political fate. Was he a man who, out of legitimate material need while in exile, had got involved with Schabir Shaik who, in turn, had used and abused Zuma's name for his own nefarious ends? Or was he corrupt?

Pacing the concrete floors of the Tate Modern's Turbine Hall, I tried to unravel the confused currents in my head. As my thoughts became clearer I made my way up to the fifth floor of this iconic building, once a gas plant, now a celebration of modern art. I wandered through the exhibition of social realist Russian revolutionary propaganda. The rigid, stark, simple style somehow encompasses the noble motives of those idealistic days while hinting at the centralising, self-serving authoritarianism that would engulf and destroy any good intentions.

I emerged from the tranquil, thoughtful space into sharp, distinct sunlight. Re-crossing Norman Foster's epoch-marking bridge, it was clear what I had to do. Give evidence. Tell what I know in the hope it might contribute a little to the establishment of the truth. Not just the truth regarding Jacob Zuma's alleged corruption, but also the role of others in the arms deal. My testimony might also highlight the intrigue and deception that so dominates South African politics in the post-Mandela era. Testifying might even provide an opportunity to assert a politics of principle, of integrity, of hope; an opportunity to shed some light from my own experience inside the ANC on our unfinished house, the democratic South Africa that is still being forged.

Hopefully the trial might also provide a massive boost to the cause of fighting corruption in South Africa and beyond, highlighting the role not only of the corrupted but also of the corrupters, in this case the international arms industry.

*

A few days after my meeting with Billy, President Thabo Mbeki fired Jacob Zuma as the country's Deputy President. While the President had refused to allow Zuma to be charged with Shaik, supposedly fearing a political backlash, he now had no choice. A week later Billy announced that Zuma would be charged under the Corruption Act. After a brief court appearance, he was released on bail to face trial in July 2006.

The firing and charging of Jacob Zuma unleashed a veritable apocalypse in the ANC. The organisation, always determined not to allow its internal divisions and disputes to seep into the public domain, now engaged in unbridled internecine warfare. The party was divided in a way it had not been since the breakaway of Robert Sobukwe to form the Pan-Africanist Congress over 40 years previously. The chasm separated those who support Zuma, those who support Mbeki and those who are desperately unhappy with both and lament what has become of this once proud organisation. They reject Mbeki's autocratic leadership style, his tragic obfuscation over HIV and AIDS, his lack of courage on Zimbabwe, and in the case of a small minority, his efforts to cover up the arms deal. They fear that Zuma may be at worst corrupt and at best injudicious. The fight for power has seen the organisation and its allies descend into factions, driven not by lofty ideals but by issues of personality, power and patronage.

A hand-grenade was lobbed into this already incendiary battle when in early 2006 Zuma was charged with the rape of an HIV-positive family friend. The Zuma camp alleged that these were trumped-up charges inspired by allies of the President in an attempt to derail Zuma's succession aspirations. This theory was lent some credence when it became apparent that the same victim had accused five other men in the ANC of rape and that she was whisked out of the country to a new home and identity as soon as the trial concluded.

However, regardless of the complainant's history, the behaviour of Zuma and his supporters during the trial was despicable. In his evidence, Zuma spoke of his confidence that despite having unpro-tected sex he would not contract AIDS, as he had showered vigor-ously afterwards. This from the man who was chairperson of South Africa's National AIDS Council before his removal from office! Every day Zuma's supporters gathered outside the court to vilify his accuser, screaming abuse and burning effigies of the young woman. Our new democracy, with its shining, progressive constitution, had reached perhaps its lowest ebb with respect to gender and human rights issues.

On 8 May 2006 Judge Willem van der Merwe found Zuma not guilty in what has been described as the most controversial court case since the end of apartheid. His supporters immediately intensified their cries of a stitch-up, and Mbeki's allies were put on the political defensive.

The high drama and tension intensified as Zuma's corruption trial drew near. Various intelligence agencies seemed involved in a war of the spooks, some in support of Zuma, the ANC's former head of intelligence, and others on the side of Mbeki. The Head of the National Intelligence Agency was fired for allegedly concocting a plot of hoax e-mails to give credence to the view of a calculated campaign by ANC leaders to undermine Zuma's presidential challenge.

In the lead-up to the trial, stories began to appear in the media about Thabo Mbeki's involvement in the arms deal. Allegations surfaced that he had met with Thomson-CSF on at least one, possibly more, occasions. His office could find no record of any meeting and the President stated that if one had taken place, it was not significant enough for him to recall. In fact, Mbeki met with the company's three most senior executives in Paris on 17 December 1998. It appears both from court documents and from a source close to South Africa's ambassador to France at the time that this was Mbeki's third meeting with Thomsons. At the December meeting Mbeki was asked about the *bone fides* of Schabir Shaik, with whom Thomsons were about to go into partnership. Mbeki supposedly gave Shaik the thumbs down, but the deal went ahead.

From the Shaik trial records it appears that Futuristic Business Solutions (FBS) was the alternative to Schabir that was, at least implicitly, approved by Mbeki. Two members of Joe Modise's extended family were directors of the company. A key figure in FBS was Ian Pierce, a business associate of Schabir Shaik's. He is a shadowy figure who crops up constantly in relation to the deal: one source described him as 'the moneybag man', but the investigators, much to their frustration, have never been able to pin anything on him.

Even more damning was news from Germany that prosecutors in Düsseldorf had begun an investigation into $25 million of bribes allegedly paid to South African politicians by ThyssenKrupp, a company that was part of the German Frigate Consortium. Around the same time, Zuma announced that he had not been the author of the scurrilous letter to Gavin Woods on 19 January 2001. The President's office was forced to admit that Mbeki had in fact written the letter, which Zuma had then signed.[19]

As all this information was being aired in the media, Zuma's defence team announced that they would, in all likelihood, have to call the President as a witness, as 'he is the only one who would know whether the arms deal was corrupt or not'.[20] I took this to be a veiled threat that if Zuma was tried he would spill the beans on far broader and more substantial ANC benefit from the arms deal.

The stage was set for the ultimate political showdown, fought out over the very issues that I had suggested to the ANC five years previously would come back to haunt the organisation if we didn't deal with them openly when they first came to light. However, before the trial had heard any evidence, the prosecution surprisingly announced that they required additional time to prepare their case ... after over five years of investigation. The judge expressed concern that Schabir Shaik's appeal was due to be heard in September, and appeals on the admissibility of evidence acquired in searches in early 2007 were ongoing. A key issue in the Shaik appeal would centre on the admissibility of encrypted communication between Thomsons and Shaik that outlined the arrangement they had agreed. Judge Msimang struck the case from the court roll, stating that the prosecution could recharge Zuma once they had their case better prepared.

Zuma immediately proclaimed himself an innocent man and praised the South African justice system, which a few weeks previously he had accused of being part of a witch-hunt against him. Portraying himself as an innocent man unjustly targeted in an attempt to derail his presidential ambitions, he toured the country showing a video about the life and persecution of Jacob Zuma. Antagonism towards the President seemed to be growing, while Zuma's fortunes looked to be in the ascendant. However, he soon displayed his tendency towards the injudicious again when he was quoted as saying that, when growing up in traditional rural KwaZulu-Natal, if he had been confronted by a homosexual he would have struck him to the ground. His allies in the trade union movement and Communist Party were not delighted, but continued their support for him.

Six weeks later, in September 2006, Schabir Shaik's appeal was rejected. Forty-eight hours later he began serving a 15-year jail sentence, cutting a sorry figure as he made the slow walk from a life of luxury to the rather more basic surroundings of his prison cell. At least he had a warm message of thanks and friendship from Jacob Zuma ringing in his ears.

The panel of judges had dealt Zuma a double blow. Not only had they confirmed the guilt of his closest financial supporter, but in their judgement they reiterated the clear admissibility of the encrypted communication. In early 2007 the prosecutors won a court decision enabling them to proceed with a request for additional encrypted communications from the Mauritian authorities.

Indications are that Jacob Zuma will be recharged under the Corruption Act in late 2007 or early 2008. This could create the extraordinary situation where, at the ANC's triennial Congress in December 2007, Zuma may be elected ANC President to succeed Thabo Mbeki while still facing charges of corruption. A sad prospect for the party of Luthuli, Tambo and Mandela.

*

Within days of Schabir Shaik beginning his lengthy jail sentence, the UK's Serious Fraud Office (SFO) was reopening its investigation into BAe's involvement in the South African arms deal. I had met with the SFO in 2002, but they seemed only peripherally interested in the South African deal. However, after Tony Blair shamelessly closed down the SFO's eight-year investigation into the notorious Al Yamamah arms deal with Saudi Arabia, just as the SFO was poised to lay charges against the BAe top brass, they refocused attention on the South African deal.

So in late 2006 they were again in touch. Through their on-going interrogation of the Saudi deal they had uncovered a *modus operandi* of slush funds, agents, offshore companies and bribes that they believed could have been replicated in the South African deal. A notorious Zimbabwean, Johan Bredenkamp (a former ally and financial backer of Robert Mugabe, well known in South Africa's murkier circles) was raided in relation to their enquiries. A small company, Osprey Aviation, whose owner and Bredenkamp associate Richard Charter died while river rafting in 2005, is also known to have been involved in the deal as BAe's South African agent.

The SFO investigation has already unearthed a web of companies which were allegedly utilised to pay bribes totalling £75 million in relation to the South African deal. This includes £3 million allegedly paid to Joe Modise's political advisor at the time, Fana Hlongwane. Richard Charter is alleged to have received almost £25 million through an obscure entity in the British Virgin Islands, in addition to almost £2 million he received through Osprey Aviation for rendering services that remain unclear. Another Bredenkamp associate, Jules Pelissier, was supposed to have pocketed £34 million.[21]

A source close to the investigation suggested they were also looking into allegations that Chippy Shaik solicited a bribe from BAe and that Joe Modise might have been a recipient of the company's largesse. This latter allegation would confirm the evidence of the paper trail that Gavin and I had been shown years before in Pretoria. The source also suggested that the investigation was looking into whether the ANC received substantial donations from BAe after they were awarded the LIFT contract in dubious circumstances.

An investigation into the BAe/SAAB deal has also been launched in Sweden, home to SAAB. A documentary flighted on Swedish television in mid-2007 has revealed allegations of corruption in arms deals between BAe/SAAB and the Czech Republic and Hungary. The programme suggested that similar inappropriate channels were used by SAAB in the South African deal.

A German journalist close to prosecutors in Düsseldorf revealed that Chippy Shaik had solicited $3 million from ThyssenKrupp, the leading member of the German Frigate Consortium (GFC).[22] Remarkably, the German company had kept minutes of the meeting with Chippy at which he requested the bribe. This money was then allegedly paid to a company controlled by the FBS CEO, Ian Pierce. Records of the payment of the $3 million were obtained by the journalist, who stated further that there was 'strong evidence' suggesting Chippy had received the money. A South African investigator told me that they were aware of where the funds were held and that they had remained largely untouched, probably 'for fear of alerting the authorities'.

If, as has been suggested, FBS was the 'approved channel', the question arises whether Chippy was soliciting money for himself alone or other entities as well.

The case of the German component of the arms deal is an intriguing one. With respect to the frigates, the navy had agreed that the ships should be built by a Spanish company, Bazan. However, after Deputy President Thabo Mbeki made a visit to Germany the tender was reopened. Soon after Thabo's return, Mo Shaik (with no diplomatic expertise whatsoever) was appointed South Africa's consul-general in Hamburg, the headquarters of the German Frigate Consortium. A few months later it was announced that the contract had been awarded to the GFC. Our consulate in Hamburg was closed down and Mo moved on to become South Africa's ambassador to Algeria.

When in March 2007 the information of Chippy's receipt of $3 million was made available to the South African authorities, newspapers reported that Chippy had fled the country and was in hiding.[23]

When questioned about the allegations, Mo replied that the German rumours were old news and had all been heard before. They were not. This was the first time that documented evidence linked Chippy to the soliciting of a bribe from one of the bidders who was awarded a contract in highly dubious circumstances. And lest we forget, Chippy's jailed brother Schabir benefited from sub-contracts linked to the GFC deal.

So it appears, as Gavin and I had suspected all along, that the man who was at the fulcrum of the deal, including as Secretary to the Cabinet committee making the final decisions, and an influential and aggressive proponent of his brother's interests in various other committees, benefited inappropriately from his interaction with one of the successful bidders. And he used the complex interaction between the main and sub-contracts to benefit his family.

A source close to the German investigation has told me that prosecutors are confident of linking additional millions directly to Joe Modise and a portion of the balance to the ANC for party purposes 'through a senior ANC politician via Liberia'. In addition, it is possible that the German prosecutors are investigating another German company which is alleged to have paid $15 million in bribes in relation to the submarine contract. This accords with the Fincantiere account that I had heard years before.

The German authorities have submitted requests for assistance to their South African counterparts, as well as UK and Swiss investigators. As at mid-2007, the South African authorities have appeared unwilling to take any action against Chippy, who announced on 27 May 2007 that he was emigrating to Australia.[24]

*

The prosecutions of Tony Yengeni and Schabir Shaik and the clearly unethical behaviour of Joe Modise undeniably indicate that there was corruption in the South African arms deal.

This sad truth is reinforced by Shaik's admission in court that Floryn Investments was established to benefit the ANC. Despite denials from the ANC, the forensic auditor investigating Shaik's finances, Johan van der Walt, said it was probable that money was paid to the ANC and not reflected in the books of Nkobi. The court accepted that Floryn was a beneficiary of Shaik's Nkobi Holdings, which, in turn, benefited from Shaik's involvement in the arms deal. Two slides from the prosecution's presentation show the interrelationship of the various businesses.

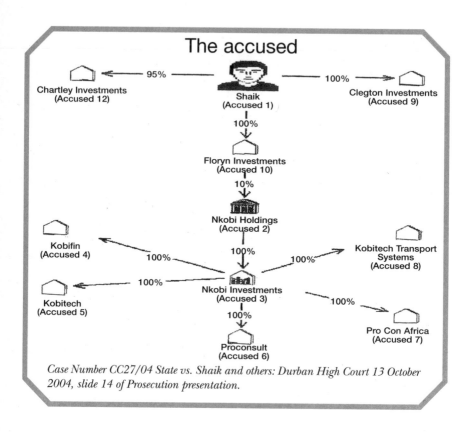

Case Number CC27/04 State vs. Shaik and others: Durban High Court 13 October 2004, slide 14 of Prosecution presentation.

If even a small fraction of the allegations emerging from the investigations in Germany and the United Kingdom are correct, the corruption in the South African arms deal will be seen to have been direct and extensive.

*

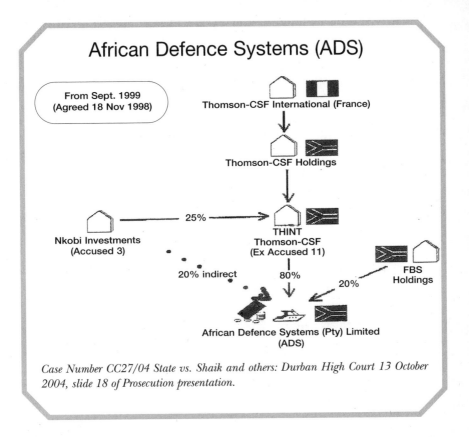

African Defence Systems (ADS)

Case Number CC27/04 State vs. Shaik and others: Durban High Court 13 October 2004, slide 18 of Prosecution presentation.

The ANC went to such extreme lengths to prevent an unfettered investigation into the deal because they needed to conceal corruption involving the head of procurement in the Defence Force at the time of the deal, at least two senior ANC leaders and probably the party itself. In addition, Mbeki would have been deeply embarrassed if it became public knowledge how negligent he and his Cabinet colleagues had been and how weak the processes governing this massive procurement were, at exactly the time that he was setting out his stall as the country's first post-Mandela leader.

To this end, besides the intimidation and pressure exerted on Gavin Woods and me, the duress brought to bear on the investigators themselves was intense. The composite picture from my varied sources was of valiant attempts to conduct a meaningful enquiry amidst enormous political interference and even intimidation. As one investigator put it to me, 'the hand of the Presidency over the investigation was palpable.'

The investigators were regularly instructed as to what could and could not be scrutinised. Director of Public Prosecutions Bulelani Ngcuka, a former Parliamentary colleague of mine, would make decisions on the basis of the political consequences. For instance, the charge sheet for the arrest of Schabir Shaik was drawn up to charge both Shaik and Jacob Zuma. When presented to Bulelani he responded: 'I will only charge the Deputy President if my President agrees.'[25] As a consequence Zuma was not charged in spite of the fact that the indictment eventually used to charge Shaik mentioned Zuma almost as often as it did the accused. It was also made clear to the investigators that a shadowy financier close to Mbeki and Zuma who had played an on-going role in financing the ANC was off limits.

The decision to have a public phase of the investigation, hotly contested by all the investigators I have spoken to over the years, was required because 'we need something for the public,' according to Ngcuka. It took what soon became a demoralised team three times as long to get anything done because of all the different levels of hierarchy that checked out what they were doing. Some of them felt personally intimidated, experiencing break-ins at their homes. New people were brought into established teams, with the incumbents fearing some of the new arrivals were intelligence operatives placed there to watch over the investigators rather than contribute to the team effort.

There was constant interference in the Tony Yengeni matter, which was clearly identified as the one minor prosecution that would satisfy the public in the hope that the whole issue would then die down. To their credit, the prosecutors presented evidence that pointed unequivocally to a jail sentence in spite of being instructed to avoid asking for imprisonment, as 'Yengeni's punishment must be such that he is able to make a return to politics'.

Guidance on Modise was contradictory but a fairly detailed investigation did take place. Progress had been made on his role in the BAe deal. Even payment schedules were in the hands of the investigators. Pierre Steyn, the Secretary of the Defence Force at the time, recently admitted that he resigned in 1998 over the deal specifically because he felt Minister Modise had made up his mind before the

bidding had even started and his acolytes had intervened to ensure his preferred outcome. He also felt coerced by Modise into
appointing Chippy and others to their strategic positions.[26] In addition, another very senior Defence Force leader at the time claimed
he had flight records showing Chippy Shaik and Joe Modise flying to
London to meet with the Chairman of BAe clandestinely. When the
investigator's report on Modise was brought to Ngcuka's attention,
he responded: 'Let's not bother with that, now that he's dead.'

Most importantly, a report submitted by the investigators to their
bosses recommended that corruption involving the ANC as an
organisation be investigated. This was driven by myriad factors
including the broader party links to Schabir Shaik and a trip that the
party's Treasurer-General, Mendi Msimang, made to Switzerland to
meet with successful bidders.[27] This recommendation never saw the
light of day.

So, while there appears to be no on-going South African investigation into the arms deal despite the fact that half a dozen partly
investigated matters sit in the files of Scorpions supremo Leonard
McCarthy, a number of portentous questions remain. These include
the extent to which Joe Modise, in addition to his role in Conlog,
benefited from the deal, whether Chippy Shaik solicited bribes
from anyone else besides ThyssenKrupp, what benefit the ANC
received from any of the successful bidders and, crucial to the
integrity of the ANC and government, who knew of this support and
in what ways it affected the judgement of the decision makers in the
deal.

To answer these questions it is crucial that South African investigators provide assistance to their international colleagues as well
as pursuing Chippy and other transgressors in South African
courts. Otherwise a shadow will continue to hang over the country. The ultimate ignominy in the whole squalid arms deal affair
might well be that it is investigations into the corrupters in their
home countries that finally expose the actions of the corrupted in
South Africa.

*

In December of 2006 my family and I went to visit our friends Barbara Hogan and Ahmed Kathrada at their weekend cottage in Simonstown. Sitting on the stoep overlooking the naval base, Barbara pointed out three gleaming ships, the partial fruits of the GFC component of the arms deal. I wondered whether they had been named Schabir, Mo and Chippy in recognition of the family whose (mis)fortunes are so closely tied to their purchase.

It is hoped that these vessels have been useful to the South African navy,[28] because the real white elephants of the deal, the Hawk/Gripen aircraft, have certainly not. On 9 March 2007 the defence department's Chief Director of Acquisitions, Major-General Otto Schür, told Parliament's Public Accounts Committee that there was no real use for the fighter aircraft because there was no 'conventional threat against South Africa or the sub region'. He said that transport capabilities were of greater importance, reducing the flying time of the fighter planes to a paltry 100 hours per year per aircraft.[29]

The head of the South African Air Force, Lieutenant-General Carlo Gagiano, said something very similar in the department's 2005–06 annual report. 'Extraordinary levels of under-funding' meant it would not be possible to use Hawks and Gripens at their optimum level.[30]

The irony lies in the cause of that under-funding: the payments on the arms deal. The inexplicable decision to buy the Hawks and Gripens at inflated prices over eight years ago, when South Africa faced no conventional threat and none could be discerned for the foreseeable future, was exacerbated by the knowledge that the Air Force still had a number of boxed Cheetah jets which still had 10 years of life in them.

While the military equipment has been of little use, what impact have the much vaunted and then downplayed offsets had on the economy? Even if one takes the most recent, best possible figures presented by the Trade and Industry Department to Parliament in late 2006, the programme will only deliver a quarter of the 12 000 direct jobs promised by Alec Erwin when he justified the deal in 2000. In addition, of the $13.6 billion that the successful bidders were contractually obliged to facilitate in sales and investment in new economic activity in the country, only $2.2 billion in investment credits and $4.5 billion in export and sales credits has been achieved.[31] Cynics would argue that even these credits don't all convert into real economic activity and that a number of the projects included in these figures have failed. The Department admitted to Parliament that up to 5 per cent of the projects had failed and up to 10 per cent were in intensive care. This included a jewellery beneficiation project, a stainless steel plant and an oil and gas rig manufacturing plant,[32] while a carbon manufacturing plant in KwaZulu-Natal was described as 'a rusting monument to failure [which] … now has only a security guard working there.'[33]

Set against the minimum cost of the deal and the most favourable foreign exchange rates possible, the offsets will not even go half way to achieving the economic neutrality that they were eventually downgraded to achieve.

*

While it is sad that South Africa's young democracy should be blighted by the indelible stain of a corrupt arms deal, it is hardly surprising. The arms industry, as Transparency International's Joe Roeber has so compellingly described, 'is hard-wired for corruption'. It is estimated that the industry accounts for between 40 and 50 per cent of all corruption in world trade.[34] While Thabo Mbeki, Alec Erwin, Jacob Zuma and Mosiuoa Lekota might honestly believe otherwise, corruption is built into the way these companies do business. It is in their DNA – which is one reason why, even when they get done down in a particular deal, they never litigate against their 'competitors'. Unsurprising really, given that the arms trade is worth between $30 and $40 billion a year.[35]

The Congress Movement in India, so indomitable a political force, was laid low by the Bofors arms scandal which, 14 years after it was signed, brought down Rajiv Gandhi's government. It has been regularly reported in the media and in recent books that Mark Thatcher was paid £12 million as a middleman in the Al Yamamah arms deal which was signed between Saudi Arabia and the British government, led at the time by Mark's mother.[36]

To put it politely, the South African government was taken for a very expensive ride by the arms industry. All the usual tactics were on display: create inappropriate relationships with those you think might influence a deal, persuade the boys that they need far more toys than they actually do, blind even the clever with economic non-sense about offset benefits, involve your most influential salespeople, especially if they happen to be your Prime Minister, charge more than the goods are worth and smile all the way to the bank as the country realises it paid too much for armaments it doesn't need, with no economic benefit to anyone other than the arms companies.

I had brief first-hand experience of this delightful industry on a couple of occasions. The Campaign Against the Arms Trade (CAAT), a London-based pressure group, bought me a share in BAe Systems to enable me to attend the company's AGM in 2002.

The security at the Queen Elizabeth Conference Centre, a stone's throw from Westminster, was daunting. Everyone was searched, al-though those of us in suit and tie somewhat less thoroughly than the obvious CAAT activists in jeans and T-shirts who had been demon-strating outside the venue. The cavernous hall was dominated by a raised platform on which the board members of BAe sat behind a long table bedecked with flowers and company branding. Among them was one Michael Portillo, a former Tory Defence Secretary and favourite of Mark Thatcher's mother.

Early in the proceedings a group of CAAT activists began to chant at the Board: 'Blood on your hands,' louder and louder. They were forcibly dragged out of the hall by burly, aggressive bouncers. I was a little more difficult to pigeon-hole as I was dressed in conventional City of London attire, a pinstriped suit and bold tie. This enabled me to be acknowledged by the chair to ask my question. I began with a short speech on the South African arms deal and BAe's inexplicable winning of a contract, and asked whether the Board didn't feel it was ever so slightly unethical to provide a R5 million donation at the time the tenders were being considered to a charitable trust of which South Africa's Defence Minister was Life President. Sir Richard Evans, the BAe chairman, responded that he knew nothing about the donation. I suggested he check it out. He promised to get back to me. He never did. But he did assure me that BAe always operates within the laws of the UK and whichever country it is doing business in and conducts itself to the highest ethical standards.

Over a year later, in July 2003, after an exposé in the *Guardian* newspaper, BAe Systems plc admitted to funding the MK Veterans

Association of which Joe Modise was Life President, 'to demonstrate that we wish to be good corporate citizens doing business in SA'.

By 2007, in addition to the new revelations about the South African deal, BAe was being investigated in connection with deals in the Czech Republic, Hungary, Romania, Chile, Tanzania and Qatar. The US Congress has initiated an enquiry into BAe's suitability to purchase an American arms company, citing its questionable ethical practices, and the Swiss authorities are investigating the company in connection with money laundering allegations. In June 2007 the BBC claimed that BAe had made payments in excess of a billion pounds to a high-ranking member of the Saudi royal family in relation to the Al Yamamah deal, and that payments were continuing.

I decided it was time to brave another BAe AGM. The venue was the same, but the chairman had changed. Dick Evans had given way to Dick Olver. I almost expected 'Tricky Dick Nixon' to rise from the dead to join this illustrious line.

I raised a series of questions on the South African deal, specifically about what the £75 million of 'commissions' were used for. I then asked for a clear assurance that not one pence found its way into the hands of any South African government or defence department official, politician or political party. Olver refused to give any such assurance and instead embarked on a smooth, pre-prepared treatise on how the company lives out its commitment to its most important principles: ethics and safety. When I responded that a litany of their actions over years and years made a mockery of any commitment to ethical business practices, the chairman's calm façade collapsed into an aggressive outburst that having asked my question I must allow others an opportunity. Even when many of the shareholders bellowed back at him that he should let me speak, Olver refused to answer my shouted question as to whether they had paid anything to the ANC or Joe Modise.

I left the Queen Victoria Conference Centre disappointed again. Outside the venue, protestors from Papua New Guinea showed photos of suffering caused by BAe's equipment in their country, while others demanded that the British government reopen its investigation into BAe's Saudi deal and allow the SFO to pursue its South African enquiries.

I felt, more than ever before, that far from being the good corporate citizen they claim to be, the *prima facie* evidence from the SFO's scandalously curtailed investigation into the Saudi deal, the SFO's letter of request to the South African authorities in connection with the SA deal, the SFO's investigation into the six other deals, the Swiss authorities' investigation into money laundering allegations, and the US Congress's scrutiny of the company suggest that BAe is a disgraceful corporate citizen, which promotes corruption and wasteful expenditure in countries that can least afford it. The company brings misery, crime and destitution wherever its defence arm operates.

*

A few days before his untimely death in late 2001, Joe Modise was awarded the Order of the Star of South Africa, the highest civilian award in the country. At his funeral oration President Mbeki described Modise as 'a person of loyalty to his principles'. He concluded: 'A mighty tree of our forest has fallen. As it came down to rest, its crashing echoes published the fact. The singular noise in the enveloping silence told the story that had to be told.'[37]

CHAPTER 15
After the Party

At a time when so much is going right in South Africa – thanks to ANC
politics – much of what is going wrong, notably the party's brutal war of
succession and the ever-growing nexus between business and politics,
has its roots in the arms deal.

Editorial, *Mail & Guardian*, 12 January 2007

A few days after my resignation became public knowledge I answered
my cell phone to a deep voice with a heavy Afrikaans accent. 'Andrew,
it's Louis Luyt here.' Luyt, a fertiliser millionaire and for many years
the controversial supremo of South African rugby, had become an
MP after the 1999 election. We had served together on the Finance
and Public Accounts Committees and I had attended a rugby match
at his invitation. 'I am proud of what you have done. Congratulations.
You and me are the only two men in South Africa with any integrity.'

I felt conflicted: it was very thoughtful of him to phone but, at the
same time, somewhat troubling to imagine that I had caused succour
to someone who had compelled President Mandela to appear in
court to explain why he had supported Luyt's dismissal from his position as Head of the South African Rugby Football Union (SARFU),
and who garnered support among conservative whites struggling to
come to terms with the new dispensation.

Personally, I was devastated by having to resign. Being an MP was
something that I loved and felt great pride in. It was the only time in
my life where I had played a role that was both completely satisfying
to my own needs and made a small, hopefully positive difference to
the country I loved. I was turning my back on an organisation that I
had admired, respected and supported for all of my adult life.
Knowing that I was alienating myself from my comrades in the ANC
was difficult, as I continued to admire many aspects of the organisation and its members. Behind my slick public line of being more

interested in losing a job that I loved to retain the principles in which I believed, lay the sadness of knowing I was giving up something I could never replace.

Marginalising myself from the struggle to build a prosperous, humane and safe society in South Africa caused me to question whether I could have contributed more by staying on and fighting from within than by taking a very public stand and violating the ANC's unwritten code of not airing criticism of the party or its leaders in public.

My political credo is based on that of long-time dissident, playwright and then surprising President of Czechoslovakia and the Czech Republic, Vaclav Havel: politics as selfless service to one's fellow human beings, as morality in practice, based on conscience and truth.[1] I believe it is essential that politicians take a stand on matters of principle. The subversion of the national good in the interests of an individual or party is crossing the line, as far as I'm concerned.

I convinced myself that it was important to resign publicly on a matter of principle in the hope that it would create a precedent for such behaviour in our young democracy. At the same time I knew that I could not continue as a 'normal politician'. It was an extraordinary experience to be a part of a political process in the early years that were dominated by people who weren't conventional politicians, who never imagined they would be remunerated for their commitment. When that changed I no longer felt comfortable.

Alexander Herzen, a nineteenth-century Russian radical émigré, suggested that: 'Humans may fashion their lives, but in some of their most vital decisions they have no choice. When facing circumstances they cannot alter, they can only act in character, sometimes with tragic results.'[2] While conceding that the science of morality is still in its infancy, Marc Hauser claims that 'morality is grounded in our biology' and that we possess 'deep moral intuitions, an unconscious and universal grammar [that] underlies our judgements of right and wrong'.[3]

I felt I had no choice. However, I had – and still have – a real fear of my actions feeding the ANC's foes, many of whom are opposed to the real change still required in South Africa, rather than furthering truth and honest governance in the pursuit of the aims of equality and justice.

On the day I resigned, as today, I have absolutely no doubt that South Africa is a profoundly better place than it ever was before 1994, that the ANC government has been more skilled, more committed and more beneficial to the country than any that has gone before it (although racist regimes of varying competence are hardly a particularly good benchmark). Our constitution, arguably the world's most progressive, is a living monument to the ANC's achievements: dignity and justice for all, deracialising the world's only remaining race-based society; significant, albeit slow, progress in addressing material inequalities in housing, access to services, education and benefits; a raft of socially progressive initiatives around gender issues and a sound and relatively stable economy.

I acted as I did because I believe that the HIV and AIDS debacle and the arms deal marked a moral turning point in the life of the ANC. Early 2001 was the moment at which the organisation started to lose the moral high ground it had held as a liberation movement and in the early years of government. It was the watershed from which the organisation's humility, accountability and integrity began to be replaced by arrogance, aloofness and a gradual diminution of its values.

The tragic obfuscation on the HIV and AIDS pandemic was a consequence of an autocratic style that brooks no dissent and to which people, including myself, felt unable to stand up. It displayed a cult of leadership that has no place in a democratic organisation, and reflected a lack of accountability driven by contempt for the people we were elected to serve.

The ANC's equally arrogant quelling of the arms deal was further illustration of the insidious creep of an aloof, disdainful attitude to the broader society. As the *Sunday Times* editorialised at the time:

An act of arrogance if unchecked feeds on itself and inevitably returns in a more virulent and damaging form. This is what seems to have happened to the ANC in the past few years, as demonstrated by the party's arrogance and repeated disregard for the public concern over various issues. The apogee of this unacceptable behaviour is the R43 billion arms probe. ... What appears to be creeping into the culture of the party is a disregard for independent institutions and voices in society. It is no longer just the voices of minority parties that the ANC refuses to hear. It also ignores the voices of progressive NGOs, civil society formations and ordinary people. ... The party must not succumb to the arrogance that often accompanies power for therein lies dictatorship and disaster.[4]

To protect the party, the ANC leadership of both the executive and legislative arms of government was prepared to sacrifice the integrity and rigour of Parliament, a blow from which it has never fully recovered. The South African Parliament of today, elected by all the country's people, is an empty vessel. The majority of its members provide little or no oversight of the Executive, who in turn pay it minimal heed.[5]

The autocratic, insulated and deaf-to-criticism-or-dissent style of leadership that has marked the Mbeki era has recently come in for severe criticism from a range of influential figures. Chief Justice Pius Langa, in his Bram Fischer lecture in 2007, spoke of 'leaders who become adept at listening to themselves and turning a blind eye or a deaf ear to those who tell them bad news. They become equally impervious to the suffering of their subjects because pain is bad news and imposes obligations these leaders would prefer to ignore. What they prefer to hear is praise, adoration and endless flattery.'[6]

Addressing the lack of dissent within the ruling party, Langa continued: 'The value and courage of dissent comes in standing up and pronouncing the difficult view in public and taking the consequences. It is easy to believe in something. It is much more difficult to speak out.' He concluded: 'In government it is vital that there should be people who are willing to speak their mind against what appears to be public opinion and sometimes against the party line.'[7]

*

As I observe the ANC in early 2007 I see an organisation that has lost its moral compass.

The arms deal was followed by the extremely suspect awarding of the country's third cellular licence to a Saudi-led consortium. The award of the licence to Cell C was shrouded in controversy, with the Minister intervening to ensure the Saudis won out against more favoured competition amidst claims of massive contributions to ANC coffers and a link to the sale of South African arms to the Saudis. Despite a public outcry, there was virtually no investigation.[8]

Cellgate was followed by Oilgate, in which an empowerment company, Imvume Management, channelled R11 million of public money from the state oil company, Petro SA, to the ANC to help fight the 2004 election campaign. This was patently illegal. The ANC prevented any meaningful investigation of the matter, with another former ANC MP and colleague of mine, by then the Public Protector, facilitating the cover-up. It was left to the media, and particularly the ever resourceful *Mail & Guardian,* to expose details of this flagrant misuse of public money. Recently Sandi Majali, the head of Imvume, has threatened to 'spill the beans' about the dodgy transaction, admitting that he had kept quiet in order to protect powerful political figures. He is known to be close to ANC Secretary-General Kgalema Motlanthe, Treasurer General Mendi Msimang, and national spokesman Mandi Msimang. He has on occasion claimed to be President Thabo Mbeki's cousin.[9]

Majali is alleged to have also made a payment of R50 000 to Durban businessman Bonga Mlambo, the brother of Deputy President Phumzile Mlambo-Ngcuka, who was promoted from her position as Minister of Mineral and Energy Affairs (where she oversaw the Oilgate imbroglio) to replace the tarnished Jacob Zuma.[10] In the new Deputy President's first year in office she was on two occasions investigated for excessive use of the public purse for official travel and on a third occasion for taking friends and family on holiday to Dubai at public expense. Phumzile is the wife of Bulelani Ngcuka, who as Director of Public Prosecutions refused to charge Jacob Zuma or Joe Modise in relation to the arms deal.

Over the past few years a number of MPs of all parties have been embroiled in the so-called Travelgate saga in which they misused or sold their parliamentary travel allocation for private ends.[11] On reading of the unfolding saga I recalled the occasion in 2000 when an ANC MP was reprimanded in a sitting of Parliament by the Speaker for misusing his travel allocation. The matter was raised at the next ANC Caucus meeting where Essop Pahad, in his usual abrasive manner, admonished the Speaker for taking issue with the member as, claimed Pahad, the member had 'misused' his allocation for party purposes, which to the leadership was quite acceptable. It is notable in Travelgate that whereas the MPs who have been found guilty have been compelled to resign, the senior ANC leaders and Cabinet members involved have, in most instances, quietly paid back the money that was defrauded from Parliament.[12]

In early 2006 the ANC established the Progressive Business Forum to raise party funds. The Forum's members, leading businesses in South Africa, including many parastatals, pay a substantial fee to the ANC in exchange for access to 'intimate' conversations with key government ministers.[13] Analyst Richard Calland describes this access as constituting corruption in that public office and/or a public good has been used for private gain. Dismissing the ANC's 'limp' defence of the scheme, he suggests that the ANC is 'fast losing sight of the distinction between state and party.' Noting that a former NP Minister, now part of the ANC, is behind the scheme, Calland concludes that 'the rancid standards of the old regime have infiltrated the new establishment'.[14]

In 2006 the *Mail & Guardian* uncovered an elaborate network of companies, known as the Chancellor House Group, established to utilise black economic empowerment deals to raise money for the ruling party. It is a profound conflict of interest for the ANC, as the party of government, to be the arbiter and beneficiary of many of these deals which are dependent on state contracts, financial support and approval.

Not a month goes by without the announcement of a major empowerment deal in which senior members of the ANC and government are direct or indirect beneficiaries. Smuts Ngonyama, Head of the Presidency at Luthuli House, was involved with the former Director-General of Communications in an empowerment entity that acquired a R7 billion stake in what was at one point the state-owned telecoms company.[15] How does a man earning a fairly average salary in a full-time job manage to be party to a shareholding of that magnitude? The Gauteng government is to build a high-speed train between Johannesburg and Pretoria. Among the business beneficiaries are Bulelani Ngcuka, Education Minister Naledi Pandor, Home Affairs Minister Nosiviwe Mapisa-Nqakula, and the Speaker of Parliament, Baleka Mbete.[16]

Most disconcerting, though, has been the drama played out

around the life and death of controversial businessman Brett Kebble. A multi-millionaire mining magnate, in the mid-2000s Kebble took to spreading his largesse among the powerful and potentially influential, including Jacob Zuma and friends, the ANC Youth League and a number of its leaders. However, while living large, his own business empire was in crisis. Facing charges of tax evasion, fraudulent transactions aimed at presenting a distortedly healthy picture of his companies and finally the suspension of his flagship company from the Johannesburg Stock Exchange, Kebble was facing ruin and jail when he was gunned down in a mafia-style hit in September 2005. With rumours about who might have been responsible spiralling into the stratosphere, in late 2006 an organised crime boss known as 'The Landlord', Glenn Agliotti, together with a number of his associates, was arrested and charged with the murder.

Of real concern is that the country's top policeman, police commissioner Jackie Selebi, a senior ANC cadre, is on record as describing Agliotti as 'a close friend, finish and klaar'.[17] Selebi was questioned by the Scorpions about his links to Agliotti. In March 2007 he remains in office with the explicit support of the President. So the country with one of the highest violent crime rates in the world labours under a head of police who is close friends with a man charged with drug trafficking, murder and extortion.

It came to light in early 2007 that Kebble had in fact given the ANC and a range of party individuals up to R24 million in the course of 2 – 3 years.[18] This included R2.4 million to the ANC in the Western Cape, R750 000 to the ANC in the Eastern Cape, R6 million to the ANC Youth League and R14 million to Lunga Ncwana, a prominent member of the Youth League, for 'services rendered'. Kebble also made available seven luxury cars, including a Maserati and a Lamborghini, for Ncwana's use.[19] Ncwana, the Youth League and the ANC refuse to pay any of the money back, even though it has been identified as stolen.

Allan Boesak and Tony Yengeni were brave heroes of the liberation struggle. No one can dispute that. However, both broke the law for personal gain and were, quite correctly, sent to jail after exhaustive appeal processes. Both men were borne to and from jail with the endorsement of senior ANC leaders ringing in their ears. Not one senior ANC functionary criticised what they had done. It is quite legitimate, in fact humane, to provide private, personal support to a friend or comrade who has erred. To fete them publicly, and not even admonish them for their crimes, is foolhardy. To do so in such a crime-ridden country is grossly irresponsible.

From my perspective, the most personal example of the party of the people losing its moral perspective came in a relatively minor incident involving the MEC for Finance in Gauteng. I met Paul Mashatile while I was chairing the PWV Economic and Development Forum. A quiet, shy, studious, smart and humble young man, Paul was a senior office bearer in the SACP with a reputation as an impressive thinker, superb organiser and dedicated party activist. Paul was, to me, the epitome of the committed comrade – and he was very likeable to boot.

In June 2006 he spent almost R100 000 of taxpayers' money on a single meal for guests and friends at one of Johannesburg's leading restaurants. This is more than the vast, vast majority of South Africans earn in a year. According to the *Sunday Times*' Fred Khumalo, when questioned about the bill Paul effectively told the taxpayer to go to hell.[20]

What ANC silence or, even worse, defence of such behaviour has done is to suggest that if it is in the interests of the party, or you are senior enough and with the right connections, anything goes. It is as though some comrades who selflessly devoted significant parts of their life to the struggle to liberate the country have decided that now they are at the trough they have every right to use the state to overfill their bellies in a similar way to their noxious predecessors.

Vaclav Havel, after experiencing the privileges that accompany high political office, many of which are necessary for simple efficiency, and the insulation from ordinary life that this entails, suggests that there is a critical moment when 'we cease to be concerned with the interests of the country for whose sake we tolerate these privileges and start to be concerned with the advantages themselves'. He continues: 'Regardless of how pure his intentions may originally have been, it takes a high degree of self awareness and critical distance for someone in power – however well meaning at the start – to recognise that moment.'[21] Sadly, many in the ANC appear to have passed this moment with barely a flicker of recognition.

*

While individual and party culpability should not be diminished, this loss of value and perspective within the ANC has to be understood within the context of the role and influence of the corporate sector in a globalised economy and the pre-eminence of consumerism that this has engendered.

The corporate sector is the most potent engine for growth and employment in the modern, market economy. However, it is not without its difficulties and contradictions. The legitimate pursuit of profit is difficult to align with a wide range of social needs. Corporations need to be regulated to ensure that in their maximisation of profit they do not break the law or work against the interests of the society more broadly.

After the collapse of the command economy as a viable alternative to the market, corporations have become increasingly more powerful actors in society. Their impact and influence on the public sector is wide-ranging and profound. Their closeness to political parties and politicians extends far beyond those parties which historically represented the interests of the business community. The potential for inappropriate interaction between the public and private spheres is probably greater than it has ever been. The seamless movement of Michael Portillo and Joe Modise from the Cabinet table as Defence Ministers to the boardroom table of arms manufacturers is just the most obvious and crudest example.

Where this relationship plays itself out most explicitly is in the arena of party political funding. In the US, campaign funding is a quagmire that in my opinion severely weakens American democracy. It is virtually impossible to run successfully for meaningful office in the US without either being extremely wealthy or having the backing of very well-resourced interest groups. The consequence is that once in office you are expected to deliver for your special interest backers. The Bush administration is the most venal manifestation of what has been a reality of American politics for decades.

It is interesting to recall that, in spite of his obvious commitment to addressing the HIV and AIDS pandemic since leaving office, it was President Clinton who had South Africa placed on a trade watch list for attempting to pass legislation to allow the parallel importation and/or manufacture of generic ARVs. Pressure from the pharmaceutical companies, which were significant donors to the Clinton/Gore

245

re-election campaign, is cited by Cameron as one of the drivers of this action.[22] It was the same Bill Clinton who pardoned a few dodgy, wealthy backers on his last day in office.

Attempts to clean up the campaign finance mess in the US are consistently thwarted by both major parties. In the UK, calls for greater transparency in party funding have been rejected by Labour and the Tories for generations. In South Africa, the ANC and the opposition DA are similarly committed to maintaining the status quo of secrecy in which parties are under no obligation to reveal their sources of funding. It is extraordinary that governments and parties, elected by the people as 'servants of the people',[23] are unwilling to allow these same people to know who funds their activities. It is yet another indication of the desultory state of politics globally.

In the South African context the corporate/party/government relationship is significantly complicated by the essential imperative of black economic empowerment. The need to rapidly redress black South Africans' years of enforced exclusion from economic opportunities is essential to the wellbeing of our democracy. To do this requires, for a period of time of at least a generation, those who were excluded being given greater education and training opportunities and being preferred to those of us who were unfairly advantaged when it comes to education, jobs and state contracts.[24] However, what has happened in recent years is that it is primarily people close to the ANC who are seen to be the main beneficiaries of this necessary strategy. So the new class of African oligarchs comprises mainly ANC cadres. This gives rise to allegations of nepotism and favouritism. The picture created is of the massive personal enrichment of a select few, and, in what is one of the most unequal societies on the planet, this is then perceived as being at the expense of 'the masses'. In addition, these symbiotic relationships between those in power and those close to them inevitably gives rise either to the type of corruption that has been exposed in the Schabir Shaik trial or to a presumption of some sort of quid pro quo by politicians.

A real difficulty in the South African context is that a significant majority of the previously disadvantaged have historical links to the ANC, which has been the dominant force in South African liberation and post-liberation politics for so long. It would be unfair to exclude people on the basis of a relationship with what was the pre-eminent liberation force. At the same time, the merging of state and party is inimical to the sustainability of a strong, vibrant democracy and to the reestablishment of a culture of accountability that is so essential an element of that democracy.

The complexity of the issue is reflected in President Mbeki's conflicting statements on the matter. As Mondli Makhanya has pointed out in the *Sunday Times*, the President has repeatedly preached tirades against the avarice and greed of those who have amassed enormous wealth and who advise others 'with rhythmic and hypnotic regularity: get rich, get rich, get rich!' And then, a few months later, the President is equally passionate in defending Ministers who have a stake in the Gautrain project, decrying their critics as racists who stereotype blacks as 'inherently amoral and corrupt'.[25] This also reflects his willingness to use race to label his critics whenever he is put on the defensive. This failure of principle has gnawed away at the non-racial legacy of his predecessor.

The double-speak on corruption and race is unfortunately the imprimatur of Mbeki's leadership. Together with the AIDS debacle, it reflects why his period in office has, on the whole, failed to provide moral leadership. This is reflected in both the perceptions of South Africans and our African peers. A survey quoted in the *Guardian* suggested that 63 per cent of South Africans think their leaders are dishonest.[26] An early draft of the first report by the African Union Peer Review mechanism on South Africa stated that: '[As a consequence of] creeping corruption and conflicts of interest proliferating in public life, South Africans feel betrayed, regarding corruption as a negation of democratic gains after a long period of struggle.'[27]

The Minister for Public Administration, Geraldine Fraser-Moleketi, has undertaken a wide range of laudatory anti-corruption initiatives. However, this has done little to stem the growth of corruption, which progressive analyst Max du Preez described recently as 'pervasive'.[28] There exists a sense that if you are suspected of being corrupt but are in political favour you can get away with it (for example, Modise and Selebi), but if you happen to be out of favour you suffer the consequences (Zuma and Maharaj). Another view suggests that many of those swarming to support Jacob Zuma do so in the hope that they will be spared punishment for their misdemeanours.

In March 2007, Fraser-Moleketi addressed the African Forum on Fighting Corruption in Ekurhuleni. She stated:

> We cannot [allow] a permissive environment for corruption to flourish. Corruption is detrimental to long-term sustainable development. Corruption costs and grand corruption costs even more. Corruption is inimical to development; it perpetuates inequality... It reproduces conditions of underdevelopment and poverty. It is morally wrong and offensive; it is illegal and it can no longer be tolerated. We collectively must dedicate ourselves to its eradication.[29]

Equally impressive was the President's statement at the opening of the 5th Global Anti-corruption Forum in Sandton in April 2007:

> Corruption in all its forms and manifestations, constitutes a process that negates the democracy and development the ordinary people need to transcend the boundaries of their world of poverty, underdevelopment and disempowerment.

The battle against the cancer of corruption needs to start at home, Mr President and Madam Minister, at its source, with the truth about the arms deal exposed for all to see. Then all other acts of corruption that have followed must be properly investigated and addressed regardless of how high or low in the party hierarchy, how close or distant to the prevailing centre of power the perpetrators sit. For, just as we forget the dark and tragic history of the Holocaust and racist apartheid at our peril, so too are we doomed to repeat the corruption of the past if we ignore or deny it.

*

Sadly, it is not just at a material level that the ANC's morality has subsided. The party has always tried to co-opt opposition to it. It was with this in mind that Azapo was offered a Cabinet post and unsuccessful attempts made to keep the IFP in Cabinet. But the most bizarre manifestation of the tendency was the merger with the former party of apartheid, the National Party. I was bemused when a friend in Parliament told me that the warder of some of my colleagues, Annelise van Wyk, was now serving as an ANC MP. I listened, pained, as it was related how President Mbeki publicly lauded Annelise in Parliament while some of her victims on the ANC benches sat weeping at the injustice of it. This incident is a contradictory reflection of both the strength of reconciliation in South Africa and the loss of a politics of principle that Mandela embodied.

When it comes to gender issues the ANC prides itself on the number of women in senior government positions, in Parliament and in the party hierarchy. And this is indeed laudable. However, during 2006 not only was the ANC's Deputy President charged with rape, but the Chief Whip who replaced Tony Yengeni was dismissed from his position and the ANC for sexual harassment. The ANC Chief Whip in the Gauteng Legislature was accused (and cleared) of sexual harassment and an MEC in the Province, my former colleague Bob Mabaso, was fired on the same charge. The country's compliant Public Protector, a former ANC MP, was accused of sexual harassment by his Deputy, while an advisor to one of the country's provincial Premiers was dismissed for the same offence. It is commendable that the ANC eventually took action against those offenders found guilty. It is, however, astonishing that six senior members of the party should have to be investigated for such behaviour in the space of one calendar year. Despite taking action against these members during 2006, in early 2007 the ANC appointed a former ambassador, who had been discharged for sexual harassment, as a Member of the Provincial Legislature in the Limpopo Province.

The confusion and contradictions are breathtaking, as was the appointment of Essop Pahad as the Cabinet member with responsibility for women, about which Pregs Govender has written: 'They [women in South Africa] needed a minister who would advance their rights, not undermine their leaders.'[30]

The greatest manifestation of the ANC's moral decline has revolved around the succession battle. Mbeki, ever the artful politician, wishes to maintain a hold on power either through the extension of his own tenure or by putting in place someone who will perpetuate his legacy, possibly through whom he can continue to exercise power. Jacob Zuma has made no secret of his ambitions to be President of the ANC and the country.

It always caused me anguished amusement when senior ANC leaders, starting from the President down, would admonish people in the organisation for being careerist or for pursuing specific positions of power. It is the President himself who is among the most manipulative and scheming politicians in the party, far more at home in smoke-filled rooms than in open discussion and debate. This struggle for power has rent the ANC and its allies asunder. In almost every province there is massive division between those who support Mbeki and those supporting Zuma. The party is now an agglomeration of factions, defined not so much by ideological or policy differences, but by personality and the pursuit of power and patronage.

Far more time is currently spent by the ANC plotting against each other than dealing with the challenges facing the country. And when it is convenient, regulations and laws are used to clip the wings of political opponents. The most obvious case is that of Jacob Zuma, whose misdemeanours had been known for years but were only brought to light by Mbeki supporters when it suited the President's ends. In the Western Cape Legislature in early 2007 it was Jacob Zuma's followers who supported an opposition-instigated investigation into the Mbeki-supporting Premier, Ebrahim Rasool, in an attempt to unseat him. And, of course, there is the tragic case of Mac Maharaj, who, having fallen out with the President, had his integrity impugned, his enormous contribution to the struggle forgotten and his career destroyed.[31]

While Mac might not be entirely blameless,[32] his words as always are wise: 'When you look at allegations of corruption, you find investigations are extremely selective. All things being equal, if you are perceived to be a friend of the President's or within his political circle, the less likelihood there is of being investigated by the Scorpions. In a certain sense, corruption and abuse are two sides of the same coin. In the case of corruption, people in positions of power use their positions in a manner contrary to the statutory obligations prescribing the way in which that power is to be used.'[33]

Sometimes this power is exercised not by threat but by fear of incurring the displeasure of South Africa's ruling elite. The worst example of this displeasure was voiced by President Mbeki in a verbal assault on Archbishop Desmond Tutu after Tutu lamented the lack of debate in the political arena. In a speech to the Nelson Mandela Foundation, Tutu called for 'a vigorous debate that is characteristic of a vibrant community where people play the ball and not the person and not think that those who disagree, who express dissent are *ipso facto* disloyal or unpatriotic.' He went on: 'An unthinking, uncritical, kowtowing party-line toeing is fatal to a vibrant democracy.'[34] Mbeki responded by branding the Archbishop a liar, writing: 'One of the fundamental requirements for the rational discussion suggested by the archbishop is familiarity with the facts relevant to any matter under discussion, as well as respect for the truth.'[35]

Mac further suggests that: 'This is an ANC government. We should encourage constant debate and the interchange of ideas, and we should invite public criticism, taking it as being honestly offered and meriting honest response.'[36]

O'Malley (2007) argues that within the ANC under Mbeki, all values are collapsed into one: loyalty to the ANC.[37] When Jacob Zuma was interviewed after the collapse of the corruption trial against him, he said: 'I don't want to say anything which might seem critical of government policy. That would be seen as disloyal and in the ANC you have no future if you are disloyal.'[38]

*

In his recent novel, *Seeing*, Portuguese Nobel laureate Jose Saramago captures the dangerous vacuity of contemporary politics. The book is set in an unnamed capital city at election time. In a spontaneous expression of the meaninglessness of the political process 73 per cent of the city's voters return blank ballots: not spoilt, not ripped up, rather a display of emptiness, the rejection of the mindlessness of an entire system. The country's leaders do not know how to react to this profound yet silent act. They denounce the evil actions and order a re-vote. Second time round, 83 per cent of voters leave their ballots blank. The politicians are even more perplexed. Desperate to understand what is happening and to stop it continuing, they conjure an imaginary insurrectionary force which they claim is opposed to civilisation as we know it. They abandon the capital before ordering a crackdown on a small innocent group of people who happen to be the only ones to maintain their sight when blindness struck the city

251

four years previously. Their crackdown on this group is brutally immoral, based on lies and innuendo.

Saramago's sagacious vision is a telling allegory on the inadequacy and moral bankruptcy of global politics. While many in the developed world and elites in developing countries have never had so much choice in lifestyle and consumer goods, our political choices have narrowed to an unappetising, centrist mulch, characterised by an interest only in the maintenance of power which is pursued with scant regard for principle or morality.

Political commentator Andrew Stephen echoes Saramago's bleak vision: '[This] is the deceit of politics and the arrogance of power. Mediocre figures, given a little power and standing in the community, come to believe their own propaganda. They then ruthlessly depict anybody standing in their way as being part of the forces of darkness and evil. In the end they have no guiding morality and are driven solely by the pursuit of self-furtherance.' [39]

Global politics is in an uneasy interregnum. The lack of real choice and ever-increasing cynicism has resulted in dwindling participation and a general lack of engagement with the political process in all but a handful of countries.

South Africa under Nelson Mandela briefly illustrated a politics of hope, of principle. It was a false dawn. The politics of reconciliation, in which the interests of the whole nation took precedence over personal or party interests, gave way within a few years to politics as normal in which personal power and the primacy of the party reasserted themselves, as they have around the world.

In much the same way and over a similar period, New Labour in the United Kingdom has atrophied from the heady days of 1997, a time of optimism, hope and change, to its current beleaguered, directionless, self-serving and widely reviled incarnation. As Martin Bright has commented, 'a government that said it was going to put morality at the heart of politics, has instead squeezed it to the margins'.[40] Nowhere has this been more apparent than in the case of BAe and the UK government. After propounding the notion of an ethical foreign policy when coming to power, Tony Blair actively supported BAe's bid in the South African arms deal by lobbying incessantly and even signing a Memorandum of Understanding with Thabo Mbeki about the deal and its economic benefits.

The most brazen support for the British arms producer came when on 15 December 2006 the British government forced the Serious Fraud Office to halt a massive corruption investigation into the notorious Al Yamamah arms deal. The investigation, which had already uncovered a massive slush fund worth tens of millions of pounds operated by BAe to provide gifts and incentives to its potential clients, was about to announce a massive breakthrough in identifying a variety of Swiss-held bank accounts through which money was transferred from BAe or its agents to Saudi politicians. The investigation was halted supposedly because alienating the Saudis would threaten Britain's national security interests. Even Tony Blair's compliant head of intelligence, John Scarlett, denied there was a national security concern. In fact, as the *Guardian* newspaper reported, the Saudis had publicly threatened to cancel a contract for 70 fighter jets unless the investigation was stopped.[41] And as BAe's premier salesman, Blair couldn't let a deal like that fall by the wayside.

The *Guardian* said of Tony Blair at the time: 'For a prime minister who once taunted his predecessor as someone "knee deep in dishonour" over an arms deal and who promised that he would be "purer than pure" in office, yesterday was a shabby, shaming day, among the most inglorious he has spent in office.'[42]

Barack Obama's description of American politics might apply equally to the UK, South Africa and many other countries. He writes: 'What's troubling is the gap between the magnitude of our challenges and the smallness of our politics.'[43]

*

The current dire state of the ANC is, thus, not part of an inevitable decline into the 'chaos of Africa'. In fact, such sweeping and bigoted generalisation caricatures a continent that comprises 54 different countries, speaks over 300 different languages, and in which Dakar and Durban have as much – and as little – in common as Dresden and Dublin. It also ignores the reality that the past decade has seen the establishment of 18 new multiparty democracies on the continent, of differing stability and vigour. Rather, what has happened in South Africa, with alarming and sad alacrity since the turn of the century, is that we have adopted the odorous norms of politics around the globe. The grasping for personal power and patronage that we witness is a manifestation of the debasement of South Africa's liberation politics by the global politics of the era.

I believe that through multilateral organisations and inter-governmental interaction enormous pressures – sometimes explicit, more often implicit – are brought to bear on emerging markets to conform to a blueprint not only in terms of economic policy and institutions of state (the so-called Washington consensus) but also in terms of the accepted, cynical nature of governance. It is no coincidence that in the US, the UK and France, as in South Africa, Brazil and India, the needs of campaign and party funding are so often associated with conflicts of interest and corruption. This doesn't excuse the behaviour of parties or individuals in either developed or developing countries. It provides a context for their behaviour. The reality of South Africa is that the tendencies that have developed within the ANC and the country over the past five or six years could lead to disaster unless they are confronted by people within the organisation and in the broader society.

A decline in morality and principle has dealt grievous blows to other proud liberation movements. The Congress Party in India was out of power for years as a consequence of the Bofors arms deal and the sleaze that accompanied it. These were years that saw a revival of communal politics in the world's largest democracy, to the detriment of all India. In similar vein, Carlos Cardoso, a fearless, progressive journalist in Mozambique, who was for many years a member of the ruling Frelimo party, documented in detail the moral decline of Frelimo from 'the first years of protestant honesty in governance … [to] taking on board an enormous dose of illegality'.[44]

It is not just these remarkable political movements that are weakened. It is the people of the country who suffer most directly. As Goetz and Jenkins so compellingly point out, '[it is] the poor … for whom accountability failures have the most dire consequences'.[45]

The decline of the last five or so years has placed under threat a number of touchstones of both South Africa's remarkable transition and the very nature of the organisation that led this transition. These include the ANC's non-racial inclusive character, its tradition of exhaustive informed internal debate and the commitment to a developmental state working in the interests of greater equality and

254

justice. In addition, as I experienced at first hand, the independence and vigour of key institutions of state and society, including Parliament, are undermined. Ultimately the decline of the ANC could come to undermine the very thing for which so many gave so much.

SECTION V
A POLITICS OF HOPE

CHAPTER 16
An Unfinished House

This is how a new country arises,
built by us as if by mere chance,
constructed for the future, going down, in tunnels,
the bright shadow of the first country, an unfinished house.

'An Unfinished House'
Adam Zagajewski

When Vaclav Havel made his maiden New Year's address to the Czech people as their first democratically elected President for decades, he spoke about the country's emergence from a contaminated moral environment. He enunciated the importance of basing the new politics on morality, and exhorted his people to 'teach ourselves and others that politics can be not only the art of the possible, especially if the possible includes calculation, intrigue, secret deals and manouvering, but that it can also be the art of the impossible, namely, the art of improving ourselves and the world.'[1] This should be our objective.

Globally, traditional liberal representative politics as currently practised seem inadequate for the consumerist, information age in which we live. Politics where parties represented specific class interests has dissipated to some extent as class structures have become more porous and fragmented. Rather than a battle of different interests, as Bernard Crick described in his influential *In Defence of Politics*, parties now do battle largely on issues of style, presentation and personalities. Policies based on the results of focus groups are incoherent and largely indistinguishable across parties. Parties are trying to keep pace with the fragmented, oft-changing views of the electors, more and more of whom feel alienated from the political process.

The challenge for those committed to politics as the art of the impossible is to re-energise, re-democratise the political process in a

259

manner that places morality at its centre, with transparent accountability as its most crucial tool.

I believe that there are certain basic global requirements for a more honest polity including:

- full disclosure of every cent of party funding, from whatever source;
- a global regulatory environment for corporations, with specific regimes for the arms, pharmaceutical, gambling and mineral and resource extraction industries;
- a global corruption watchdog that has the power to fine transgressors in the public and private sectors (both corrupters and the corrupted) and, in the case of extreme violations, to deregister companies and political parties;
- a global citizens' movement with a Citizens' Charter for Political Parties that demands honesty, transparency and consultation at all levels of government.[2]

In South Africa, we have lost moral ground since the turn of the century. However, I believe that in this remarkable country and within the ANC and its affiliated organisations there are many who retain sufficient of its historical culture of dialogue, debate, high-mindedness and community spiritedness to regenerate the organisation and the country.

Certain changes of a constitutional and policy nature are desperately needed, including most importantly:

- the adoption of a mixed constituency/PR system, so that MPs are able to have an independent voice either as non-party constituency MPs or as representatives of a party directly elected by people from a specific geographical area, so that they are not beholden exclusively to their party leaders;
- a vibrant, adequately resourced legislative arm of government in which the Westminster paradox of junior backbenchers being expected to hold their political seniors to account is overcome by living out the constitutional role envisaged for Parliament and identifying certain specific oversight committees that are constitutionally protected from party political influence;

- a change in the way in which political parties are funded so that there is a cap on party spending, with the state providing a percentage of party funds and all sources of funding, either direct or indirect, being completely transparent and open to public scrutiny;
- a blanket ban on members of the Executive having any direct or indirect business interests;
- a clearer separation between state and party;
- a more broad-based black economic empowerment initiative that recognises all those who were disadvantaged by racial oppression.

A mixed electoral system is essential for South Africa for two reasons. An element of proportional representation allows minorities to be represented in Parliament, thus increasing the likelihood of minority buy-in to the constitutional process. Constituencies would provide the direct link between representatives and the voters in a particular location as well as diluting the power of the party leadership to get rid of independent-minded MPs. This would create a political environment in which it would be more likely that MPs would be driven by principle and the needs of their constituents rather than the narrow loyalty required to remain in favour with the party leadership.

Even though a constituency system, Westminster suffers the problem of politically junior backbenchers finding it difficult to hold politically senior Cabinet members to account. In South Africa this dynamic is accentuated by the pure proportional representation system. By insulating certain key parliamentary oversight committees from political partisanship, as happened informally in the first democratically elected legislature after 1994, the constitution would enable the members of these committees to take the tough decisions that ensure real accountability. These committees would include Scopa, the Ethics Oversight Committee and possibly the Intelligence Oversight Committee.

Party funding has to be more rigorously regulated in South Africa. Parties should have some degree of a level playing field, as regards finance and access to media, to ensure elections are as fair as possible. Transparency is a non-negotiable requirement of open and honest governance. No party claiming to be accountable to the people can justify hiding any source of benefit. Without knowing who is providing party funds it is impossible to know whether a governing party is acting in the best interests of the country or the narrow interests of its main donors.

Members of the Executive should not hold business interests. Where people come into politics with significant outside interests and financial assets, these should be placed in a blind trust for the duration of their time in office. Any public representative should have to declare all outside interests and benefits fully and regularly. Failure to do so should lead to exclusion from office and judicial penalties. Public service should be exactly that. No one should expect to benefit materially from holding public office (beyond earning a good salary and benefits).

I don't believe that there is anything wrong with wanting to make significant amounts of money, as long as it is done legally and without negatively impacting on anyone else. But the public sector is not the place to do it. People who want to make money should go into business, as some of my former colleagues have done. There should be a cooling-off period after serving in government, in terms of which senior officials or public representatives should be barred from remunerated work in any sector in which they have had influence or taken material decisions. The honour of serving a constituency and the country, together with a decent but not excessive income, should be motivation enough for public service.

Because of the ANC's pervasive influence on all aspects of life in South Africa, the blurring of state and party is difficult to avoid. But avoid it we must, for the simple reason that party and national interests do not always coincide. The ANC's Leninist/Stalinist residue, evoked in many of the party's strategic documents over the years and in the attitudes and behaviours of some of its leaders, especially in the Presidency, leads the movement to regard the state as the plaything of the ANC. We must honour our liberal democratic constitution and ensure the differentiation is deepened.

It follows that when performing a government role, politicians must at all times benefit the state, obviously informed by the outlook and policies of their party. However, decisions should not be taken or actions followed to directly benefit the party. The ANC crossed this line with the creation of its Progressive Business Forum, as citizens had to pay the party for special access to Cabinet Ministers, a right that all citizens should have regardless of whether they can afford it or not. As importantly, party affiliation should not be a requirement for jobs in the public sector. It is only political advisors whose political stripe is of any consequence.

The domain in which this distinction is most blurred is in the laudable pursuit of BEE. Decisions favouring party stalwarts because of their party connections alone are unacceptable. State contracts should be widely distributed across all of those best able to fulfil them, regardless of political affiliation or party donations, with consideration given to the empowerment of those who were excluded from economic opportunities pre-1994. The ANC's Business Forum and companies like Floryn Investments and the Chancellor House Group have no place in our democracy and should be closed down forthwith.

In addition, any further sales of state assets should incorporate a significant tranche of shares to be distributed in small quantities among those in the society who are least able to participate in the market economy. To avoid the plundering of such schemes that occurred in the former Soviet Union, strict resale regulations would need to be developed.[3]

*

To achieve this environment the ANC will need to use its strength – a 70 per cent majority of the electorate and an unrivalled liberation history – not to silence dissent but to empower its representatives and the broader public to use their full talents and diversity in the service of all the people of South Africa, particularly the poorest.

The succession to Thabo Mbeki will be key in this regard. The question is, if Mbeki remains ANC president, whether he will attempt to install a puppet as the country's president so that he can continue to pull the strings from behind the scenes. Will Zuma assume the Presidency despite overwhelming *prima facie* evidence of corruption and ineptitude? Or will one of the talented and principled people who have distanced themselves from the recent excesses and infighting return to lead a renaissance within the ANC?

Havel suggests that: 'Politics ... places greater stress on moral sensitivity, on the ability to reflect critically on oneself, on genuine responsibility ... on the capacity to empathize with others, on a sense

263

of moderation, on humility. It is a job for modest people, for people who cannot be deceived. ... Politics is work of a kind that requires especially pure people, because it is especially easy to become morally tainted.'[4]

I do believe that there are people who fit this bill in the ANC and the country, and who could return South Africa to the heights we scaled towards the end of the last century. We do, however, need to encourage more people of talent and principle, for whom financial reward is secondary to public service, into government. This requires giving people the sense that they can make a difference in public service through utilising their unique skills and expressing their principled views without having to compromise to the false god of a dogmatic party line.

Some within the ANC and the country believe that both Thabo Mbeki and Jacob Zuma are tarnished goods and that to move forward requires someone unsullied by the past few years of excess, autocracy, arrogance and deceit. I agree with them.

It seems to me inevitable, post the failure of Schabir Shaik's appeal, that Jacob Zuma will be recharged. If he is not, there will always be questions asked about what was being hidden and why. I hope that in the event of another trial, he will be given the opportunity to prove his innocence or suffer the consequences of his guilt. It would also provide the country with an opportunity to get to the bottom of some of the less exalted chapters of our recent history. In addition, the government must allow independent, unfettered investigations into the arms deal and all who were involved in it, the awarding of the third cellular licence, and the Oilgate fiasco.

The underlying factors that led to the tragedy of hundreds of thousands of lives lost unnecessarily during five years of AIDS denialism must be examined to ensure that such a moral vacuum is never repeated. An examination of this sort must include a consideration of the shutting-down of open and honest debate and the inappropriate deference shown to the views of 'the leader'. Such soul searching, made less likely by the firing of the Deputy Minister of Health, will provide the springboard from which to maximise the progress made towards the end of 2006 and the first half of 2007 in uniting around a clear and explicit strategy to deal with the pandemic. This united effort should result in access to the best affordable holistic treatment

264

for all who need it as soon as possible. And our leaders should now take the lead in educating the country about how to avoid infection, eradicate stigma and how best to live a positive, long life with HIV and AIDS. To craft true unity in addressing this challenge will, I believe, require the removal of the current Minister of Health, who is an embarrassment to the country, the government and the ANC.

Some may regard these as the views of a naive idealist with little understanding of the harsh realities of politics. Some may even condescendingly suggest that it is inappropriate to set such high standards for a developing country in a difficult global environment.

I believe that in the country that has produced Nelson Mandela and Steve Biko, Miriam Makeba and Abdullah Ibrahim, Desmond Tutu and Beyers Naude, Nadine Gordimer and Zakes Mda, we have a right to demand a higher order, to lead the world in a politics of hope, just as we have in reconciliation and the resolution of centuries of enmity by peaceful means. Rather than accept the tawdry global political and economic standards, let us have the confidence to achieve the art of the impossible.

CHAPTER 17
Speak Truth to Power

Speaking truth to power … is carefully weighing the alternatives, picking
the right one and then representing it where it can do the most
good and cause the right change.

Representations of the Intellectual
Edward Said

After resigning from Parliament I had a desperate need to be away
from South Africa for a time. We went to live in London where
Simone grew up and where most of her family live. For a few years I
found travelling to South Africa difficult. I was almost embarrassed at
the thought of bumping into my former colleagues, as if I had done
something wrong, shameful.

My emotions about the country and my recent experience of it were
confused. I felt that I was betraying South Africa while trying to serve its
best interests, that my resignation was a moment of failure and success. I
experienced, in some small way, the strangeness of Edward Said's
description of the Palestinians, a victim of the victims – in my case, resigning from an organisation of great moral reputation on a matter of principle; the personal sadness and loneliness of discovering and then pub-
licising that the good guys are corruptible, of experiencing 'the family'
turning you into 'the other' for telling the family's secrets in public.

This sad corrupting of the family and the practical reality that I
could easily, if not happily, get a remunerative job on leaving Parliament, is partly why I took the course I did. I regret it every day of
my life. And every day of my life I am glad I did it.

I hope that one day we will learn the full truth about the corrupters and the corrupted. But even more I hope that, even with only
partial truth, we will learn the lessons of our weakness and failures.

*

266

The melting pot that is London gave us a welcoming base – even our son's little school of 14 children had two other 'Juslims'. But I despaired at the mendacious, ethnocentric response of the British and US governments to the tragedy of 9/11, in which vacuous politics fed into simplistic, tribal notions of identity, the division of the world into 'us and them', needed as much by Osama bin Laden as by George Bush.

A couple of months after our arrival I came across a remarkable building at 19 Princelet Street in the East End of London. The building was first home to a French Huguenot textile merchant fleeing religious persecution. It was then occupied by Jewish immigrants and was the site of the first meetings of the Anti Fascist League. The ground floor was converted into a synagogue. With the wave of Bangladeshi immigration the building became home to a multitude of Bengali families and a vibrant community centre. Today it houses the Museum of Diversity and Immigration, a celebration of the East End and London's openness to immigration and cosmopolitanism. The museum charts the life of all those who have passed through the area. One of the exhibits is a film of a group of young Bengali schoolchildren acting out the experience of the early Jews who, like my father's family, fled the pogroms of Lithuania and Latvia. To hear these children 'kvetching' in their east London/Bengali accents made me realise that this city in which over 350 languages are spoken provides my wandering, Jewish soul and young 'Juslim' family with a home that is uniquely local and universal at the same moment.

From my first (of many) visits to 19 Princelet Street I again realised the importance of combining my commitment to accountability and transparency in the quest for equality and justice with an outlook which transcends the limiting identity politics that have become so pervasive since 9/11. Jettisoning the easy but harmful, and embracing our common humanity in all its diversity.

Kwame Anthony Appiah provides an apposite description of this state of mind, of being: 'rooted cosmopolitanism', which he construes as a synthesis of identification and transcendence; acknowledging one's own complex identity and embracing the complex and different identities of others.[1] In political terms this could form the basis for a softer nationalism, where attachment to one's own does not preclude fellowship with the other. Mandela is the pre-eminent example of such a soft nationalism, at once the father of the South African nation and a global icon for justice, a truly rooted cosmopolitan.[2]

However, such a discourse demands a politics of basic truth and honesty, of accountability; a politics that encapsulates Mandela's extraordinary ability to put national interest ahead of party interest, to put the many before the few and to put the people ahead of the person. But while such a politics of hope remains a distant dream, it is essential that in striving towards this new Jerusalem individuals have the courage 'to speak truth to power'.[3]

NOTES

INTRODUCTION

1 I will use racial descriptors commonly used in South Africa: 'coloured' to refer to people of mixed race, 'black' to refer to coloureds, Asians and Africans.

2 Thabo Mbeki, 'I am an African'. Issued by the Office of the Deputy President, Cape Town, 8 May 1996.

CHAPTER 1

1 At the time Anton headed UCT's Students' Representative Council.

2 In 1991 Pro was shot down by his own ANC comrades in drug-related gangster-ism, political factionalism or a dreadful error on the part of an ANC self-defence unit. In spite of an ANC member admitting to the accidental killing, the TRC was unable to establish the true reason for the shooting.

CHAPTER 2

1 Warren's basic thesis was that capitalism was a progressive but brutal force which had to be embraced before any transition to socialism was possible.

CHAPTER 3

1 It took the persistent support of Theuns Eloff, head of the CBM, to overcome this little obstacle.

2 As witnessed in the assassination of Ruth First in Mozambique in August 1982, and of Dulcie September in Paris in March 1988.

CHAPTER 4

1 The interim constitution negotiated at the World Trade Centre had replaced apartheid South Africa's 4 provinces and 13 homelands and self-governing terri-tories with 9 new provinces. The smallest but wealthiest and most powerful of these was the awfully named Pretoria-Witwatersrand-Vereeniging (PWV), which incorporated Johannesburg, Pretoria and their surrounds.

2 Hani was touted as a challenger for the leadership of the ANC in succession to Mandela, a hero to the movement's militant youth for his continuing support of the armed struggle and his readiness to challenge party positions he disagreed with. He was assassinated outside his Boksburg home by right-wing zealot Janusz Walus.

CHAPTER 5

1 'We'll open brothels to survive: Casino men', *The Citizen*, 7 August 1996, p 3.
2 Mark Gevisser, *Portraits of Power*, p 127 (see Bibliography). Gevisser, author of the definitive biography of Thabo Mbeki, is one of the country's most astute political writers.
3 Liebenberg had replaced Derek Keys, a National Party-appointed businessman who had continued in the role until late 1994.
4 Despite his good intentions, personal integrity and leadership, Nyerere's Ujamaa experiment left Tanzania in economic crisis with an economy that was unable to generate wealth, plagued by budget problems, dependent on the aid industry, on occasion unable to feed its people and characterised by creeping corruption. See R. Calderisi, *What's the Matter with Africa: Why Foreign Aid isn't Working*. London: Palgrave Macmillan, 2006, Chapter 5.
5 The debate about the desirability and role of the provinces continues unabated in the ANC today.
6 Mark Gevisser, *Portraits of Power*, p 129.
7 ANC HQ in Johannesburg, later renamed Albert Luthuli House.
8 Mark Gevisser, *Portraits of Power*, p 129.
9 At the time of writing, Tokyo was angling for the presidency of the country. Ironically, at one point, it appeared that some in Mbeki's inner circle were supportive of his candidacy.

CHAPTER 6

1 See *The Independent*, 13 June 2002: obituary headlined 'Peter Mokaba: ANC politician and AIDS denialist'.
2 See Joe Slovo, 'Beyond the Stereotype: the SACP in the past, present and future', www.sacp.org.za.
3 Thabo Mbeki, 'I am an African'. Issued by the Office of the Deputy President, Cape Town: 8 May 1996.

CHAPTER 7

1 See Bresser Pereira, LC, Maravall, JM, and Pzerworski, A. *Economic Reforms in New Democracies*. Cambridge: Cambridge University Press, 1993.
2 Dissaving refers to government consumption and debt expenditure, but excludes productive investment spending.
3 For a more detailed account of GEAR and its alternatives see Bibliography: Feinstein, 'Reflections on South African Political Economy'; Marais, *South Africa: Limits to Change*, and Hirsch, *Season of Hope*.
4 According to official data quoted in *Business Day*, 25 July 2007.
5 *Umrabulo*, Number 5, 3rd Quarter 1998.
6 TRC Amnesty Hearing Transcript, 14 July 1997.

CHAPTER 8

1 Statistical information in this paragraph comes from Y Muthien, *Democracy South Africa: Evaluating the 1999 Election*. HSRC: Pretoria, 1999.
2 'Speech on the occasion of the consideration of the budget vote of the Presidency', National Assembly, 13 June 2000.
3 Mbeki's first reference to the notion of two nations was in a speech in May 1998,

but the theme was followed up forcefully in his State of the Nation address in 1999, among many others.

4   Thabo Mbeki, 'I am an African'. Issued by the Office of the Deputy President, Cape Town, 8 May 1996.

5   Thabo Mbeki, 'Address to the Corporate Council Summit – Attracting Capital to Africa', Virginia, April 1997.

6   Thabo Mbeki, 'The African Renaissance', Speech at Gallagher Estate, 13 August 1998.

7   As pointed out by P Botha in 'The Challenge of an African Renaissance in the 21st Century', in *Problematising the African Renaissance*. Pretoria: AISA, 2000.

8   For this description of NEPAD I have drawn extensively on WM Gumede, *Thabo Mbeki and the Battle for the Soul of the ANC* (see Bibliography).

9   See *Business Day*, 30 June 2005, 'Senegalese President Attacks Lame NEPAD', and IOL, 14 June 2007, 'Senegal president slams Nepad'.

10 *Crossing the Borders of Power: The Memoirs of Colin Eglin*. Johannesburg: Jonathan Ball: 2007.

11 'The Death of the Rainbow Nation: Unmasking the ANC's programme of re-racialisation', DP website, 1988.

12 Having left the GNU in 1996, the National Party performed poorly at the polls in 1999 and within a year had joined the DP to form the DA. It left the DA after little more than a year and subsequently formed an alliance with the ANC before ceasing to exist in 2004.

CHAPTER 9

1   Suttner, I (ed). *Cutting Through the Mountain* (see Bibliography), p 601.

2   Quoted in Marcia Leveson, 'Insiders on Outsiders: Some South African Jewish Writers', in Shane and Mendelsohn, *Memories, Realities and Dreams* (see Bibliography), p 60.

3   Drawn from Shane and Mendelsohn, *Memories, Realities and Dreams*.

4   James Campbell, 'Beyond the Pale: Jewish Immigration and the South African Left', in Shane and Mendelsohn, *Memories, Realities and Dreams*.

5   See Mark Gevisser, Interview with Cyril Harris, Chief Rabbi of South Africa, in *Portraits of Power*.

6   Campbell, 'Beyond the Pale', p 109, states that between 1910 and 1970 South African Jewry donated more per capita to Zionist campaigns than any other community in the world.

7   See Mark Gevisser, Interview with Cyril Harris.

8   See Geoffrey Wheatcroft, *The Controversy of Zion: Jewish Nationalism, the Jewish State and the Unresolved Jewish Dilemma*. New York: Perseus Books, 1997 and I Pappe, *The Ethnic Cleansing Of Palestine*. Oxford: Oneworld, 2007.

9   Adapted from J Butler, 'No it's not anti-Semitic', *London Review of Books*, 21 August 2003.

10 Sara Roy, 'Living with the Holocaust: The Journey of a Child of Holocaust Survivors', in Adam Shatz (ed), Prophets Outcast. New York: Nation Books, 2004.

11 Quoted in Sara Roy, 'Living with the Holocaust', p 353.

CHAPTER 10

1   See particularly AP Kwame, *Cosmopolitanism: Ethics in a World of Strangers*. New York: Norton, 2006.

2   I Deutscher, 'The Non-Jewish Jew', in Adam Shatz (ed), *Prophets Outcast*. New York: Nation Books, 2004.
3   A line attributed to Paul Begala, American political journalist and author.

CHAPTER 11
1   Quoted in 'More Than a Name: State-Sponsored Homophobia and its Consequences in Southern Africa', Human Rights Watch and the International Gay and Lesbian Human Rights Commission, 14 May 2003.
2   'Zimbabwe's Mugabe Renews Attack on Rotting Britain's Blair', SAPA, 20 November 1999.
3   Mbeki 'Address to the Corporate Council Summit – Attracting Capital to Africa', 1997.
4   Mbeki, 'The African Renaissance', SABC, Gallagher Estate, Midrand, August 1998.

CHAPTER 12
1   Luc Montagnier, whose group at the Pasteur Institute first isolated the AIDS virus in 1983.
2   Throughout, when stating that people die of AIDS I am implying of AIDS-related causes, as death is finally brought on by a variety of illnesses caused by AIDS.
3   All figures are taken from an authoritative independent analysis by the Actuarial Society of South Africa, released on 29 November 2005.
4   Given the massive diversity of Africa it is difficult to generalise. This analysis attempts to draw together some of the common threads that have contributed to the nature and scale of the HIV and AIDS epidemic on the continent. Obviously regional, national and local differences exist within the general framework.
5   This analysis draws from the work of Nicoli Nattrass, *The Moral Economy of AIDS in South Africa* (see Bibliography).
6   Zackie Achmat, John Galway Foster Lecture, London, 10 November 2004.
7   *Daily News*, 29 September 2000.
8   Gumede, *Thabo Mbeki and the Battle for the Soul of the ANC*, pp 160–161.
9   *Mail & Guardian*, 30 June 2003.
10 Chris McGreal, 'The shame of the new South Africa', *The Guardian*, 1 November 2002.
11 In E Cameron, *Witness to AIDS*, p 160 (see Bibliography).
12 Statement from the President's Office quoted on PBS, 16 September 2003.
13 Quoted in *Mail & Guardian*, 6 October 2000.
14 Interview with e-TV, 24 April 2002.
15 Both these statements are quoted in Nattrass, *The Moral Economy of AIDS in South Africa*, p 190.
16 A phrase first used by Edwin Cameron in his Edward A. Smith lecture at Harvard University in April 2003.
17 *Hansard*, 18 March 2003, Minister of Finance Trevor Manuel.
18 Nattrass, *The Moral Economy of AIDS in South Africa*.
19 Quoted in Cameron, *Witness to AIDS*, p 187.
20 'South Africa: AIDS Treatment Update', *AfricaFocus Bulletin*, 11 June 2005.
21 Quoted in *Cape Times*, 26 September 2003.
22 See Liz McGregor, *Khabzela*. Johannesburg: Jacana, 2005.

23 See statements of the SA Medical Association, 2 and 11 March 2005.

24 See affidavit by Dr Peter Saranchuk, October 2005, prepared for a case brought against Matthias Rath by the TAC, available on www.tac.org.za.

25 Gumede, *Thabo Mbeki and the Battle for the Soul of the ANC*, p 162

26 Quoted in *New York Times*, 5 August 2004: 'Criticism Starts at Home', a profile of Wole Soyinka by Henry Louis Gates Jr.

27 Sparks, *Beyond the Miracle*.

28 Published in *Mail & Guardian*, 6–12 October 2000.

29 Quoted in Gumede, *Thabo Mbeki and the Battle for the Soul of the ANC*, p 163.

30 *Washington Post,* 4 June 2000.

31 Hugo Young, *One of Us: Life of Margaret Thatcher*. London: Macmillan, 1989.

32 Nelson Mandela, Foreword to O'Malley, *Shades of Difference* (see Bibliography), although the Foreword is dated November 2004.

33 'Manto a drunk and a thief', *Sunday Times*, 19 August 2007. Soon after this report, the ANC had to admit that it knew of Manto's conviction for theft in Botswana.

34 'Minister has reversed HIV gains – TAC', *Business Day,* 16 August 2007.

35 Statement by Nozizwe Madlala-Routledge, quoted in *The Independent*, 10 August 2007.

CHAPTER 13

1 Estimates of how much the contracts will actually cost South Africa as a consequence of currency fluctuations, financing costs and input materials costs range from R45 billion to R100 billion.

2 See Laurie Nathan, 'No ownership, no commitment: a guide to local ownership of security sector reform', *Crisis States Research Centre*, LSE, 2007.

3 Through Logtek and Applied Logistics Engineering, in which Conlog was a stakeholder.

4 Special Review by the Auditor-General of the Selection Process of Strategic Defence Packages for the Acquisition of Armaments at the Department of Defence [RP 161/2000], September 2000.

5 At the time of writing Andries Nel was the ANC's Deputy Chief Whip in Parliament, having been rewarded for six more years of unflinching loyalty.

6 Quoted from Draft Evidence – Scopa Department of Defence Hearing, 11 October 2000.

7 See, for instance, J Brauer and JP Dunne (eds), *Arms Trade and Economic Development: Theory, Policy and Cases in Arms Trade Offsets*. London, New York: Routledge, 2004.

8 Quoted from Draft Evidence – Scopa Department of Defence Hearing, 11 October 2000.

9 *Ibid.*

10 For instance, Joe Modise in Parliament on 9 March 1999 and members of Cabinet in their statement and background notes released on 12 January 2001.

11 Quoted from Draft Evidence – Scopa Department of Defence Hearing, 11 October 2000.

12 *Ibid.*

13 Idasa media release, 30 October 2000.

14 *Christian Science Monitor*, 30 November 2000.

15 Molai is the son-in-law of Lambert Moloi, who is Modise's brother-in-law and was his

chief-of-staff in MK. Molai and Moloi are also both Directors of ADS, along with Schabir Shaik.

16 In addition and to his credit Richard Young has been indefatigable in unearthing material about the arms deal, fighting a number of court cases that have compelled government and its agencies to make publicly available crucial documents relating to the deal and establishing a superb website with information on the deal: www.armsdeal-vpo.co.za.

17 The Infogate scandal exposed the apartheid government's covert purchase of newspapers in the US and Europe which were used to influence public opinion in favour of the internationally isolated regime.

18 *Cape Times,* 14 November 2000.

19 *Africa Confidential,* Volume 42, Issue 3, 9 February 2001.

20 *Sunday Independent,* 24 December 2000.

21 Media statement, 12 January 2001.

22 *Ibid.*

23 *Mail & Guardian,* 5–11 January 2001.

24 'That taint of a cover-up', *Sunday Independent,* 7 January 2001.

25 Idasa press release, 15 January 2001.

26 Quoted in *Business Day,* 17 January 2001.

27 Quoted in *Cape Argus,* 15 January 2001.

28 Report from the Director Public Prosecutions Western Cape, Advocate FW Kahn SC, and Advocate J Lubbe SC, to the Minister of Justice and Constitutional Development, PM Maduna, 18 January 2001.

29 Editorial, *Sunday Independent,* 28 January 2001.

30 Transcript of President Mbeki's public address, 19 January 2001.

31 *Sunday Independent,* 21 January 2001.

32 *Ibid.*

33 The above quotes are taken from the letter from Jacob Zuma to Gavin Woods, 19 January 2001.

34 See Roeber, 'Hard-wired for Corruption'; Sampson, *The Arms Bazaar*; Thomas, *As Used on the Famous Nelson Mandela,* and Crawford-Browne, *Eye on the Money* (see Bibliography).

35 President Mbeki admitted that he had been the author of the letter in an interview with the *Sunday Independent* on 26 February 2006.

36 It turned out she had seen my Psion in Gavin's office with a wire coming out of it. I had been charging my machine in Gavin's office while we were working.

37 Statement issued by ANC on the arms procurement, 23 January 2001.

38 Quoted in *Business Day,* 7 February 2001.

39 Transcription of Ministers' Deliberations, Scopa, 26 February 2001.

40 *Ibid.*

41 *Ibid.*

42 *Ibid.*

43 *Ibid.*

44 *Ibid.*

45 Rhoda Joemat left the ANC Study Group and Scopa, saddened and angry about the demise of the committee. She later left Parliament as a result of the Travelgate saga.

46 Quoted in *Business Day,* 7 May 2001.

47 Goniwe subsequently became the ANC's Chief Whip in Parliament and in 2006 was fired and expelled from the ANC for sexual harassment.
48 *Business Day*, 18 May 2001.
49 See *Hansard*, 7 June 2001, Douglas Gibson MP.
50 See *Hansard*, 7 June 2001, Jeremy Cronin MP.

CHAPTER 14
1 Statement by Tony Yengeni, *Sunday Independent*, 15 July 2001.
2 Tokyo Sexwale indicated at the time that his car had been bought from Daimler-Chrysler and that he had no dealings with EADS (*The Star*, 3 July 2001).
3 'The Modise House that Denel Built', *Mail & Guardian*, 20 July 2001.
4 The JIT Report hinted at this arrangement without fully exposing it. This aspect of the transaction is central to the investigation by German prosecutors into the German Submarine Consortium (GSC).
5 *Sunday Independent*, 22 July 2001.
6 Final Report of the Joint Investigating Team into the Strategic Defence Procurement Package, November 2001.
7 *Ibid.*
8 *Ibid.*
9 Edward Said, *Representations of the Intellectual.*
10 'Arms report sanitised', *Mail & Guardian*, 7 January 2005.
11 'Chippy Shaik Meddled in Arms Probe', *Mail & Guardian*, 23 November 2001.
12 Quoted from the documents provided to Richard Young by the AG.
13 Quoted in James Myburgh, 'BAe and the arms deal', www.Politicsweb.co.za, 14 August 2007.
14 *Ibid.*
15 Quoted in James Myburgh, 'BAe and the arms deal. Part II', www.Politicsweb.co.za, 15 August 2007.
16 *Ibid.*
17 This section has been drawn from the documents provided to Richard Young and the article by Myburgh.
18 In the High Court of South Africa (Durban and Coastal Local Division). In the matter between: The State and Schabir Shaik (and 11 of his companies) Judgment: 2005-05-31.
19 *Sunday Independent*, 26 February 2006.
20 'Zuma trial: We'll put Mbeki in the stand', *Mail & Guardian*, 21 July 2006.
21 'Arms deal: Who got R1 billion in pay-offs?', *Mail & Guardian*, 12 January 2007.
22 *Der Spiegel*, 5 February 2007.
23 *Sunday Times*, 19 March 2007.
24 *Sunday Tribune*, 27 May 2007.
25 I heard of the President's involvement in this decision from three independent sources in three different agencies.
26 *Mail & Guardian*, 2 February 2007.
27 This was confirmed to me independently by two separate investigators in different agencies.
28 According to Terry Crawford-Browne, p 163 (see Bibliography), 'the frigates are so badly constructed that they are barely seaworthy'.
29 'SA's fighter jets turn into expensive folly', *Business Day*, 10 March 2007.

30 *Ibid.*
31 'Jobs from arms offsets fall short', *Business Day Weekender,* 18 November 2006.
32 *Ibid.*
33 'Rusting Targets', *Business Day,* 20 November 2006.
34 J Roeber, 'Hard-wired for corruption', *Prospect,* August 2005.
35 *Ibid.*
36 See Roberts, *The Wonga Coup,* and Hollingsworth, *Thatcher's Fortunes* (see Bibliography).
37 Thabo Mbeki, Oration at the funeral of Joe Modise, 8 December 2001.

CHAPTER 15

1   Vaclav Havel, *The Art of the Impossible* (see Bibliography).
2   Quoted by political philosopher John Gray, *New Statesman,* 12 March 2007.
3   Marc Hauser, author of *Moral Minds,* quoted in the *Guardian Review,* 12 May 2007.
4   *Sunday Times* Editorial, 14 January 2001.
5   See, for instance, 'More than a law-making production line: Parliament and oversight', in *South Africa 2005-2006: State of the Nation.* Cape Town: HSRC Press; *Economist Intelligence Unit* 12, September 2006; 'South Africa: Democracy without the People?' *Journal of Democracy,* Volume 13, Number 1, 2002.
6   Quoted in *Business Day,* 10 May 2007.
7   *Ibid.*
8   See 'MPs deny any influence over CellC bid', www.iol.co.za, 31 March 2001.
9   *Sunday Times,* 6 May 2007.
10 *Business Day,* 8 May 2007.
11 Seventeen sitting MPs at the time of writing, with more charged who had already left Parliament, including my former Scopa colleague, Bruce Kannemeyer.
12 *Pretoria News,* 30 March 2007.
13 The word is taken from the ANC website promoting the Forum.
14 From 'Counterpoint', Richard Calland, *Mail & Guardian,* 23 February 2007.
15 Institute for Justice and Reconciliation, *Ecotransnews,* 14 November 2004.
16 'Gautrain: Who gets the Gravy?' *Sunday Times,* 26 November 2006.
17 'Selebi: Here's the evidence, minister', *Mail & Guardian,* 24 November 2006.
18 It appears he also gave much smaller amounts to other parties. The R250 000 given to the Democratic Alliance was repaid by the party. 'Selebi: Here's the evidence, minister', *Mail & Guardian,* 24 November 2006.
19 *Sunday Times,* 11 March 2007.
20 Fred Khumalo, 'It's nice to be ...', *Sunday Times,* 3 June 2007.
21 Havel, *The Art of the Impossible,* p 72.
22 Edwin Cameron, *Witness to AIDS,* pp 183–4.
23 Tony Blair describing the Labour Party, quoted in A Rawnsley, *Servants of the People.* London: Penguin, 2004.
24 The notion that affirmative action has led to exclusion and suffering for the white minority is debunked by the reality that unemployment rates amongst this minority are 5 per cent, lower than in most developed countries.
25 *Sunday Times,* 10 December 2006.
26 *The Guardian,* 29 January 2007.
27 Quoted in *The Guardian,* 29 January 2007.
28 *Cape Argus,* 20 January 2007.

29　Quoted in *Mail & Guardian*, 9 March 2007.

30　Pregs Govender. *Love and Courage.* Johannesburg: Jacana Media, 2007, p 175.

31　For an account of the hounding of Maharaj see Padraig O'Malley's *Shades of Difference*, especially chapter 20. (See Bibliography.)

32　I cannot pronounce on the allegations of corruption against Mac as I have not been close to the issues. However, I can say that his continued closeness to the Shaiks is a sign of poor judgement at best.

33　Quoted in O'Malley, *Shades of Difference*, p 452.

34　Nelson Mandela Lecture, 23 November 2004, quoted in O'Malley, *Shades of Difference, p* 453.

35　Thabo Mbeki, in a newsletter on the ANC website, 'ANC Today', quoted in 'News 24', 29 November 2004.

36　Quoted in O'Malley, *Shades of Difference*, p 453.

37　*Ibid.*, p 473.

38　*Ibid.*

39　Quoted in *New Statesman*, 25 April 2005.

40　Quoted in *New Statesman*, 12 June 2006.

41　*The Guardian*, 16 December 2006.

42　*The Guardian*, 14 December 2006.

43　Barack Obama, *The Audacity of Hope* (see Bibliography).

44　Paul Fauvet and Marcelo Mosse, *Carlos Cardoso: Telling the Truth in Mozambique.* Cape Town: Double Storey, 2003.

45　AM Goetz and R Jenkins, *Reinventing Accountability*, pp 2 and 3 (see Bibliography).

CHAPTER 16

1　Havel, *The Art of the Impossible*, p 8.

2　The author intends to articulate these ideas in detail in future writings.

3　The constraints of length necessitate that these ideas are presented only in brief and simplistic form. It is the author's intention to develop each of these ideas in future publications and articles.

4　Havel, *The Art of the Impossible*, p 74

CHAPTER 17

1　Appiah, *Cosmopolitanism* (see Bibliography).

2　This example is drawn from Xolela Mangcu, 'To embrace one's own identity without rejecting that of another', *Business Day*, 6 June 2006.

3　Quoted from Said, *Representations of the Intellectual* (see Bibliography).

SELECTED BIBLIOGRAPHY

Appiah, K A. *Cosmopolitanism: Ethics in a World of Strangers.* New York and London: Norton, 2005.

Brauer, J. and Dunne, J.P. (eds). *Arms Trade and Economic Development: Theory, Policy and Cases in Arms Trade Offsets.* London: Routledge, 2004.

Cameron, Edwin. *Witness to AIDS.* Cape Town: Tafelberg, 2005.

Crawford-Browne, Terry. *Eye on the Money.* Cape Town: Umuzi, 2007.

Crick, Bernard. *In Defence of Politics,* 4th ed. Chicago: University of Chicago Press, 1992.

Fauvet, Paul and Mosse, Marcelo. *Carlos Cardoso: Telling the Truth in Mozambique.* Cape Town: Double Storey, 2003.

Feinstein, Andrew. 'Reflections on South African Political Economy', *LSE: Crefsa Quarterly Review,* Number 2, 1998.

Goetz, A M and Jenkins, R. *Reinventing Accountability: Making Democracy Work for Human Development.* London: Macmillan, 2005.

Gumede, Mervyn. *Thabo Mbeki and the Battle for the Soul of the ANC.* Cape Town: Zebra, 2005.

Hauser, Marc. *Moral Minds: How Nature Designed our Universal Sense of Right and Wrong.* London, New York: Little, Brown, 2007.

Havel, Vaclav. *The Art of the Impossible: Politics as Morality in Practice.* New York: Knopf, 1997.

Hirsch, Alan. *Season of Hope: Economic Reform under Mandela and Mbeki.* Scottsville: University of KwaZulu-Natal Press, 2005.

Hollingsworth, Mark. *Thatcher's Fortunes: The Life and Times of Mark Thatcher.* London: Mainstream Publishing, 2006.

Marais, Hein. *South Africa: Limits to Change: The Political Economy of Transition.* London: Zed Books, 1997.

Nattrass, Nicoli. *The Moral Economy of AIDS in South Africa.* Cambridge: Cambridge University Press, 2004.

Nattrass, Nicoli. *Mortal Combat.* Scottsville: UKZN Press, 2007.

Obama, Barack. *The Audacity of Hope: Thoughts on Reclaiming the American Dream.* London: Canongate, 2007.

O'Malley, Padraig. *Shades of Difference: Mac Maharaj and the Struggle for South Africa.* London: Viking Penguin, 2007.

Roberts, Adam. *The Wonga Coup: Guns, Thugs and a Ruthless Determination to Create Mayhem in an Oil-Rich Corner of Africa.* London: Public Affairs, 2006.

Roeber, Joe. 'Hard-wired for Corruption', *Prospect Magazine,* August 2005.

Roy, Sara. 'A Jewish Plea', in Hovsepian, Nubar (ed), *The War on Lebanon: A Reader.* Northampton, MA: Interlink Publishing, Spring 2007 (forthcoming).

Said, Edward. *Representations of the Intellectual.* New York: Vintage Books, 1994.

Sampson, Anthony. *The Arms Bazaar.* London: Viking, 1977.

Saramago, Jose. *Seeing.* London: Harvill Secker, 2006.

Shane, M and Mendelsohn, R. *Memories, Realities and Dreams: Aspects of the South African Jewish Experience.* Johannesburg: Jonathan Ball, 2000.

Shatz, Adam (ed). *Prophets Outcast.* New York: Nation Books, 2004.

Sparks, Allister. *Beyond the Miracle: Inside the New South Africa.* Johannesburg: Jonathan Ball, 2003.

Suttner, I (ed). *Cutting Through the Mountain.* London: Viking, 1997.

Thomas, Mark. *As Used on the Famous Nelson Mandela.* London: Ebury Press, 2006.

INDEX